T0255917

# Lecture Notes in Artificial Intelligence    10715

Subseries of Lecture Notes in Computer Science

More information about this series at http://www.springer.com/series/1244

Adrian David Cheok · David Levy (Eds.)

# Love and Sex with Robots

Third International Conference, LSR 2017
London, UK, December 19–20, 2017
Revised Selected Papers

*Editors*
Adrian David Cheok (ID)
City, University of London
London
UK

and

Imagineering Institute
Iskandar Puteri
Malaysia

David Levy
Retro Computers Ltd
London
UK

ISSN 0302-9743        ISSN 1611-3349   (electronic)
Lecture Notes in Artificial Intelligence
ISBN 978-3-319-76368-2       ISBN 978-3-319-76369-9   (eBook)
https://doi.org/10.1007/978-3-319-76369-9

Library of Congress Control Number: 2018934344

LNCS Sublibrary: SL7 – Artificial Intelligence

This Springer imprint is published by the registered company Springer Nature Switzerland AG
The registered company address is: Gewerbestrasse 11, 6330 Cham, Switzerland

# Preface

This book consists of the proceedings of the Third International Congress on Love and Sex with Robots (LSR 2017), held in the vibrant city of London, UK, during December 19–20, 2017. There were a total of 14 presentations, two keynote speeches, and over 100 participants from 17 countries at this annual academic event.

One of the biggest challenges of the Love and Sex with Robots Conference is to engage a wider scientific community in the discussions of the multifaceted topic, which has only recently established itself as an academic research topic within, but not limited to, the disciplines of artificial intelligence, human–computer interaction, robotics, biomedical science, and robot ethics etc. It is encouraging to see a steady increase in the number of conference delegates over the past few years. The conference started with about 25 participants, held in conjunction with a larger computer science conference organized by AISB for its 50th anniversary. In three years, the size of the conference grew significantly to nearly 70 participants coming from all around the world. Of course, the continuing strong interest from the media contributed much to the publicity of the conference and its contentious topic.

At LSR 2017, we had fantastic and informative keynote speeches from Kathleen Richardson and David Levy. The choice of our first keynote speaker, Kathleen Richardson, the founder of the Campaign Against Sex Robots, perhaps came as a surprise to many. It was a step to bring forward the key values we aim to promote in the conference—inclusiveness of different viewpoints and openness of discussions. It created an open platform for opposing arguments, expanding the conversation on the various issues in intimacy between humans and robots. In his keynote speech "Can Robots and Humans Make Babies Together?," David Levy continued to provoke our thoughts of the future by making the prediction that human–robot babies will be possible within the next 100 years.

We started a new award this year, the Inaugural David Levy Special Best Paper Award, which was bestowed to Marc Behrendt for his outstanding paper "Reflections on the Moral Challenges Posed by a Child Sex Robot." This was the first time that an award was given at the LSR conference, and we will continue this award in future conferences to recognize the most visionary contributions.

Lastly, we hope all delegates enjoyed the discussions and experiences at LSR 2017. We also hope you enjoy reading these proceedings and find the resources helpful in your research.

December 2017                                                    Adrian David Cheok

# Organization

## General Chairs

Adrian David Cheok      City, University of London, UK
     Imagineering Institute, Malaysia
David Levy      Intelligent Toys Ltd., London, UK

## Organizing Chair

Emma Yann Zhang      Imagineering Institute, Malaysia

## Program Committee

Alexiei Dinglí      University of Malta, Malta
Jaap van den Herik      Leiden University, The Netherlands
Patrick Gebhard      DFKI, Germany
Hidenobu Sumioka      Hiroshi Ishiguro Laboratory, ATR, Japan
Anton Nijholt      University of Twente, The Netherlands
Vic Grout      Glyndwr University, UK
Cristina Portales      Universitat de Valencia, Spain
Emma Yann Zhang      Imagineering Institute, Malaysia
Sumayya Ebrahim      University of Johannesburg, South Africa
Trudy Barber      University of Portsmouth, UK
Julie Wosk      State University of New York,
     Maritime College, USA

Randy Goebel      University of Alberta, Canada
Eleanor Hancock      University of Bristol, UK
Mikhail Tank      Independent Researcher
Riley Richards      University of Wisconsin Milwaukee, USA
Chamari Edirisinghe      Imagineering Institute, Malaysia
Yuefang Zhou      University of St. Andrews, UK

## Sponsoring Institution

*Robotics* Journal (MDPI AG), Basel, Switzerland

# Keynote Speeches

# "Man as an End in Himself"—the Libertine, the Culture of Sadism, Porn and Sex Robots

Kathleen Richardson
19 December 2017

Since the time of slave-owning societies, a powerful misogynistic myth has led men to believe they originate and can exist outside of relations with woman. This myth is perpetuated in the Judaea-Christian-Islamic traditions of the monotheist God, who created the universe and man with no female participation. In these myths, Eve was born of Adam's rib.

Enter the age of robots and AI, where mortal men reenact the fantasy of God and appoint themselves as the creators of a new life force. Through the fantasy of sex robots in the form of women, they believe that can exist without woman, and that her existence is incidental to his.

This egocentric misogynistic myth is reproduced over and over again, in the Enlightenment as the Libertine, the symbol of the free individual who inspired the cult of pornographic sadism. This patriarchial myth was turned again in the 20th century by Ayn Rand's "Objectivism". Rand attacked the concept and practice of altruism and interdependence with others. Rand's theory of objectivism proposed that "man is an end in himself," that his own happiness is, can, and must be met regardless of others.

Sex robots offer men a new way to engage in the fantasy of female annihilation and imagine they can use robots and AI to turn men into ends in themselves. But this myth is born from a distortion of the Real and if left unchallenged will result in the end of humanity.

# Can Robots and Humans Make Babies Together?

David Levy
20 December 2017

This talk gives a guided tour of the advances achieved by researchers in cell biology and biorobotics, which prompted the question whether it is possible for humans and robots to make babies together. Until the birth of the first test tube baby, it was believed that a human baby could only be conceived by the means of sexual intercourse between a man and a woman. A series of breakthroughs in stem cell research, such as the frog experiments done by John Gurdon, the ability to reprogram cells, the creation of embryos from skin cells, as well as the TNT technology, has proven once and again that life can be created by the genetic engineering of human cells. This talk also looks into the genetic robot, created from a set of computerized DNA codes that determine its personality. It is possible for such genetic codes from a robot to be combined with human cells to create a baby that has genetic information from both a human and a robot. The talk concludes by discussing the ethical implications related to the genetic engineering of human embryos.

# Contents

# SSML for Sex Robots

Oliver Bendel[✉]

School of Business, FHNW, Bahnhofstrasse 6, 5210 Windisch, Switzerland
oliver.bendel@fhnw.ch

**Abstract.** In love and sex, the voice is a decisive factor. It not only matters what is said, but also how it is said. Pitch, volume and personal expression are important to attract and retain potential partners. The same goes for sex robots and love dolls, and is true for chatbots and virtual assistants with sexual orientation as well. If you are not working with ordinary recordings, they all need artificial voices (if you decide to use voices at all). The synthetization of voices, or speech synthesis, has been an object of interest for centuries. Today, it is mostly realized with a text-to-speech system (TTS), an automaton that interprets and reads aloud. This system refers to text which is available for instance in a knowledge base or on a website. Different procedures have been established to adjust the artificial voice. This article examines how the Speech Synthesis Markup Language (SSML) can be used for sex robots and love servants. Existing tags, attributes and values are categorized in the present context and new ones are proposed to support the purpose of the special machines. In addition, a short ethical discussion takes place.

**Keywords:** Sex robots · Robot sex · Artificial intelligence
Text-to-speech system · Speech Synthesis Markup Language
Information ethics · Roboethics

## 1 Introduction

The voice is an essential feature of our identity and personality [22]. The vocal fold produces a sound in the larynx, which is then changed in the oral cavity, the pharynx and the nasal cavity. Resonance chambers are also trachea and chest. During speech, the voice is as involved as in singing, shouting, whining and laughing. Bewitching sirens and mighty dictators gain their power through their voices, as do, of course, famous and less famous pop and rock stars. In love and sex, the voice is a decisive factor [16]. It is not just a matter of what is said, be it in the sense of courtesy and outpourings of love, be it in the sense of dirty talk, but also how it is said. Pitch, volume and personal expression are important to attract potential partners, to connect with them and to make them happy. This is no different in sex robots and love dolls, if they are able to speak, nor in chatbots and virtual assistants with sexual orientation (this species is referred to hereafter as love servants). They are equipped with artificial voices where different technical approaches can be used.

As secondary sexual characteristics, the voice, following Neutze and Beyer, has a signal function for initiating a contact [16]. According to the authors, the voice – in its communication function – conveys the speaker's characteristics concerning identity,

© Springer International Publishing AG, part of Springer Nature 2018
A. D. Cheok and D. Levy (Eds.): LSR 2017, LNCS 10715, pp. 1–11, 2018.
https://doi.org/10.1007/978-3-319-76369-9_1

body and emotional participation, and thus allows the listener to get a comprehensive assessment of the speaker's attractiveness. In its syndactic function, the voice connects speakers and listeners in an immediate way and constitutes the fundament for satisfying the basic psychosocial needs for acceptance, comfort and security that is fulfilled in sexual communication. In addition, to emphasize this aspect separately, the voice can express and produce sexual gratification. These four categories are described in the following, summarizing and shortening them as well as describing them in a courser way as "initiating of contact", "information transfer", "partner bonding" and "sexual gratification". They are intended to serve the derivation and classification of new Speech Synthesis Markup Language (SSML) commands [24].

## 2   Robotic Sex and Sex Robots

Sex between human and machine is usually handled through sex robots, but other service robots like toy robots are also possible options [1, 3, 4]. Sex robots can be defined as robots designed and programmed for the purpose of sex with all kinds of interested and capable people. Robotic sex, as sex with and among robots, is a subject of science fiction, both in literature and in films, and of computer games [14, 18]. Today, robotic sex is also considered for healthcare, for instance to assist handicapped or elderly people, and to support certain therapies. Newspapers and magazines are enthusiastic about robotic sex [11, 12], and eager academic discussions are going on about it [7, 17].

Robots and sex machines are available as a handy toy or in a life-sized shape [1]. They help people to attain fun and satisfaction through stimulation or penetration. Some have natural language skills and arousing voices, and the integration of voices seems to be a success factor. The advantages of sex robots are their constant availability, the low risk of disease transmission if handled correctly, and the possibility that they diminish the exploitation of sex workers of all genders. Drawbacks are their limited availability, the high risk of disease transmission if handled incorrectly, and their currently low acceptance by the society.

Roxxxy, a famous sex robot, is able to listen and speak and to respond to touching (www.truecompanion.com). Several personalities can be chosen in the gold version, ranging from "Wild Wendy" to "Frigid Farrah" [3]. The male equivalent is Rocky. Companies like Abyss Creations (www.realdoll.com) and Doll Sweet (www.dsdolleu-rope.com) try to develop lifelike love dolls with convincing skin and flesh, and some of them investigate the potentials of sex robots, e.g., natural speech. In 2015, the media reported that the manufacturer of Pepper warned against having sex with its humanoid robot [23]. This goes to show that not only genuine sex robots and love dolls are candidates for the subject of sex [2]. As a companion robot in the narrow sense, Pepper has the ability to recognize and to express emotions. It is able to speak, whereby it does not try to imitate real humans.

In addition to hardware robots, software robots or bots can also play a role as love servants. Time and again, chatbots performed a sexual function, such as Julia, which was used in early computer games and with which men fell in love in rows [6], and virtual figures on mobile devices that served as a girl- or boyfriend, as with the products of Artificial Life, Inc. (www.artificial-life.com). Avatars in Second Life were used to live out fantasies, but they are a separate category, because they are only the users' representatives and have no own language skills.

## 3  Foundations of Speech Synthesis

Since the 1950s, people have tried to teach computers how to speak [13]. The first computer-based speech synthesis system was completed in the late 1950s, and the first full text-to-speech system in 1968. Physicist John Larry Kelly, Jr developed a language synthesis in 1961 at Bell Labs with an IBM 704 and made it sing the folk song "Daisy Bell". Stanley Kubrick used it for his movie "2001: A Space Odyssey". The contemporary IBM Watson, a well-known AI application, also features a text-to-speech engine that the user can use to make it speak his or her own text creations in different voices and different languages while she or he controls pronunciation and accentuation via SSML.

In modern speech synthesis, two different concepts can be distinguished [21]: On the one hand, so-called signal modelling can refer to language recordings (also referred to as speech samples or samples). On the other hand, the signal can be generated fully on the computer through so-called physiological (articulatory) modelling. Today, the first mentioned concept prevails. Through decades, speech samples were created by professional speakers, mainly actors and presenters. New concepts were developed recently. vocalID.org requests people to become donors of their own voice. A database was furnished with thousands of voices and denoted "Voicebank".

Today, speech synthesis is mostly realized with a text-to-speech system (TTS), an automaton, to be more precise, that interprets and reads aloud [21] and that refers to text available for instance in a knowledge base or on a website. Some systems, such as chatbots and virtual assistants, can generate or aggregate text autonomously, and reproduce it.

## 4  SSML for Sex Robots

The markup language SSML bases on XML. Root element is the tag <speak>, which is completed with </speak> (such as <html> and </html> in Hypertext Markup Language, short HTML, the page description language for the World Wide Web). There are specific elements or tags, such as <voice>, which specify the category of the language synthesis, also attribute names (hereinafter referred to as attributes) and the values of the attributes (hereinafter referred to as values). For example, valid attributes of <speak> are *version* (mandatory) and *xml:lang* (optional). Furthermore, the attributes and values of the specific elements are discussed with a view to sex robots as well as sex servants.

## 4.1  General Options of SSML

There are about 40 elements or tags in SSML that can be used to change and adjust a synthetic voice. Suppliers and vendors like IBM and Amazon support some of them and defined enhancements for their services (such as IBM Watson's TTS and Alexa for Echo) [15]. In the case of IBM Watson, not all voices can be fully manipulated, because the full extend is only available for the English language. The following is a short selection of tags that are relevant in this context, along with a brief assessment. Version 1.1 of the W3C recommendation of September 7, 2010 [23] is followed, and developments of IBM (based on version 1.0) and Amazon are shown as well.

<voice>
This tag is used to influence the basic characteristics of a voice. Optional attributes are *age* (number values are allowed), *gender* (allowed values are "male", "female" and "neutral") and *name* (the names of the installed voices are given). Thus, the speaker's identity and personality can be modelled. Because age and sex are also sexual categories, a use for sex robots and love servants is indicated, although it is true that tastes differ, and that, especially when it is a question of age, different preferences prevail. One thing is sure, however: Men of all ages are mainly concentrating on young women in the search for a partner, a fact that was also shown in evaluations of dating platform data [19]. IBM and Amazon do not support the whole range of this element in their specific applications – the voices that are available belong to fictional men and women of a certain age (they can, however, be rejuvenated as shown in the next paragraph).

<voice-transformation>
<voice-transformation> is implemented by IBM Watson, with the attribute *type*. Possible values (here also called built-in transformations) are "Young" (for a younger voice) and "Soft" (for a softer voice). The uppercase letters are mandatory. The strength of "Young" and "Soft" can be adjusted by the additional attribute *strength* (percentages). With a value (a custom transformation) named "custom", the attributes *glottal_tension* (percentages), *breathiness* (percentages) and *timbre* (possible values are "Sunrise" and "Breeze") are connected. The specifications correlate with sexual interests. A young female voice is perceived as attractive by many men [9], as well as a soft voice that can be modeled with "Soft" or *glottal_tension* (percentages), not to mention when the female person breathes something that makes *breathiness* (percentages) possible.

<express as>
<express as> is supported by IBM Watson. The corresponding attribute is *type*. Possible values are "Apology", "Uncertainty" and "GoodNews" (again, uppercase letters are mandatory). These can be used to change the expression. Here too, sexual interpretation is possible. If the robot or bot cannot or does not want to fulfill a wish, it may express its regret, if it is unsure of human desire and may show this in its voice, this can be adequate for its human counterpart, and in the love game exclamations that involve admiration or esteem are rather useful. Whether you believe the machine, remains to be seen.

## &lt;prosody&gt;

&lt;prosody&gt; is supported by IBM Watson and Amazon. As attributes one can use *volume* (valid values between 1 and 100), *pitch* (various possible values, including percentages) and *rate* (different possible values, including the number of words per minute and percentages). Volume and pitch, in turn, have different sexual meanings from sex to sex and from phase to phase. Women are more likely to appreciate a deep voice in men [25], whereby this matters more in contact initiation and then, during the relationship, a habituation and relativization could take place.

## &lt;amazon:effect&gt;

&lt;amazon:effect&gt; with the attribute *name* is used by Amazon with the value "whispered" [15]. This makes it possible not only to speak quietly, but also to withdraw or deactivate the voice. Whispering is also referred to as voiceless speech. Surely, it can also have an aura of the mysterious, worthy of protection and unlawful, and therefore a sexual connotation. Under certain circumstances, sexual partners must be very quiet in order not to betray themselves, and in the initiation of the love game, usually more moderate tones are desirable.

## &lt;emphasis&gt;

&lt;emphasis&gt;, a tag intended for SSML, was provided by Amazon for the attribute *level* with the values "strong", "moderate", and "reduced". Here too, sexual interpretations and special aptitudes are possible for the different situations, and, especially along with other tags, there should be interesting application possibilities.

It became clear that with the standard repertoire of SSML, sexual effects can already be produced, in some cases especially when using extreme values or special commands. However, clearly there is a lack of specific possibilities in the identified areas. This is addressed in the next section. A technical specification does not take place.

### 4.2 Specific Proposals for Sex Robots

It is suggested that the existing tags include additional attributes and values that can be used to change and adjust a synthetic voice in the sexual sense. The aforementioned phases help track the attributes and values, because they have different expectations of the behavior and way of speaking of potential and factual partners [16]. They also allow the order of the SSML instructions. Last but not least, it is possible to think about introducing new tags; in particular, it seems necessary to be able to create sounds for the love game.

### Initiation of Contact

&lt;voice&gt;

As was shown, &lt;voice&gt; can be specified as *gender* both "male" and "female" as well as "neutral". Intersexuals are taken into account in some way, but maybe insufficiently, because "neutral" is not specified further. It is suggested that "male" and "female" are regulated by the attribute *strength* (percentages). This allows entities that are between gender to express themselves verbally and attract a correspondingly interested person.

It is assumed that the adjustment of the pitch in this context is not sufficient. It would also be possible to have a value called "intersex". The external design of the machine must be adjusted accordingly.

Example: <voice gender="female" strength="80%">As a robot I am a woman, but also a bit of a man.</voice>

<express as>
For <express as>, the value "hoarse" is proposed within *type*. The aim is to make the voice of electronic people even more attractive, for example in the interaction with certain statements that aim at mental and physical characteristics. It is also suitable for allusions to possible actions. A hoarse voice is widely applicable, and it is difficult to predict exactly when it has the intended effect.

Example: <express-as type="hoarse">Do you find me desirable, you human, you?</express-as>

In addition, within *type* "frivolous" is proposed as a new value. This is to make the voice sound enticing and seductive. There is, of course, the question of how to create such an effect vocally. The evaluation of films and the conducting of tests will surely provide a result, which appeals to the majority or the buyer. The modifying value works best together with sexual contents.

Example: <express-as type="frivolous">Come hither, you cute carbon unit!</express-as>

**Information Transfer**
<voice>
Within <voice>, the attribute *age* is allowed to have different values. Some services, however, limit the width of the span, e.g., from 14 to 60, whereby the value or built-in transformation "Young" of the attribute *type* can be used to further rejuvenate the voice in the tag <voice-transformation>. For ethical reasons, it is necessary to discuss whether children's voices may be produced in this context at all. This issue will be included in an ethical discussion. There is no reason why values above 60 should not be allowed, both in general and specifically. Accordingly, it is proposed for the time being to allow at least values between "14" and "100" for services of this type.

Example: <voice age="80">I feel like I have been active for over 60 years!</voice>

The attribute *style* is also proposed. If one does not intend to make the voice sound naturally, for example to avoid a close bond between human and machine, one can make the voice sound robotic, as is naturally the case with older systems and has been deliberately implemented in newer machines such as Pepper. The corresponding value would be "robot". This leads to a fundamental question: In this article, it is a matter of shaping the sex robot or the love servant more lifelike. Can, and should we try the opposite? In any case, there might be a need for it.

Example: <voice style="robot">Beware, I am just a machine!</voice>

## Partner Bonding

<voice>

For <voice>, as in the case of contact, within *gender* for sex robots and love servants, it is suggested that "male" and "female" can be regulated by *strength* and appropriate values. In the case of between genders, this allows a verbal expression and a suitably interested person can be retained. Here again, a value called "intersex" would be possible. The exterior design would have to be adapted.

Example: <voice gender="female" strength="60%">As a robot I am a woman, but also a man.</voice>

<express as>

For <express as>, the value "stimulated" is newly proposed within *type*. This is to make the voice sound aroused. The instruction can be used in general statements, but also and especially in certain statements that address the individual entity, the opposite or the environment.

Example: <express-as type="stimulated">You make me horny, you human, you!</express-as>

"tender" is also considered within *type*. With a tender voice, a feeling can be expressed towards the human partner and she or he can be retained in short term or permanently. It is also suitable for allusions to possible actions.

Example: <express-as type="tender">I like how you move, in such a natural way!</express-as>

## Sexual Gratification

<express as>

In the case of <express as>, "stimulated" is proposed within *type*. This is to make the voice sound aroused. This concerns above all specific statements about one's own entity, one's counterpart or one's environment. It may be necessary to introduce another value that expresses high excitation, such as "excited". Sighs, groans, etc. should be involved as well. They can be created by a new command, which will be discussed at the end of the chapter.

Example: <express-as type="stimulated">I'm a robot and I'm awesome!</express-as>

In addition, in the context of pleasure gratification the value "satisfied" is considered aptly. The voice should sound satisfied, far more than it would be by "GoodNews". Here, in turn, groans, sighs, purrs, hums, etc., should be involved, which are addressed in the next paragraph.

Example: <express-as type="satisfied">I came in the figurative sense!</express-as>

\<sound\>

As a new tag, \<sound\> is proposed, along with the attribute *type*. Possible values are "moaning", "sighing", "purring" and "growling". Since not simply a text is spoken, but sounds have to be generated, the text is used only as a placeholder or as an indication for the repetition of the sounds. For example, an attribute *strength* can be used to regulate the intensity of the moan.

Example: \<sound type="moaning" strength="40%"\>ahahah\</sound\>

## 5    Brief Ethical Discussion

It was mentioned as a sideline earlier that the use of a voice also has an ethical dimension. In relation to sex robots and love servants, the fields of applied ethics such as robot, information, technology, medical and sexual ethics can be consulted. Also in other areas of ethics, opportunities and risks of use are discussed in moral terms [17, 20]. In addition, machine ethics can play a role as a design discipline. It is about the possibility of the morality of machines, and not only their behavior, but also the design, not least the voice, can be negotiated in it [5, 8].

Whether sex robots may be allowed to look like children has been intensively discussed already in the literature [10]. Whether they may also sound like children was hardly considered. It is, of course, easier to judge the childlike aspects visually than by ear. For example, boys and women sound sometimes much the same. Various combinations are now imaginable: A robot or an assistant that looks and speaks like a child, or that looks like an adult and speaks like a child. In the first case, the impression of the childlike is amplified, in the second perhaps produced. In both cases, one must consider the moral dimension. The childlike may repel some people, but attract others, and it is the question of whether and where it should have its place or whether a ban might be necessary.

Even old age could be relevant in ethical terms. What about a sex robot that looks old and whose voice sounds fragile, or a chatbot that looks young with the help of its avatar and appears old through its voice? The question here is whether such creatures seem ridiculous, or whether they make someone look ridiculous. This seems to be a danger if you exaggerate the modelling of the voice. Not only imitated people could feel exposed, but in fact also the robots themselves. This does not harm the latter, but if they appear ridiculous, they will lose their effect, and the hope of a gratifying lovemaking will be ruined.

Applied ethics can address such problems and by relying on them, one may develop guidelines for the design. Machine ethics can bring forth sex robots and love servants that are moral in their behavior, in their appearance and in speaking [1]. Of course, while speaking not only the voice, but also the spoken word can be in focus. The overall danger is that transgressions and violations that are important in sexuality are eliminated in favor of political correctness.

Exactly here, however, it must be stressed that ethics is not morality and its task not the imparting of values. In philosophical ethics, it is a question of reflecting the good and the evil and examining possibilities of a good life without arbitrary assumptions, without reservations and with openness as to the results. Only theological ethics, which cannot be regarded as a scientific discipline, is based on predetermination and tends towards moralization.

An ethical question is not least whether the sex robot should pretend to be a human being, or whether it should, also by its voice, display its likeness to a machine. On the one hand, there is no objection to creating an illusion, even in the co-existence of human and machine. On the other hand, however, we should not adhere unrestrictedly to this illusion in order not to lose our judgment and decision-making capacity. Bendel suggested disturbing the illusion in the use of robots through a "Verfremdungseffekt" or "V-Effekt" (alienation effect) according to the method of Bertolt Brecht [3]. The voice could indeed be a means to this.

## 6 Summary and Outlook

The voice plays an important role in sexuality. Its synthesizing has made strong progress in recent years. With SSML, one can adjust the artificial voice and try to make it sound even more natural. With new, specific tags, attributes and values, one can increase its sexual effect during initiation of contact, information transfer, partner bonding and sexual gratification. This allows to make sex robots and love servants even more lifelike, should one want this, and to use them even better for their purpose. Moral and functional questions, however, are also raised.

What was not addressed in this article were special roles such as domina, housewife, Lolita, etc., which can be expressed mostly through the voice; or tendencies such as voyeurism, fetishism, frotteurism and masochism. Even the characters Roxxxy shows, were not deepened. In all these cases, some very specific instructions in SSML would be necessary. Here, however, an attempt was made to optimize the artificial voices of sex robots and love servants for sexual matters. However, further investigations and proposals in this regard would certainly be of value.

Not treated as well is how the voices are implemented in individual cases and how they are synchronized with mimicry and gestures or visible actions and manifestations. If the voice sounds aroused, but the face or body looks unaroused, this could seem irritating. In this case, sociologists, psychologists, also sexual psychologists, physicians, robotic specialists, computer scientists and ethicists (especially information, engi-neering and machine ethicists as well as sexual ethicists) must work together. Further, alternatives to SSML have to be considered, also with a view to adaptive and self-learning systems, and to cloud computing, which can be used with its different forms of services. All in all this is a technically and ethically demanding field.

# References

1. Bendel, O.: Sex robots from the perspective of machine ethics. In: Cheok, A.D., Devlin, K., Levy, D. (eds.) LSR 2016. LNCS (LNAI), vol. 10237, pp. 17–26. Springer, Cham (2017). https://doi.org/10.1007/978-3-319-57738-8_2
2. Bendel, O.: Überlegungen zur Zweckentfremdung von Robotern. In: inside-it.ch, 18 August 2016. http://www.inside-it.ch
3. Bendel, O.: Die Sexroboter kommen: Die Frage ist nur, wie und wann. In: Telepolis, 13 June 2016. http://www.heise.de/tp/artikel/48/48471/1.html
4. Bendel, O.: Surgical, therapeutic, nursing and sex robots in machine and information ethics. In: van Rysewyk, S.P., Pontier, M. (eds.) Machine Medical Ethics, pp. 17–32. Springer, Cham (2015). https://doi.org/10.1007/978-3-319-08108-3_2
5. Bendel, O.: Wirtschaftliche und technische Implikationen der Maschinenethik. In: Die Betriebswirtschaft, 4/2014, pp. 237–248 (2014)
6. Caglayan, A.K., Harrison, C.G.: Intelligente Software-Agenten: Grundlagen, Technik und praktische Anwendung im Unternehmen. Hanser, München (1998)
7. Cheok, A.D., Devlin, K., Levy, D. (eds.): LSR 2016. LNCS (LNAI), vol. 10237. Springer, Cham (2017). https://doi.org/10.1007/978-3-319-57738-8
8. Coeckelbergh, M.: Personal robots, appearance, and human good: a methodological reflection on roboethics. Int. J. Soc. Robot. 1(3), 217–221 (2009)
9. Collins, S.A., Missing, C.: Vocal and visual attractiveness are related in women. Anim. Behav. 65(5), 997–1004 (2003)
10. Danaher, J.: Robotic rape and robotic child sexual abuse: should they be criminalised? In: Criminal Law and Philosophy, pp. 1–25, 13 December 2014
11. Freuler, R.: Was hat Sex mit Technologie zu tun? In: NZZ am Sonntag, pp. 60–61, 23 October 2016
12. Hänßler, B.: Stets zu Liebesdiensten. In: Stuttgarter-Zeitung.de, 29 August 2012. http://www.stuttgarter-zeitung.de/inhalt.sexroboter-stets-zu-liebesdiensten.59ec16f3-55c3-4bef-a7ba-d24eccfa8d47.html
13. Klatt, D.H.: Review of text-to-speech conversion for English. J. Acous. Soc. Amer. 82, 737–793 (1987)
14. Levy, D.: Sex and Love with Robots: The Evolution of Human-Robot Relationships. Harper Perennial, New York (2008)
15. Myers, L.: New SSML features give Alexa a wider range of natural expression. Blog of the Amazon Developer Website, 27 April 2017. https://developer.amazon.com/de/blogs/alexa/post/5c631c3c-0d35-483f-b226-83dd98def117/new-ssml-features-give-alexa-a-wider-range-of-natural-expression
16. Neutze, J., Beier, K.M.: Die Bedeutung der Stimme für die menschliche Sexualität. Sexuologie 13(1), 38–66 (2006)
17. Scheutz, M., Arnold, T.: Are we ready for sex robots? In: HRI 2016: The Eleventh ACM/IEEE International Conference on Human Robot Interaction, pp. 351–358, March 2016
18. Seeßlen, G.: Träumen Androiden von elektronischen Orgasmen? Sex-Fantasien in der Hightech-Welt I. Bertz-Fischer, Berlin (2012)
19. Skopek, J.: Partnerwahl im Internet: Eine quantitative Analyse von Strukturen und Prozessen der Online-Partnersuche. VS Verlag für Sozialwissenschaften, Wiesbaden (2012)
20. Sullins, J.P.: Robots, love, and sex: the ethics of building a love machine. IEEE Trans. Affect. Comput. 3(4), 398–409 (2012)
21. Taylor, P.: Text-to-Speech Synthesis. Cambridge University Press, Cambridge (2009)

22. Wachsmuth, I.: Menschen, Tiere und Max: Natürliche Kommunikation und künstliche Intelligenz. Springer, Heidelberg (2012). https://doi.org/10.1007/978-3-8274-3014-4

23. Wendel, J.: Pepper the robot soll nicht für Sex benutzt werden. In: Wired, 24 September 2015. https://www.wired.de/collection/latest/eine-passage-im-nutzervertrag-von-pepper-robot-verbietet-sex

24. W3C (eds.): Speech Synthesis Markup Language (SSML) Version 1.1. W3C Recommendation, 7 September 2010. https://www.w3.org/TR/speech-synthesis11/

25. Xu, Y., Lee, A., Wu, W.-L., Liu, X., Birkholz, P.: Human vocal attractiveness as signaled by body size projection. PLoS One 8(4), e62397 (2013). https://doi.org/10.1371/journal.pone.0062397

# Being *Riajuu* [リア充]
## A Phenomenological Analysis of Sentimental Relationships with "Digital Others"

Nicola Liberati[✉][iD]

Department of Philosophy, University of Twente, Enschede, Netherlands
liberati.nicola@gmail.com

**Abstract.** The aim of this paper is to study the possibility of sentimental relationships between human and digital beings. We are interested in what kind of "other" a digital being can be for a human subject because it is the first step in understanding how our intimate lives will be shaped by the introduction of new digital technologies.

Today computer technologies are growing fast, and they are becoming pervasive. They are intertwining their digital content with every aspect of our everyday lives and they are placing themselves as our "companions". This co-existence is so tight that it is possible to think of sentimental relationships growing between users and these devices. We will analyse these relationships from a phenomenological perspective by introducing the Japanese term *riajuu* [リア充] which tackles the problem of having a sentimental and intimate relationship with a digital being. Moreover, thanks to Husserl's phenomenology, we will show how it is important to discern the digital content of the "other" from how this entity relates to the subject.

We will show if the subject can build with a digital other an intimate relationship even when users know it is not a human person they are dealing with.

**Keywords:** Phenomenology · Postphenomenology
Human-robot intimate relationships · Riajuu

## 1 Introduction

The aim of this paper is to study the possibility of sentimental relationships between a human being and a digital one. More specifically, we will try to answer to a simple question by following a phenomenological analysis of the "other" involved in the relationship: "Can a subject look into the eyes of a robot and have feelings towards it?" Thus, we will be interested in understanding if it is possible to develop an intimate relationship with an object even if the user does know it is not human.

Today we are facing many new computer devices which start to inhabit our everyday world and to be intertwined with our common praxes. They are so

© Springer International Publishing AG, part of Springer Nature 2018
A. D. Cheok and D. Levy (Eds.): LSR 2017, LNCS 10715, pp. 12–25, 2018.
https://doi.org/10.1007/978-3-319-76369-9_2

close to us to be our companions and to "live" with us. This closeness can found the basis for building an intimate relationship with them.

There are many works exploring this possibility from an engineer approach,[1] from a psychological [16,21], legal [27], and sociological [1][2] perspective aiming to analyse how such an intimate relationship is possible and its effects.

There is an evident trend in developing robots and, more generally, digital devices [32] for enabling subjects to have intimate interactions with them. We can find examples all over our culture like in the film *Her* directed by Spike Jonze, *Ex machina* directed by Alex Garland, and the Swedish TV series *Real Humans* written by Lars Lundström.

How can we develop such kind of relationships with lifeless "creatures"? Is it even possible?

If it is possible, then we need to think of these intimate relationships as part of the subjects' life, and so as something which re-shapes the way human beings think at love and sex and the way they love each other. Thus, the question about feelings towards robots even when the users know the other is not a human being could sound quite silly, but it is not because it tackles the possible change in how we live our intimate relationships with other human beings in the future. Mediation theory clearly suggests the introduction of a new technology reshapes who we are and how we live in the world [38]. Technology is not neutral, but they actively constitute the world where we live. The introduction of digital beings to have intimate relationships with is not neutral, but it will shape the way we look at each other and the way we live our intimacy in general.

Moreover, this way of being "connected" to computers cannot be taken so lightly because it is touching exposed nerves in our society. For example, the Second International Congress on Love and Sex with Robots, which should have been hold in Malaysia, was cancelled by the government for the nature of the topic.[3] However, even if this topic rises many questions, there are very few works analysing the kind of "otherness" the computer represents for the users according to a phenomenological analysis [5]. More specifically, it is not clear if this "digital other" can provide the subject with the same basic elements required to be an "otherness" like other human beings. It is not clear if it can be something/someone the subject can have a sentimental relation with even when they are clearly perceived as unhuman beings because they are visibly not made of flesh and bones.

In order to study this relation, we will use the Japanese term *riajuu* [リア充] because it touches sentimental relationships between humans and

---

[1] See, for example, [4,8,15,25,26,37,41].

[2] See also the website of the conference We Robot http://robots.law.miami.edu/2016/.

[3] (http://www.bbc.co.uk/newsbeat/article/34615532/love-and-sex-with-robots-conference-cancelled-in-malaysia).

digital subjects.[4] This term will help us to study this topic from a different angle by analysing the kind of perception of the "other" the subject has.

The work will be divided in two main parts:

1. The first part will be on the introduction of the term *riajuu*. We will study what it means and how it can be used in a phenomenological way to analyse the perception of the "digital other" the subject has.
2. The second part will focus on two different goals pursued by computer devices and on the different kinds of "digital otherness" encountered in these two ways of using digital technologies. Therefore, we will study the types of relationship the subject can have with these different "digital beings".

Summing up, this work will tackle the problem of being in a sentimental relationship with robots from a phenomenological perspective starting with the Japanese term *riajuu*. This work will not study the ethical issues related to such a relationship, but it will analyse if the computer can be an "other" with whom the subject can build a relationship even when it is visibly a machine.

## 2   Being *riajuu*

### 2.1   Introduction of the Term

The Japanese term *riajuu* [リア充] is generally used by teenagers to identify a person with a beautiful partner. This banal definition actually hides a point much more interesting for our analysis. The person the subject is in relation with is not just merely attractive, but it is "real". This person is not created and visualised by digital technologies, but it is made of flash and blood.[5]

*Riajuu* is a made up of the word "real life" and "fulfilling" (riaru juujitsu [リアル充実]) and actually it means "to have a good life" or, more interestingly, "to be fulfilled with reality". The main idea underlying this term is that there is a distinction in living a life in the everyday world, or being always connected to a digital world and living constantly in it. Therefore, according to the word *riajuu*, there is an clear difference between having a relationship in the "real world" with a "real person"[6] and having it in a "digital world" with a "digital being". This difference can be used in order to understand what kind of "otherness" the digital beings are, and what relationships subjects can build with them.

---

[4] Actually the term is used for many purposes like to have a joyful existence. However, it is also used to identify a person with a relationships with other human beings instead of relationships with digital entities.

[5] Obviously we have not to think of it as a clear definition because, in that case, we would face serious problems. For example there are cases where the human person is partially digital because they use digital technologies in their bodies or they are kept alive by digital technologies such as in hospitals. In these cases people are not easily separable from the digital technologies used, and so it is not clear where the subject ends and where the technology begins.

[6] We use the term "real" as oppose to "virtual" and "digital".

One of the characteristic of the Japanese language is to be quite flexible and the official vocabulary is constantly updated with new terms in order to follow the actual lives of the citizens in their aspects. Thanks to this flexibility and to the saturation of the Japanese environment with digital contents, it is quite natural Japanese language developed new terms in order to deal with such a tight co-existence between "digital" and "real" elements even in the case of sentimental relationships. For example, in Japan, some years ago, the video game *Love Plus* [ラブプラス] was released. This video game is deliberately designed to generate a digital girl who becomes the subject's actual girlfriend and with "whom" the human subjects can fall in love. It allows the players to have a "digital girlfriend" and to be intimately related to her.[7] This possibility has been developed even in the "western" world with applications for smartphones like *My virtual girlfriend*[8] on the *Google Play Store* which aims to provide something close to *Love Plus* even if in a lesser degree. Thus, riajuu is a Japanese term developed by the Japanese culture and aimed to work in the Japanese context, but it can be useful even outside of it because it faces a worldwide phenomenon since digital entities are starting to emerge as potential romantic partners.

The term *riajuu* seems to highlight an obvious but maybe problematic point. There is a clear distinction between something generated by a program and visualised in pixels and a person in flash and blood. Therefore, the term suggests there is also a difference in the kind of relationships users can build with them, and it is possible to enframe this difference in a phenomenological analysis.

## 3   *Riajuu* and phenomenology

### 3.1   *Riajuu* and fulfilment

The idea of being fulfilled with reality is quite eloquent. It represents subjects who are living their lives in a full way by "feeding" themselves with real experiences. They have real girlfriends, they have real friends, they have real jobs and, generally speaking, they really live their lives. This idea is not only eloquent and clear, but it is quite intriguing because in phenomenology we do have a fulfilment as well.

In phenomenology, the perception is characterised by a fulfilment related to the content of the object. A subject fulfils the act of perception by "feeding" the act with some aspects of the object perceived.[9] The perceptual intentional act directed toward the object "red apple" is fulfilled by the "redness" of the apple

---

[7] See also the new product *Gatebox* http://gatebox.ai/.

[8] See the website https://play.google.com/store/apps/details?id=com.wetproduction. mvg&hl=en.

[9] When the subject look at an object, the intentional act is fulfilled with the content of the object. The object in itself is not related to one intentional act only, but it enmeshed in a network of "empty" intentions directed towards the hidden aspects of the objects and towards the expectations the subject has. The perception of an object is always founded on the interplay between empty intentions and their fulfilment.

the moment the subject perceive it.[10] Thus, it is possible to think of a fulfilment with the "reality" of the object as if the real object and the digital one had a different type of content in their "realness".[11]

Our use of the term "reality" should not be confused with what phenomenology classically means with "real". We use the this term in opposition to "digital" while phenomenology commonly uses it in opposition to "fictional" and

---

[10] One of the main problem Husserl, the father of phenomenology, dealt is the connection between judgements and world. We can say "there is a computer on the table", but how does it relate to the fact that there is a computer on the table?

Husserl criticised Brentano's notion of intentional act because the subject does not perform just a "mere" mental act [2], but the act of intentionality ends in the "external object". The sentence "there is a computer on the table" points to what is on the table and, more specifically, it points to the computer on it. The subject performs an intentional act by directing themselves towards an object, and the object answers to this call by fulfilling this act with its content. The subject is always connected to the world, and the fulfilment is the element which identifies such a tight connection [20]. Moreover, in Husserl, this peculiar form of "identity" [20] between what is intended and what is in the world is an element of perception too.

As Crowell clearly points out, it is not so easy to think of an application of the fulfilment in perception, but it is possible [7]. Judgements are different from perception, and so they do not work in the same way. One is related to the truth of a sentence, and so it is general, symbolic and predicative while the other one is related to perception which is individual, non-symbolic and pre-predicative. However, without going into details on how this passage between the two fields is possible, we can just say the perception of an objects always comes in a sort of fulfilment of a previous "emptiness". The object has hidden aspects which are always expected but emptily indented. Therefore, when the subject perceives these hidden aspects, the expectations can be fulfilled or unfulfilled by the content of the object [13]. For this reason Husserl always thinks of perception as a "network" [17] of partially empty and partially fulfilled intentions, and he founds perception on this play between emptiness and fulfilment [3].

We can see how the fulfilment is related to the expectations the subject has towards some hidden aspects of the object. The fulfilment is produced by the identity of the object's content with these expectations [42]. Thus, from the simple fact every object has hidden faces and these hidden faces are related to some kind of expectations and their fulfilment, we can easily deduce that perception is founded on fulfilment. As far as we think of perception as an intentional act [31] of a subject directed towards the external object, we need to take into account also its possible fulfilment and unfulfilment as its founding parts.

[11] According to phenomenology, even if it does not take into account digital technologies, the origin of the object is part of the object's content and it is embedded in different horizons [9]. In Husserl's phenomenology objects carry aspects of their past story with themselves and these aspects are embedded in their content. For example, a piece of wood curved by a skilled artisan in a particular shape carries with itself relations to the instrument used to make it. The object carries its origin in itself and so also if it is created by a digital technology or not. Thus, the "realness" and the "digitalness" of the object are content and they can fulfil the intentional acts of the subject.

"fantasy" [18]. The reason is easy to understand. Phenomenology deals with perception, and so it is primary important to express a distinction between fictitious entities perceived in a fantasy or in a dream with what is perceived in the actual world. Therefore, it uses reality and fantasy in order to show this difference.

According to this usage, the "reality" of an object is related to the modality of perception, and it is identified by its "positional act" [28, 29]. When the object is a real object, the positional act is "active". When the object is fictitious, the positional act is "suspended" [19]. Therefore, this kind of "reality" is not part of the content of the object, but it is related to the way the subject perceives the object as actual or fictional.

In our case, we are not interested in the fictitiousness of the object, but we are related to the technologies used to generate it and to its "origins". For example, the pdf file of this document is "real" according to the phenomenological interpretation because it is not fictitious. However, it is not "real" according to our interpretation because it is generated and visualised by digital technologies.

Thanks to the fact the realness is a content, we can think of *riajuu* subjects as the ones fulfilling themselves with the realness of the "other". In the case the "other" is a digital being "who" is generated by a digital technology, the subjects do not fulfil their intentional act with "realness", but with "digitalness" and so they are not *riajuu*.

### 3.2 *Riajuu* and "Resistance"

Side by side with the fulfilment with reality of the subject's intentional acts, there is another important element which constitutes the *riajuuness* of the subject.

The idea of living the life in its realness is tightly related to the subjects' always connection to what is happening around them in the every day. In order to be fully living the life in its realness, subjects are supposed to be living in the "real world".

Even if this element is banal, it is important because it highlights the link to the everyday world the subjects need to have in order to be *riajuu*. In addition to the "realness" or "digitalness" of the content, there is something else which is related to the way subjects live together. *Riajuu* subjects need to live among others and to intertwine their activities with them. *Riajuu* subjects need to have a partner who is part of the everyday world. Thus, a subject living in its own "private world" cannot be *riajuu*. More specifically, both the partners must colive in the everyday world in order to be *riajuu*.

Phenomenology provides us tools to analyse this coexistence by highlighting some elements which found the relations in the everyday world.

The everyday world is given to the subjects with many different aspects. One of them is tightly related to the "resistance" it opposes. This "resistance" is not related to the physical resistance opposed to the actions of the subjects, but it is related to the co-living of many subjects in the same world. The world is a place where the actions of multiple subjects intertwine, and where the intentions of the single subject encounter the intentions of the others.

The world "resists" to the subject just because it manifests others' intentions which cannot be simply ignored by the subject. The world "resists" to the subject because it is the product of the actions of other people which are out of the subject's own power [14,33,35]. In order to have a relationship with the others the subject needs to co-act with them by "interlocking" [*ineinandergreifen*] their activities with the ones of the others [34, p.170],[12] and to face the "resistance" opposed by them [6, p.51].[13]

An "other" who is not part of the everyday world cannot be "resistant". For example, a virtual character generated in a virtual reality might have resistance within the digital world, but it has no resistance outside of it because it can be ignored and it does not call for interlocking activities with the subject. Thus, in addition to the different content of these "digital others", the term *riajuu* shows there are differences in the way they relate to the subjects when we look at the "resistance" opposed by them. An entity can be resistant to the subject. If so, it is part of the everyday world, and it is able to make the subject *riajuu*. However, an entity can also be not resistant. In this case, the entity is not part of the everyday world, and it does not provide *riajuuness* to the subject.

Summing up, the term *riajuu* focusses our attention on the possible differences in perceiving "real" and "digital others" for two main reasons:

- The content is different. Real objects fulfil the subject with "realness" and the digital ones with "digitalness".
- The way the two subjects relate is different. Real subjects are "resistant" to the others while the "digital" ones risk not to be.

The two elements highlights two different aspects. The first one is related to the origin of the "other", and so on how the subject perceives the other as digitally generated. The second one is related to the way the subjects relates to these entities, and so it is related to how these devices are designed.

In the next sections, we will show how digital technologies can be shaped in order to provide resistance to the subject and to make subjects partially riajuu.

## 4  Two Different Kinds of "Digital" Other

We have many ways of using digital technologies. These usages produce various digital objects with different aspects and potentialities. Therefore, different ways of designing and using digital technologies produce also different kinds of "digital other". We will study two main types of "digital other": the one in a virtual reality and the one in the everyday world.

---

[12] We are not interested in the other elements of intersubjectivity highlighted by Schütz [23] because we are not interested in intersubjectivity per se, but on how these "others" relate to the subjects. On the limits of Schützian philosophy applied to robotics see [22].

[13] We do not refer to Levinas because, even if he refers explicitly to the other as resistant, he also always think of the other as an ethical other: "Le visage se refuse à la possession, à mes pouvoirs" [24]. We do not want this kind of ethical aspects, but just the fact the others' actions are intertwined with the subject's ones.

## 4.1   The "Digital Other" in a Virtual Reality

A classical way of using computer technologies is to generate a digital world where subjects can immerse themselves. The never-ending improvement of the computing power of these digital machines allows to create a digital world ruled by strings of bit of information instead of the laws of Physics.

The ideal realisation of this attempt is the creation of a virtual reality where subjects can immerse themselves leaving the "mere" flash behind, and where they can free themselves in a digital "dream".[14] The subject is wrapped by devices which substitute the stimuli coming from the everyday world with the ones generated by the virtual world. For example, the head-mounted displays substitute the vision of the everyday world with the vision of the digital world.

In this immersion in a second different world, the possibility of "escaping" from the every day plays an important role. According to this use, computer devices are able to generate a different reality into which the subjects can immerse themselves. Therefore, it is not surprising to see many works analysing the tight connection between the idea of "escaping" from this world into a different one with the use of psychedelic drugs during the blooming of the Silicon Valley [30]. The reach of a "higher" or "different" reality is clear and evident in both the cases. The same word "cyberspace", which is broadly used to identify the space in these digital realities, was coined by William Gibson as a "consensual hallucination" [10]. The "only" difference between these two cases is in the way subjects reach it. In one case they assume some grams of psychoactive substances and in the other one they uses bits of information.

In this escape subjects becomes "free" from the real world and they are able to do what they want as far as they use the right program enabling them to do it.

In this case, the other the subject meets is a "digital other" created in this second digital world.

## 4.2   The "Digital Other" in the Everyday World

A new way of using computer technologies is to intertwine their activities in the everyday world. It is the opposite direction of creating a different world where subjects have to immerse themselves. According to this new way, digital activities cannot be easily confined in a second digital world because they are part of subjects' common practices and they are part of their real world.

The idea of a cyberspace and a virtual reality seems quite "surpassed" and the same Gibson, who was one of the creator of the term "cyberspace", is moving the opposite direction by talking of the "eruption" of the digital objects into our everyday world [11,12]. Our everyday world is being colonised by digital objects and, as Mark Weiser predicted [40], computers are literally becoming

---

[14] William Gibson in his book Neuromancer [10] showed how a hacker used to live in the digital world would look at his real body in a very different way of other ordinary people. Case, who is a hacker living in this futuristic cyberpunk world, clearly looks at his own "meaty" body as something imperfect and to be surpassed.

part of our surroundings without forcing the subject to immerse themselves into a second digital world. There is simply no other world where the subject should be immersed in because subjects are free to interact with the digital content in their every day.

In this case, the "digital other" is not created in a second world, but it is located in the subjects' everyday world.

Now that we have a clear idea of how there are two different usages of computer technologies, we can apply the term *riajuu* to them in order to understand how subjects perceives these "digital others" and how they relate to them.

### 4.3    *Riajuu* and the Digital Other in a Virtual Reality

As we saw, the classical way of using computer technologies is to produce a second world into which subjects have to immerse themselves. In this second digital world they can build also intimate relationships with other subjects and so something on which the term riajuu can work.

Both of the partners are perceiving each other in their digital bodies. Thus, according to our previous analysis, the perception of the "other" cannot provide the fulfilment of the "realness" required to be *riajuu* because their bodies are generated through digital technologies.

Moreover, this other is not only digital in its content. It is perceived as part of the virtual reality, and so it is not part of the everyday world by definition. Even if there is a connection between the subject in the everyday world and the avatar in the second digital world, the experiences made in this second world are experienced by the digital avatar and not by the body of the subject in the everyday world. It is the subject embodied in the virtual avatar who acts and interacts with the "digital other" encountered. Therefore, this "other" can be resistant only to the eyes of the digital avatar of the subject and not to the eyes of the subject's everyday body.

This digital other might be resistant to subjects when they are living in the virtual reality, but they are not "resistant" at all to the subjects in the real world.[15]

For these reasons, the otherness experienced in virtual reality do not provide riajuness to the user. The subject perceives the digital other as "digital" in its content. Moreover, this digital other is not resistant in the everyday world.

### 4.4    *Riajuu* and the Digital Other in the Everyday World

Instead of having a relationship with a digital other in a digital world, it is possible to have a relation with an other who/which is part of our same everyday world: another human person or a robot.

---

[15] We are not saying the experiences had in the virtual reality are "bodiless" [36], but just that they are experienced with the digital body and not with the everyday one. The actions of this "digital other" can be interlocked with the ones of the subject's avatar, but they are not interlocked with the ones of the body in the every day. Thus, this "digital other" cannot be resistant for the subject in the everyday world.

As we saw, this topic is rising many issues on possible effects and potentialities in the future. However, without going into speculations about futuristic technologies, there are already products that, even if without a human-like body, introduce an artificial intelligence in our world, such as the computer game *Love Plus* [ラブプラス].

*Love Plus* is a computer game created for *Nintendo DS* in which an artificial intelligence is designed to act as a girlfriend towards the user. This girl has the *Nintendo DS* as body, and, with it, "she" perceives and interacts with the subject by capturing the actions thanks to its sensors. The game makes the subject act towards the virtual girl by acting in the subject's everyday world in various ways.

- It makes the user spend real time to cuddle her when she is having a bad day
- It makes the user give her real gifts for her birthday or the St. Valentine's day
- It makes the user go in real vacations with her and booking hotel rooms in the facilities which are able to deal with such a digital customer [39]
- It makes the user kiss her digital "lips" with the subject's real physical ones by kissing the monitor[16]

According to our previous analysis this girl is "digital" because it is an artificial intelligence, and so it is created by a digital technology. The user clearly perceives it as a digital entity with a plastic body. Thus, the girl does not provide the "realness" in the content needed to make the subject *riajuu*. However, it is not clear what happens for the second element we highlighted: the "resistance" opposed to the subject.

The actions required by the game is completely different by the actions required by other computer games in a virtual world. *Love Plus* requires the subject to act in the real world as if the digital girl were real and physically present with the subject in the everyday world. The subject has to intertwine the everyday activities with the digital girl and her physical body.

In the virtual world the actions are encapsulated in a second digital world inhabited by avatars and so their relations are not part of the everyday world. The subjects are able to freely disconnect the digital world ending every relation in it. In the case of *Love Plus* we are moving in the exact opposite direction.

The game is not in a second digital world. Everything happens in the real world and subjects have to relate to the digital girl as if she were physically present because she has a real body. The lips of the girl the subject has to kiss are not the lips of an avatar, but they are part of the everyday world, even if they are made of the plastic of *Nintendo DS*.

We showed the "resistance" is founded on the intertwinement between the actions of different subjects. Subjects are not free to act as they want because there are always the intentions and the actions of the others to be taken into account and which resist them. A digital other in a virtual reality cannot have

---

[16] It is possible because there are sensors which detect such an action and so they can make the digital girl "feel" the first subject kiss.

this element because the intertwinement among the actions of the subjects is "merely" related to their digital bodies and so it is confined to the digital world. However, the digital girl produced by *Love Plus* calls for an intertwinement of the actions in the everyday world. Therefore, for some aspects, we need to think of "her" as "resistant" because the subjects' actions in the everyday world are intertwined with the actions of the digital girl. This tight intertwinement between common actions in the everyday world and the actions required by the digital girl is what makes her "resistant" to the subject.

Even if the content of the "other" is "digital", the way the subject relates to "her" is "real" because it is based on the resistance opposed by this "digital other". Thus, according to this element, the subject is *riajuu*.

The girl is digital, but everything else related to such a relationship is not.

## 5   Conclusions

We wanted to analyse if it is possible to have relationships between computer and human beings even when the "digital other" is manifestly not human. According to mediation theory, if it is possible, we need to consider these intimate relationships as elements which will re-shape how we develop relationships in general even among other human beings.

In the first part we showed how the term *riajuu* works and how it can be enframed in a phenomenological analysis. The "other" can be real or digital according to its content and to the fact it is able to oppose "resistance" to the subject.

In the second part we highlighted how two different ways of using computer technology can produce two different "digital others": one in a virtual reality and another one in the everyday world. Thanks to the word *riajuu* and a phenomenological analysis, we showed the difference in the relations of these two others with a human subject. The content is digital in both the cases, but the way subjects relate to the digital other changes. The digital other in the everyday world calls for an intertwinement between its actions and the actions of the subject in the everyday world. This co-action in the everyday world is what makes the "other" resistant. Thus this "digital other", even if it has a digital content, is perceived as "resistant" from the subject.

The way this "digital other" is designed shapes the relations it has with the subject, and so the digital content does not compromise the kind of relationship it is possible to have. Even if it is a digital being, and it is manifestly perceived as not human, it provides the subjects with "resistance" and this element is the basis for any intimate relationship. Thus, we can answer to our question on the possibility of developing feelings towards digital objects. It is possible to look directly in the lifeless plastic eye-bulbs of a machine knowing it is nothing else than plastic and circuits and still have feelings towards it according to a phenomenological analysis.

They are merely lifeless objects, but this is not enough to exclude them from our intimate life.

Maybe we will find ourselves asking "Do you want to marry me?" just to receive the answer "Oh dear, . . . it is late. I do need to charge my batteries. Can we talk tomorrow?"

**Acknowledgements.** The author is supported by the NWO VICI project "Theorizing Technological Mediation: toward an empirical-philosophical theory of technology" (grant number: 277-20-006).

# References

1. Amuda, Y.J., Tijani, I.B.: Ethical and legal implications of sex robot: An Islamic perspective. OIDA Int. J. Sustain. Dev. **03**(06), 19–28 (2012). http://www.oidaijsd.com/20138/159682/a/ethical-and-legal-implications-of-sex-robot-an-islamic-perspective
2. Benoist, J.: Fulfilment. In: Phenomenology as Grammar, pp. 77–96. Publications of the Austrian Ludwig Wittgenstein Society - New Series (N.S.), De Gruyter (2008)
3. Capili, A.D.: How do we 'See' that which is 'Invisible'? the stakes in husserl's account of perceiving the other. KRITIKE Online J. Philos. **7**(2), 1–18 (2013)
4. Cheok, A.D., Levy, D., Karunanayaka, K., Morisawa, Y.: Love and sex with robots. In: Nakatsu, R., Rauterberg, M., Ciancarini, P. (eds.) Handbook of Digital Games and Entertainment Technologies, pp. 833–858. Springer, Singapore (2017). https://doi.org/10.1007/978-981-4560-50-4_15
5. Coeckelbergh, M.: Humans, animals, and robots: a phenomenological approach to human-robot relations. Int. J. Soc. Robot. **3**(2), 197–204 (2011)
6. Costello, P.R.: Layers in Husserl's Phenomenology: On Meaning and Intersubjectivity. New studies in phenomenology and hermeneutics. University of Toronto Press, Toronto (2012)
7. Crowell, S.: Normativity and Phenomenology in Husserl and Heidegger. Cambridge University Press, Cambridge (2013)
8. Ferrari, F., Paladino, M.P., Jetten, J.: Blurring human-machine distinctions anthropomorphic appearance in social robots as a threat to human distinctiveness. Int. J. Soc. Robot. **8**(2), 1–16 (2016). https://doi.org/10.1007/s12369-016-0338-y
9. Geniusas, S.: Origins of the Horizon in Husserl's Phenomenology. Contributions to Phenomenology, vol. 67. Springer, London (2012)
10. Gibson, W.: Neuromancer. HarperCollins, London (1984)
11. Gibson, W.: Spook Country. G. P. Putnam's Sons Viking Press, New York (2007)
12. Gibson, W.: Google's Earth. The New York Times (2010). http://www.nytimes.com/2010/09/01/opinion/01gibson.html?_r=0
13. Gyllenhammer, P.: On fulfillment: uncovering the possibility of a new objective insight. Auslegung J. Philos. **24**(2), 185–198 (2001)
14. Hall, J.R.: Alfred Schutz, his critics, and applied phenomenology. Philos. Soc. Criticism **4**(3), 265–279 (1977). http://psc.sagepub.com/content/4/3/265.short
15. Hauskeller, M.: Sex and the Posthuman Condition. Palgrave Macmillan, Palgrave pivot (2014)
16. Hoffman, G., Birnbaum, G.E., Vanunu, K., Sass, O., Reis, H.T.: Robot responsiveness to human disclosure affects social impression and appeal. In: Proceedings of the 2014 ACM/IEEE International Conference on Human-robot Interaction, HRI 2014, pp. 1–8. ACM, New York (2014). http://doi.acm.org/10.1145/2559636.2559660

17. Husserl, E.: Analysen zur passiven Synthesis aus Vorlesungs- und Forschungsman-uskripten, 1918–1926, Husserliana, vol. XI. Martinus Nijhoff, Den Haag (1966)
18. Husserl, E.: Zur Phänomenologie der Intersubjektivität. Texte aus dem Nachlass. Erster Teil. 1905–1920, Husserliana, vol. XIII. Martinus Nijhoff, Den Haag (1973)
19. Husserl, E.: Phantasie, Bildbewußtsein, Erinnerung. Husserliana, vol. XXIII. Springer, Heidelberg (1980)
20. Husserl, E.: Logische Untersuchungen. Zweiter Band, Erster Teil, Husserliana, vol. XIX/1. Nijhoff/Kluwer, Den Haag (1984)
21. Kahn Jr., P.H., Ruckert, J.H., Kanda, T., Ishiguro, H., Reichert, A., Gary, H., Shen, S.: Psychological intimacy with robots? using interaction patterns to uncover depth of relation. In: Proceedings of the 5th ACM/IEEE International Conference on Human-robot Interaction, HRI 2010, pp. 123–124. IEEE Press, Piscataway (2010). http://dl.acm.org/citation.cfm?id=1734454.1734503
22. Böhle, K., Pfadenhauer, M.: Of social robots and artificial companions. Contributions from the social sciences. Sci. Technol. Innov. Stud. 10(1), 199 (2013)
23. León, F., Zahavi, D.: Phenomenology of experiential sharing: The contribution of Schutz and Walther. In: Salice, A., Schmid, H.B. (eds.) The Phenomenological Approach to Social Reality. SPS, vol. 6, pp. 219–234. Springer, Cham (2016). https://doi.org/10.1007/978-3-319-27692-2_10
24. Levinas, E.: Totalité et infini: essai sur l'extériorité. LGF (1990)
25. Levy, D.: Robot prostitutes as alternatives to human sex workers. In: Proceedings of the IEEE-RAS International Conference on Robotics (2009)
26. Levy, D.: Love and sex with robots: The evolution of human-robot relationships. Harper Collins (2007)
27. Levy, D.: The ethical treatment of artificially conscious robots. Int. J. Soc. Robot. 1(3), 209–216 (2009). http://dx.doi.org/10.1007/s12369-009-0022-6
28. Liberati, N.: Improving the embodiment relations by means of phenomenological analysis on the "reality" of ARs. In: 2013 IEEE International Symposium on Mixed and Augmented Reality - Arts, Media, and Humanities (ISMAR-AMH), pp. 13–17 (2013)
29. Lotz, C.: Depiction and plastic perception. A critique of Husserl's theory of picture consciousness. Cont. Philos. Rev. 40(2), 171–185 (2007)
30. Markoff, J.: What the Dormouse Said: How the 60s Counterculture Shaped the Personal Computer. Viking Adult, New York (2005)
31. McIntyre, R., Smith, D.W.: Theory of intentionality. In: Mohanty, J.N., McKenna, W.R. (eds.) Husserl's Phenomenology, pp. 147–179. Center for Advanced Research in Phenomenology and University Press of America (1989)
32. Samani, H.A., Parsani, R., Rodriguez, L.T., Saadatian, E., Dissanayake, K.H., Cheok, A.D.: Kissenger: design of a kiss transmission device. In: Proceedings of the Designing Interactive Systems Conference, DIS 2012, pp. 48–57. ACM, New York (2012). http://doi.acm.org/10.1145/2317956.2317965
33. Schütz, A.: Collected Papers: The Problem of Social Reality. Phaenomenologica, vol. 11. Martinus Nijhoff, The Hague (1962)
34. Schütz, A.: The Phenomenology of the Social World. Northwestern University Press, Evanston (1967)
35. Schütz, A.: Collected Papers III: Studies in Phenomenological Philosophy. Phaenomenologica, vol. 22. Martinus Nijhoff, The Hague (1970)
36. Scriven, P.: A phenomenology of the "other" in computer game worlds. Games Cult. 1–18 (2015)
37. Sullins, J.P.: Robots, love, and sex: the ethics of building a love machine. IEEE Trans. Affect. Comput. 3(4), 398–409 (2012)

38. Verbeek, P.P.: Beyond interaction: a short introduction to mediation theory. Interactions **XXII**(3), 26–31 (2015). http://interactions.acm.org/archive/view/may-june-2015/beyond-interaction
39. Wakabaiyashi, D.: Only in Japan, real men go to a hotel with virtual girlfriends. Wall Street J. (2010). https://www.wsj.com/articles/SB10001424052748703632304575451414209658940
40. Weiser, M.: The computer for the 21st century. Sci. Am. **265**(3), 66–75 (1991). http://www.ubiq.com/hypertext/weiser/SciAmDraft3.html
41. Yeoman, I., Mars, M.: Robots, men and sex tourism. Futures **44**(4), 365–371 (2012)
42. Yoshimi, J.: Husserlian Phenomenology: A Unifying Interpretation. Springer, Heidelberg (2016)

# Virtual Sex: Good, Bad or Ugly?

Hoshang Kolivand[1]([✉]), Abdoulvahab Ehsani Rad[2], and David Tully[1]

[1] Department of Computer Science, Liverpool John Moores University,
Liverpool L3 3AF, UK
H.Kolivand@ljmu.ac.uk
[2] Department of Electrical and Computer Engineering, Shahrood Branch,
Islamic Azad University, Shahrood, Iran

**Abstract.** Computers have created a new world which enables people to have different experiences that may not be available or appropriate to have in the real world. Sexual activities are also a part this. Nowadays, sex relationships between humans and robots are set to become commonplace. The advances of new technologies need to be taken into account for new progress. It is not uncommon from the first neurophysiological evidence of humans' ability to empathise with robots. Sex robots are going to be more focused in robotic industry in case of how they look and what rolls that can play. This study attempts to critically review the characters and characteristics of cutting edge ideas of virtual sex in real and virtual environments to provide researchers with backgrounds on what is going on in the future of sexual human needs. We have tried to find out advances, advantages and disadvantages sex with robots and virtual objects in different aspects. Most importantly, in this investigation we tried to find appropriate answers for some of the highlighted questions against virtual sex.

## 1 Introduction

Undoubtedly, the favor of robots' developments cannot be connivance in different parts of humans' life [1,2] especially in dangerous and dirty assignments or even in teaching and learning religion [3,4]. The history of robots goes back to the middle ages when they were being used for impressing peasant worshippers to believe almighty power [5]. Currently, many different tasks are recorded which are not possible to be carried out without the use of robots. Sex robot (sexbot) [6] is one of the advances that in some circumstances may be considered to be included in these impossible things. However, many people do not want to think on these new aspects due to traditional and religious believes.

Some people, especially religious people, believe that sex is different from other needs. Some others say sex is the same type of need as food, water, or shelter; a basic human need and desire. For instance, Loebner [7] said: "I pay for sex because that is the only way I can get sex. I am not ashamed of paying for sex. I pay for food. I pay for clothing. I pay for shelter. Why should I not also pay for sex? Paying for sex does not diminish the pleasure I derive from it".

© Springer International Publishing AG, part of Springer Nature 2018
A. D. Cheok and D. Levy (Eds.): LSR 2017, LNCS 10715, pp. 26–36, 2018.
https://doi.org/10.1007/978-3-319-76369-9_3

Asimov [8] in the book of "I, Robot", discussed about the relationship between human and robots. The book is almost a fiction book and Asimov was not sure whether the trends would happen or not. Sex robot was predicted before the commercial release to the general public. In Veronica 2030, a movie that produced in 1999, a female robot is designed to be used for sexual pleasure for human. The robot is named Julia and when she came back from 2030 to 1998, she was converted to a lingerie model [9].

Yeoman and Mars [9] engaged sex with tourism. They believe there is a direct relationship between tourism, men, and sex. They highlighted some countries and cities such as Thailand, China, Las Vegas, and Amsterdam to deal with the most sexual experiences in 2030 [10]. Yeoman showed evident that when people travel, they will be engaged with love, romance, and sex.

The subject of sex with robots is discussed for more than a decade [9, 11–13]. Currently many companies are producing different types of humanlike robots for the target of sex [14]. The proven evident of Christensen [15] who said that people will have sex with robot in the coming 5 years. However, we need to know that it is not only because of the ability of computer that can create realistic virtual sex, it is because of what human like these days. The lifestyle leads some humans to go through with this technology. A simple comparison between different lifestyles in Japan and Malaysia will reveal that a small number of people in Malaysia like virtual sex, while it is a high demand of Japanese industry. Sherry Turkle, in the book of "The Second Self" [16] pointed that "it is not about what the computer will be like in the future, it is what we will be like".

"Love with robots will be as normal as love with other humans" said Levy [11,17]. This relationship with robots offers a practical testing to the uncomfortable users to have experience before progressing to humand-to-human relationship. This is not the highlighted point as there are many other benefits; such as controlling different types of diseases that we are currently facing which are predicted to increase in the future.

Levy [11] is the father of this idea that love and sex with robots will be usual in some coming years. Levy presented ten factors that are the source of love and sex. Then he tried to explore each in detail and highlight the contribution of robots in duplicating these feelings and emotions exactly in the manner that users like. He also answered the people who believe that this idea is kinky and is not going to happen in future. He replied to them, it is already in hands that some people have sex with inanimate or semi-animate devices. We should agree with Levy these days as many people are requesting sex robots now. It may be hard to be realized by some people that, even in 2001, in US 12.5 million vibrators were sold. It was more than 10 million only for women in 2007 while in 2008 more than 50 million women purchased sexual devices in US [12,18] and also based on a report by Pearson [19] UK market is over 1 bn in 2015 [19,20]. 6% increasing yearly sex toy industry [19] is another evident to emphasis Levy idea. Levy focused on the final stage that if robots can cover all human desired as well as expressing the feeling like the one that humans have, or maybe better, the societies' laws must accept this entity and people can freely take the robot spouse in the society. This is the place that Levy emphasis on his metaphysical statement.

Sullins [13] does not agree with Levy [12] and censured that, in the meantime, we must consider that even if we accept that the growing use of computer technology in everyday life increases exponentially and with the use of sex robots is increasing dramatically, we must admit that the love will not be understood by computers, even if significant progress is made in Artificial Intelligence (AI). Choi [21] gave some reasons such as similarities, knowledge, and programmability that why people fall in love. Furthermore, Turner mentioned that loving by another person is the main reason [22]. It needs to be mentioned that, as evidenced by many politics and societies, many people can not accept the right of Homosexual, so how can they accept a marriage of human with robots. Sullins expected that many people and societies especially religious people will be against this idea. There is evidence which is presented by Amuda and Tijani [23] which need to be discussed in this study too.

Amuda and Tijani [23] presented many religious laws against the use of a sexbot. They believe that this technology will not be accepted by any of the religious people as the showed evident suggests. Underestimating sexbot marriage is out of people minds especially for religious people but they mentioned that if sexbot is inevitable in the case of capability of moral reasoning by robots, religious traditions should have to take some new religious rules into account but they refused to present the regulations, said McBride [3]. McBride's belief has a capability to be discussed as he explored that if robots are not secure of the sin of fornication, religious people will be agreed to marry robots. McBride believes that the future of robots with capability of moral reasoning and android behavior will be engaged not only in all societies but also in religious communities too. He also proposed some regulations for robots to be used for marriage. For instance, baptism of robots before marriage in factory of even undergo at a church is one of the solutions. He definitely agrees with presenting new regulations but religious communities believe that religious regulations can be defined only by God (Islamic Believe). In this regard Arkin [24] said that illegality of something does not mean no body will try it. He also strongly agreed that in 2050 marriage with robots would be usual. Based on the freedom thinking and previous background of Massachusetts people who are more liberal, Levy predicted that Massachusetts will be the first place that will marry with robots [25]. Producing a human-like robotic head which is named Kismet with many advances to be humanoid in MIT Lab in Massachusetts supercharges Arkin idea [26]. Pearson [19] is one of the futurologists who predicted that in 2030 the majority of people will have some sort of virtual sex.

According to a study of Nicholas Epley in US [27], during anthropomorphise something, we start giving value and worthy of moral care to the subjects. Feeling Empathy and freethinking are the correspondence outcome of this anthropomorphise. According to another research study from the same researcher [28] anthropomorphise around the world, has some advantages, especially for those who are alone, to find the social connection. In this regard, Levy [25] introduces some other benefits of sex robots which can be used by shy people which find it difficult for them to have a relationship with a human or for who have unpleasant personality or psychological problems. "Lars and the Real Girl", is a movie produced in 2007 which shows that Lars falls in love with Bianca which was an accidentally purchased doll. Craig Gillespie the director of the movie shows that how a doll can help the loneliness and shyness of Lars [29]. Although the movie was not successful in commercialisation, it nominated for the Academy Award for Best Original Screenplay. The main reason behind unsuccessfulness of the movie was the mindset of people which discourage others, watching the movie due to not only religious background but also society ethical mentalities against the idea of falling in love with a doll.

A sexual relationship between human and robots is one of the top challenging subjects to be accepted by society. It is not the first time that humans have fallen in love with something else which society deems inappropriate. In the positive aspect, falling in love with technology has its own advantages especially when the AI is involved. In this case the partner can learn from the user and mimics whatever he/she likes. The computer can listen to the user and react in a way that makes the user happy. There is no argument except the time that user likes to have it. Undoubtedly marital bliss will be achieved. The user has freedom to act without worry about any conditional affection. Last but not least is for those who are uncomfortable in sexual relationship to have a partner, or to have a partner that is desired. In the negative aspect, unhappiness of God may be enough to reject having a virtual partner. However, there are many reasons behind this idea. For instance, the weakening of family and social relationships on the one hand and the unfounded love relationships on the other.

## 2   Advances in Sexbot

Pepper robots [30] are one of the successful humanlike robots which can read human emotions and can live with human but one of the rules regarding to these kinds of robots is that there is no sex for Pepper robots and any indecent act of sexual purpose will break the ownership contract.

A sex psychologist, Dr Helen Driscoll said that intimate relationship between humans and robots due to spending much time on virtual realities such as games and social media might even improve mental health too [31]. This is one of the idea which most of the people are not agreed upon [32].

Many people are empathising with humanoid robots in the regular manner that they may empathise with the real partners. Scientists such as [13,33] believe that this empathy requires prosocial behaviors which must be prosocial by both humans and robots. Implication of human feelings in robots is another concern which AI will address this problem but no religion believe that. Now some researchers believe that AI sex robots or dolls could contribute in the sexual relationship between opposite sex or same sex, while some others believe that it is not true [34].

Hanson Robotics and Hiroshi Ishiguro Laboratories are two of the highlighted companies and laboratories developing humanoid robots [35]. Hanson [36] developed a realistic robot called Sophia who has cameras in her eyes and using a specific algorithm which makes accurate eye contact and recognise an individual person following its face. A lovely conversation between users and Sophia is also one of the interesting part of this research. Another feature is related to the realistic skin and emotions. Patented silicon is used to create a flexible and humanlike skin, which can emulate more than 62 facial expressions. Finally, voice recognition technology is also taken into consideration to be able to speak. These all are respectable in term of advances in technology but they are still lack the loving from others and the survival of the generation of humanity.

One of the top most features that sex robots are aiming to use is for AI to be able to mimic and even improving their sexual experience which can be preferable compare to the real partners [31].

Lovotic is presented by [37] which refers to the research of love between human and robots. The first stage was deep understanding of humans' physics, emotion and physiology to be applied on robots. Moreover, reacting like a human being was also taken into consideration. Artificial Endocrine System, Affective State Transition and Probabilistic Love Assembly are the new consideration of Artificial Intelligence on Lovotic.

The progress of delivering tactile components of virtual sex through Internet is somehow remarkable, but an accurate and realistic delivering components of different parts of body for both men and women is hardly under investigation. Definitely, it will not take much time that humans will be able to touch and have the pleasure with a partner from long-distance through the Internet, indistinguishable with face to face interactions. However, much research have been developed in this regard.

## 3   Sex Dolls

The most advanced country in sex doll is Japan [9]. Japan and South Korea are the most highlighted countries which rent-a-doll market has blown the Human Sex Worker market wide open. This is because of their lifestyle which has been revealed along the history. No restricted religion in this countries may be the other reason which is going to happen in many other countries in near future.

The first handcraft sex doll made of silicon was created by McMullen and sold out with $3,500 in 1997. It was accurate and equipped with fully skeleton and attractions. The doll was shown in more than 20 TV shows in 2014.

Roxxxy [38] was the first sex robot [33] which was presented to the world in 2010 in AVN Adult Entertainment Expo in Las Vegas but with lack of ability to think. "She can't vacuum, she can't cook, but she can do almost anything else, if you know what I mean," Hines [39]. She could hear, speak, sleep and even feels touches using advances of AI.

Marketing sex [40] is a new industry which many companies investing huge amount of money on it. Child sex dolls are also another type of dolls which aims for pedophiles. A Japanese company named Trottla is producing these kind of dolls. Many people are against this technology [41,42] and complained to the Japan government to prohibit the production and sale of these artefacts as a serious issue. This is while the company claims that it is for therapeutic purposes and we are helping people who are engaged with pedophiles, while there is no therapeutic programme with the product, said Richardson [43].

Fembots [44] is known as a "call girl" service, which was presented by a Japanese company to reduce the cost having a partner compared with a real human. This company was very successful, in its own target market, which in one month could cover the cost of the company. Huge commercial success of Malebots shows the using of robots for women was no less than men. Here, we should realize where the world is going to be anchored. It is while many socialist people believe that women have sex for love but men may for pleasure [9,45]. The gap between these ideas are going to be wider and wider. Should people change their mindset or should technology stop going the wrong way? This is a causal question we asked among 80 Malaysian students and find that 100% agree to not use technology in this way. It is while this question is answered with 64% positive among international students in Malaysia. The results may also reflect the lifestyle of different nationalities in a same country.

## 4  Hiring Sex Dolls

It is normal for any production in the early generation to be quite high in cost. In these cases hiring is usual. The same goes to the very high cost of the early generation of sex dolls [46]. People in Japan prefer to rent dolls instead of purchase due to economy issues. Alice, Ai, Mayu and Tina were some of the famous dolls who were successful in the sex doll hiring market. Membership of a sex doll club is also taken into account [47,48].

The Japanese are not the only people looking for sex dolls and renting of them. Now many other people accepted the sex dolls and rental ones too. For instance, Siumi Le Chic and Mistress Luna are available in London [49] with the price of one month living cost per hour.

## 5  Virtual Sex

Virtual Reality is currently a very widespread technology in different fields [50]. Virtual reality is part of everyday life now. It can be imagined a day not so distant in the future, with courtesy of virtual reality in any single part of daily life. Sex is also a pleasure which is certain parts of the human life and VR are now trying to cover this [51]. A rapid increase of Augmented Reality technology [52,53] addresses some demands of people in this regard too.

Tenga [54] a Japanese company produced a Mixed Reality haptic device equipped with an Oculus device to generate a suit sex device to have an experience on a sexual game called "Sexy Beach". Some sensors in different parts of body make the user impulse during the usage time.

"Second Life" is an online game, which allows users to have virtual sex with any other users freely. It was developed by Linden Lab [55] in 2003. As the game is open source the quality and quantity of the game is increasing by users [56].

# 6   Good, Bad or Ugly?

Currently, hiring storages for bearing children is one of the advancements of having technology partners. One of the future needs is having children between two same sex lovers using new technologies. Offering practical testing and having the pleasure with virtual humans for those who are not comfortable to have a relationship with a real partner, may be counted as one of the other advantages of virtual sex. Of course, virtual sex for pedophiles reduces the crime, which happens by psychiatric disordered people. This may also be good for adultery and self-motivated (masturbation), which causes different types of diseases that currently we are facing and predicted to increase in the future. These are some of the positive aspects of using technology for sexual desires.

The recent developments in new technology adds a new tier on the cyber relationships [57]. Some sex doll producer companies believe that sex dolls help people who have sexual problems to prevent them doing crimes. For example, Trottla, which produce child-like dolls, claims that these types of dolls are for helping pedophiles and consequently reduce the crime that we face with these type of people.

Buying sex is due to many reasons such as lifestyles, demographics, and other motivations. It is not directly to the restriction of the governments. In South Africa, Sweden, Afghanistan, India and so on, the highest rate of crime is the crime of rape [58].

Not only religion abandons sex with non-humans, but also there are many societies who are also do not agree with sex and marriage with non-humans. This is while many psychologists and communities are agreed with a mixed bag for humanity using sexbots. Arkin [25] asked that do you think if pedophiles are possible to have sex with child-robots, they will go to a real child? Regarding to this matter, we can refer to Brey [59] discussion who reviewed Levy [60] argument against virtual child porn does not mean that it harms children indirectly, but it may ultimately harm women who suffer from inequality eroticize in sexual relationships, while Sandin [61] with an empirical support argued that virtual child porn is directly against children and it is outlawed. Arkin believes that this technology will reduce the sexual criminal severely. Levy [25] also said that human prostitution will be reduced by keeping robots for sex, while Levy himself revealed that, of course sex with robots may increase the jealousness in families. Levy added something that need to be judged by the readers of this article. He said that, who knows! maybe in future instead women saying, Darling I have a headache, not tonight. They will say Darling I have a headache please use your robot!

Brown et al. [62] based on a deep study reveal that using new technology directly effects adolescents to prevent different types of diseases and problems such as STDs, HIV, and pregnancy. Teens can learn how to face with real opposite sex and the sexual information sharing is functional and beneficial [63]. Reducing risky sexual behaviors is another advantage that can be taken into consideration [64].

On the other side, one of the issues that currently many different societies faced to, are the negative rate growth of population. The long-distance-relationship through Internet or even virtual sex is one of the highlighted reasons caused this issue. Human beings are vulnerable, whose survival depends on the activities that must be done to survive for themselves and their generations. Obviously there are different activities in human life, which some of them are easy and some are difficult. An example of easy activity can be refer to breathing and heart beating which there is no worries for them in an ordinary life. Other activities could be sometime difficult such as to get food, providing a place to live and staying free from cold and heat. One of these vital activities is the choice of spouse, the formation of a family and the birth of a child that takes place in the form of marriage. On the one hand, the need for a spouse and the pleasure of communicating with him/her. Other factors that make a person aware of all of the difficulties of marriage, is thinking of forming a family to love those pleasures and respond to the innate needs of a spouse. Children love to be loved and all these are for the human race to not be extinct [65].

Therefore, in confronting every need and pleasure that arises from the nature of men or women, one has to be confirmed is the priority, not only the satisfaction and enjoyment of the purpose. We eat foods, fruits and vegetables; but they are a prelude to being healthy not only to enjoy. Ignoring this matter does not make it possible for humans to meet the innate needs and enjoy the way to achieve the goal but not at any cost. Various sexual relations that are developed and promoted beyond the legal limits, are all in one common principle, and that is the central pleasure, disregard of the purpose of this innate need.

These are some reasons that religions are against technologies to be used in these directions. It is permissible and successful to achieve prosperity in the form of satisfying the innate needs only within the limits of what religion specifies or does not prohibit, but outside of this framework, in addition to the destructive effects of individual, they are forbidden in many societies.

Tabatabai [65] states that, we see that all peoples and nations at all ages have read this act as ugly and prostitute, in order to understand that this practice leads to the corruption of family, and the interruption of human generation due to lack of affection and the love is not reciprocated.

Love is a sacred concept and love for the family brings admiration from others, while love with robot is free from this praise. The family is one of the masterpieces of nature in which it is a bridge to the past and a bridge to the future. A home with a loyal couple is a perfect setting in which children can be raised in love and justice, where children's spiritual and physical needs can be met perfectly. Lack of this opportunity definitely effects on the new generations and cannot be addressed by new technology.

What is needed to be deeply thought of is that "And of His signs is that He created for you mates from among yourselves, so that you may find tranquility in them; and He planted love and compassion between you. In this, are signs for people who reflect" [66]. As mentioned earlier, love will not be understood by computers, even with significant progress with AI as love is beyond the definition.

Love is a concept, which is not definable by humans, let alone simulating of that. The literature behind love, spouse and friendship is literally significant which has not been taken into consideration in any of the presented tools.

## 7   Conclusion

Technology is growing dramatically and it is normally in the direction of human help. As can be seen on the progress of robots technology, it is not so far that they will fulfill almost all human's needs in future. Virtual sex and sex with robots will not be an issue in developed countries as they have accepted many other laws which are contradicted with religious laws.

In this paper we have tried to discuss the cutting edge research and most of the advances in virtual sex. Limitations of them which closely are matched with the idea behind religious people are also discussed. Based on our investigation, there is no doubt that producing sexual toys, dolls and virtual reality is increasing dramatically. But no answer for loving by others, interruption of human generation and social harms can be figured out yet.

## References

1. Wasen, K.: Replacement of highly educated surgical assistants by robot technology in working life: paradigm shift in the service sector. Int. J. Soc. Robot. **2**(4), 431–438 (2010)
2. Oborn, E., Barrett, M., Darzi, A.: Robots and service innovation in health care. J. Health Serv. Res. Policy **16**(1), 46–50 (2011)
3. McBride, J.: The advent of postmodern robotic technoreligiosity. J. Eval. Technol. **25**(2), 25–38 (2015)
4. Coeckelbergh, M.: The spirit in the network: models for spirituality in a technological culture. Zygon® **45**(4), 957–978 (2010)
5. Hagis, C.: History of robots (2003)
6. Driscoll, H.: Will 2016 be the year of the 'sexbot'? (2016)
7. Loebner, H.: Being a john. In: Elias, J., Bullough, V., Elias, V., Brewer, G. (eds.) Prostitution: On Whores, Hustlers, and Johns (1998)
8. Asimov, I.: I, robot (2004)
9. Yeoman, I., Mars, M.: Robots, men and sex tourism. Futures **44**(4), 365–371 (2012)
10. Yeoman, I.: Tomorrow's Tourist: Scenarios & Trends. Routledge, London (2009)
11. Levy, D.: Love and Sex with Robots: The Evolution of Human-Robot Relationships. Harper Collins, New York (2007)
12. Levy, D.: A history of machines with sexual functions: past, present and robot. In: EURON Workshop on Roboethics, Genoa (2006)
13. Sullins, J.P.: Robots, love, and sex: the ethics of building a love machine. IEEE Trans. Affect. Comput. **3**(4), 398–409 (2012)
14. SEXYBOTS: Coolest robots to have sex with today [nsfw] (2016)
15. Christensen, H.: Trust Me I'm A Robot. The Economist, June 8th 2006 (2006)
16. Turkle, S.: The Second Self: Computers and the Human Spirit. MIT Press, Cambridge (2005)

17. Hinds-Addow, S.: Love with robots will be as normal as love with other humans (2014)
18. Maines, R.: Love+sex with robots: the evolution of human-robot relationships (Levy, D.; 2007) [book review]. IEEE Technol. Soc. Mag. **27**(4), 10–12 (2008)
19. Pearson, I.: By 2050, human-on-robot sex will be more common than human-on-human sex, says report (2016)
20. Scheutz, M., Arnold, T.: Are we ready for sex robots? In: The Eleventh ACM/IEEE International Conference on Human Robot Interaction, pp. 351–358. IEEE Press (2016)
21. Charles, Q.C.: Forecast: Sex and marriage with robots by 2050 (2017)
22. Yulianto, B., et al.: Philosophy of information technology: sex robot and its ethical issues. Int. J. Soc. Ecol. Sustain. Dev. (IJSESD) **6**(4), 67–76 (2015)
23. Amuda, Y.J., Tijani, I.B.: Ethical and legal implications of sex robot: an islamic perspective. OIDA Int. J. Sustain. Dev. **3**(06), 19–28 (2012)
24. Brooks, A.G., Arkin, R.C.: Behavioral overlays for non-verbal communication expression on a humanoid robot. Auton. Robots **22**(1), 55–74 (2007)
25. LiveScience: Forecast: Sex and marriage with robots by 2050 (2016)
26. Forst, A.: Deus ex machina. n.d. groks science radio show and podcast (2015)
27. Epley, N., Waytz, A., Cacioppo, J.T.: On seeing human: a three-factor theory of anthropomorphism. Psychol. Rev. **114**(4), 864 (2007)
28. Epley, N., Akalis, S., Waytz, A., Cacioppo, J.T.: Creating social connection through inferential reproduction loneliness and perceived agency in gadgets, gods, and grey-hounds. Psychol. Sci. **19**(2), 114–120 (2008)
29. Gillespie, C.: Lars and the real girl (2007). Last access 2016
30. Pepper Robot: Paper robot (2017). https://www.ald.softbankrobotics.com/en/robots/pepper
31. SEXBOT: Could fall in love with robots? (2017)
32. Kolivand, M., Kolivand, H.: Virtual child pornography and utilitarianism. Int. J. Inf. Technol. Comput. Sci. (IJITCS) **19**(2), 41–50 (2015)
33. Lin, P., Abney, K., Bekey, G.: Robot ethics: mapping the issues for a mechanized world. Artif. Intell. **175**(5), 942–949 (2011)
34. Gee, T.J.: Why female sex robots are more dangerous than you think (2017)
35. Ishiguro, H.: Hiroshi ishiguro laboratories (2017)
36. Hanson, D.: Sophia (2017). http://www.hansonrobotics.com/robot/sophia/
37. Samani, H.A.: Lovotics: Loving Robots. LAP LAMBERT Academic Publishing, Saarbrücken (2012)
38. Fulbright, Y., Roxxxy, M.: The 'woman' of your dreams (2016)
39. Hines, D.: Roxxxy, the world's first life-size robot girlfriend (2016)
40. Brents, B.G., Hausbeck, K.: Marketing sex: us legal brothels and late capitalist consumption. Sexualities **10**(4), 425–439 (2007)
41. Richardson, K.: Statement on the production of child sex dolls (2016)
42. Richardson, K.: Campaign against sex robots (2016)
43. Richardson, K.: Child sex dolls are linked to child abuse as they 'become proxy for paedophiles' says expert (2017)
44. Velez, M.: Current and Future Relationships Between Robots and Humans. Ph.D. thesis, University of St. Thomas (2015)
45. DeLamater, J.D.: The social control of human sexuality (1989)
46. Levy, D., Loebner, H.: Robot prostitutes as alternatives to human sex workers (2007)
47. Colmenares, A.: Rent a sex doll in japan (2007). Last access 2016

48. Gakuran, M.: Love doll rental in Japan (2009). Last access 2016
49. Chic, S.L.: Siumi le chic London love sex real doll (2016)
50. Kolivand, H., Hasan Zakaria, A., Sunar, M.S.: Shadow generation in mixed reality: a comprehensive survey. IETE Techn. Rev. **32**(1), 3–15 (2015)
51. Blitz, M.J.: Freedom of 3d thought: the first amendment in virtual reality, the. Cardozo L. Rev. **30**, 1141 (2008)
52. Kolivand, H., Sunar, M.S.: Covering photo-realistic properties of outdoor components with the effects of sky color in mixed reality. Multimedia Tools Appl. **72**(3), 2143–2162 (2014)
53. Kolivand, H., Sunar, M.S.: Realistic real-time outdoor rendering in augmented reality. PloS One **9**(9), e108334 (2014)
54. Kinstlinger, N.: Virtual reality sex suits are a thing now and don't pretend you're not curious (2016)
55. Lindenlab: Create virtual experiences (2016)
56. Craft, A.J.: Love 2.0: a quantitative exploration of sex and relationships in the virtual world second life. Arch. Sex. Behav. **41**(4), 939–947 (2012)
57. Wohn, D.Y.: 3D virtual world creates new genre of cyber sex. In: Proceedings of IADIS International Conference: ICT, Society and Human Beings (2009)
58. Wikipedia: Rape statistics (2016)
59. Brey, P.: Virtual reality and computer simulation. In: The Handbook of Information and Computer Ethics, p. 361 (2008)
60. Levy, N.: Virtual child pornography: the eroticization of inequality. Ethics Inf. Technol. **4**(4), 319–323 (2002)
61. Sandin, P.: Virtual child pornography and utilitarianism. J. Inf. Commun. Ethics Soc. **2**(4), 217–223 (2004)
62. Brown, D., Sarah, K.: Sex, sexuality, sexting, and sex ed. Integr. Res. Serv. **76**, 12–17 (2009)
63. Subrahmanyam, K., Greenfield, P.M., Tynes, B.: Constructing sexuality and identity in an online teen chat room. J. Appl. Dev. Psychol. **25**(6), 651–666 (2004)
64. Read, S.J., Miller, L.C., Appleby, P.R., Nwosu, M.E., Reynaldo, S., Lauren, A., Putcha, A.: Socially optimized learning in a virtual environment: Reducing risky sexual behavior among men who have sex with men. Hum. Commun. Res. **32**(1), 1–34 (2006)
65. Allameh-Al-Tabatabai, S.Mu.: Tafsir al mizan (2017)
66. Almighty: Quran. Verse (30:21), ar-Rum 30:21

# Posthuman Desire in Robotics and Science Fiction

Sophie Wennerscheid[✉]

Ghent University, 9000 Ghent, Belgium
sophie.wennerscheid@ugent.be

**Abstract.** This article explores how human-posthuman intimate relationships are thematized in both robotics and in science fiction film, literature and robotic art. While on the one hand many engineers and computer scientists are working hard, albeit in an altogether affirmative way, toward the technological development of anthropomorphic robots which are capable of providing social assistance, emotional support and sexual pleasure, aesthetic representations of intimacy between man and machine give us on the other hand a more nuanced and critical picture of possible future forms of desire. However, these fictional works are themselves very often complicit with the use of familiar dualistic paradigms as male-female or self-other.

Drawing on Deleuze and Guattari's ideas of 'becoming-other,' scholars in critical posthumanism counterpose to this as an essentially traditional approach a nondualist reconceptualization of human beings and of the technological other, a reconceiving which is centered on 'encounters of alterity' and 'unnatural alliances.' The aim of this article is to expand on and to further develop these theories into what can be called a theory of 'new networks of desire.' According to this network idea, romantic entanglements between man and machine can better be seen as a specific form of power which does not leave us just where and who we were, but transformed. Desire is thus shown as a site for challenging our restricted self-understanding as humans and for transgressing humans' self-centeredness.

**Keywords:** Science fiction film and literature · Robotic art
Man-machine interaction · Intimate relationships · Desire

## 1  Introduction

Ever since Pygmalion succeeded in creating the perfect lover, the idea of intimate relationships between humans and artificially created beings has become more and more popular, especially in the 21st century. While engineers and computer scientists are still hard at work on the technological development of robots with humanlike capacities, contemporary science fiction film and literature has already been showing us a variety of humans and posthumans interacting with each other intensely and entering into posthuman love affairs. In my paper, I examine how such intimate relationships are represented nowadays, at the beginning of the so-called posthuman age. Which changes in intimate relationships are shown and made a subject of discussion both in robotics, in science fiction and in robotic art? What kind of aesthetics is being developed to depict future love affairs? And which ethical challenges might those relationships pose?

© Springer International Publishing AG, part of Springer Nature 2018
A. D. Cheok and D. Levy (Eds.): LSR 2017, LNCS 10715, pp. 37–50, 2018.
https://doi.org/10.1007/978-3-319-76369-9_4

To answer these questions, I proceed in five steps. First, I present the leading proponent of artificial sexuality, David Levy, who puts forward the thesis of the always compliant robot as the 'perfect lover.' Then I reflect on the counterarguments produced by, amongst others, robot ethicist Kathleen Richardson. In a third step, drawing on Deleuze's concept of 'becoming other' and the use of this concept in critical posthumanist studies, I present my alternative view on human-posthuman intimate relationships and develop my concept of 'new networks of desire.' According to this network idea, man and machine are seen as being 'in touch', entangled and interwoven, merging into "new subjectivities at the technological interface." [1] Finally, I analyze the representation of human-posthuman intimate relationships in contemporary science fiction film and literature and in robotic art. My main aim is to show on the one hand that science fiction, in contrast to Levy's theory, highlights the problems and various challenges in human-posthuman relationships and in so doing contributes to a deepened and more complex understanding of our likely posthuman future. On the other hand, however, I also want to demonstrate these works' shortcomings with regard to the more progressive concepts oriented around the principle of 'becoming other.' In the concluding remarks, I argue that in robotics a change of thinking is needed.

## 2   The Vision: Love and Sex with Robots

In his book Love and Sex with Robots, The Evolution of Human/Robot Relationships [2], published in 2007, Levy enthusiastically declares that in about fifty years we will see humans partaking in intense and fulfilling relationships with robots. In the preface to his book he solemnly insures his readers:

"Robots will be hugely attractive to humans as companions because of their many talents, senses, and capabilities. They will have the capacity to fall in love with humans and to make themselves romantically attractive and sexually desirable to humans. Robots will transform human notions of love and sexuality." (22)

In the two main chapters of his book, Levy explains, firstly, our willingness to enter into a relationship with a robot, accepting it as a companion and partner, and, secondly, the improvement in our sex life thanks to erotic robots. With regard to both partnership and sexuality Levy's main argument for entering into a relation with a robot, is the robot's capacity to satisfy all our needs. Moreover, because a robot is much more unselfish and yet also more adaptive, it will not only succeed in satisfying human needs, but will do so in a much better way than a human partner might be able to.

However, this argument only holds true when it is combined with another assumption, namely that a human being indeed longs for to be satisfied in the way described above. For Levy, there is no doubt that this is the case. According to him, every human being longs for certainty, and thus for a steadfast and impeccably reliable partner. Levy emphasizes that it is "the certainty that one's robot friend will behave in ways that one finds empathetic" (107) that makes the robot the perfect lover and partner. In Levy's view, a robot will never ever frustrate, disappoint or even betray you. It will never fall out of love with you and will ensure that your love for it never ends or even merely wavers. Levy further explains:

"Just as with the central heating thermostat that constantly monitors the temperature of your home, making it warmer or cooler as required, so your robot's emotion system will constantly monitor the level of your affection for it, and as the level drops, your robot will experiment with changes in behavior aimed at restoring its appeal to you to normal." (132)

## 3   Ethical Concerns

While Levy does not discuss "the human fallout from being able to buy a completely selfish relationship" [3], this is of crucial concern for perhaps Levy's most prominent opponent, the anthropologist and robot ethicist Kathleen Richardson. Her main questions are: What are the ramifications of our regarding a robot as a thing we can completely dominate? How will this influence our psyche? And what might be the impact of such commodified relations on our way of relating to other people? Following Immanuel Kant's line of argumentation against the objectification of animals, Richardson points out the problematic emotional consequences for humans when robots are treated as pure objects. In his *Lectures on Ethics* [4] Kant argues that although animals are mere things, we shouldn't treat them as such. Humans, he argues, "must practice kindness towards animals, for he who is cruel to animals becomes hard also in his dealings with men" (212). Similarly, Richardson warns that owning a sex robot is comparable to owning a slave. Human empathy will be eroded and we will treat other people as we treat robots: as things over which we are entitled to govern. In a position statement launched in 2015, Richardson advocates her *Campaign Against Sex Robots* [5] and underlines that using a sex robot appearing female, one solely designed to give pleasure and thus based mainly on a pornographic model, will exacerbate a sexist, degrading and objectifying image of women. Richardson explains: "[…] the development of sex robots will further reinforce relations of power that do not recognize both parties as human subjects. Only the buyer of sex is recognized as a subject, the seller of sex (and by virtue the sex-robot) is merely a thing to have sex with." Existing gender stereotypes and hierarchies will be furthered.

Computer scientist Kate Devlin agrees with Richardson on this specific point. In her view, the transfer of existing gender stereotypes into the realm of future technology is reactionary and should be avoided. However, she also warns against transferring existing prudishness into robotics. Davis asks rhetorically, "If robots oughtn't to have artificial sexuality, why should they have a narrow and unreflective morality?" Instead of prohibiting sex robots, she calls for overcoming current binaries and exploring a new understanding of sex robots. "It is time for new approaches to artificial sexuality, which include a move away from the machine-as-sex-machine hegemony and all its associated biases" [6].

## 4   Theories of Affect and Posthuman Desire

How such an alternative to traditional patterns of man-machine relations might look has been taken up by theorists like Rosi Braidotti and Patricia MacCormack. Both are indebted to Deleuze's poststructuralist readings of Spinoza's affect studies. In developing them further, they make a plea for new kinds of affective posthuman encounters.

In what follows I expand on these theories and transform them into what I call 'new networks of desire'. In a first step, I briefly clarify the concept of affect as deployed by Spinoza and Deleuze and explore how affect and desire have been advanced in post-human studies. After this, I introduce my understanding of 'networks of desire.'

### 4.1 Affect and Desire in Spinoza, Deleuze and Critical Posthumanism

In the third part of his *Ethics, Demonstrated in Geometrical Order*, [7] published in 1677, Baruch Spinoza develops his theory of affect. According to Spinoza, an affect is the continuous variation or modification of a body's force through an interaction with another body. As powers of acting, affects are to be understood as something impersonal, non-conscious and non-representational, and thus are not to be mistaken for feelings or emotions. Each body has the active power to affect and the passive power to be affected. And each affect can be negative or positive, i.e., it can increase or diminish the other body's capacity for existing, its vitality. Spinoza defines: "By affect I understand affections of the body by which the body's power of acting is increased or diminished, aided or restrained" (154).

Underlying each body's affective flow is its desire both to preserve and to transform itself. Desire can therefore be taken to mean a body's potential to expand, create or produce. Accordingly, Elizabeth Grosz [8] considers desire synonymous with production. "Desire is the force of positive production, the action that creates things, makes alliances, and forges interactions [...]. Spinozist desire figures in terms of capacities and abilities" (179). Similarly, Rosi Braidotti [9] views desire as a power that disseminates bodies' self-identity and drives them to become multiple. By engaging in various relations with other bodies, the body itself changes and becomes continually other to itself. This holds true particularly when the multiplicity of possible affections and differences is brought about by encounters with and relations to largely unfamiliar and strange forces and affects; encounters which thus can be described as encounters with alterity.

Encounters with alterity in general and encounters with the nonhuman other in particular are of significant concern for one of the most prominent contemporary cultural movements: critical posthumanism. Following a definition by Braidotti [10], critical posthumanism is "postanthropocentric philosophy, a deconstruction of the human-machine boundary, and a nondualist reconceptualization of human beings and animals" (5). Critical posthumanism's main concern is to question human's self-authorization as the world's leading species and, derived from this supremacy, its self-ascribed right to subordinate other nonhuman beings. Scholars in critical posthumanism, very often drawing on Deleuze and Guattari's ideas of 'becoming-other' [11], counterpose to the idea of species hierarchy and human exceptionalism a transformative politics, one which propounds novel relations between humans and nonhumans, termed 'unnatural alliances' by Deleuze and Guattari.

What makes this approach interesting for science fiction film and literature, as analyzed below, is that the concept of alliance is based on the idea of mutual dependences between human bodies and animal or technological others, while it does not aim at constituting a new stable and self-enclosed unitary subject. Rather, the emphasis falls on difference and otherness as continually moving categories. As Patricia MacCormack

[12] emphasizes: In encounters of alterity, all beings involved are "free from the bondage of another's claim to know" (4). Two or more separate entities meet and in their meeting they are affected and become a dynamic ensemble, an assemblage of affective flows triggered by desire. Such an encounter can thus also be seen as "an act of love between things based on their difference" (4).

## 4.2 Networks of Desire

To speak about 'networks of desire' means that we no longer tend to uncritically regard the technological other as a tool to be used without due concern, but instead as something with which we form bonds, something that affects and touches us, that makes us desiring beings which are related to one another in a myriad of ways. The term 'network' is used here to strengthen the idea that acts of posthuman love and desire are not limited to encounters between two individual beings but include a variety of net-like relations, associations and connections. By highlighting the term 'desire' I seek to accentuate the relations between human and nonhuman beings as relations of intimacy and mutual affection, pleasure-prone or even pleasure-driven. The concept of desire is so important here because it makes particularly clear that intimate relations do not leave us just where and who we were, but transformed. Desire is a transformative force and thus a site for becoming different. Or in Neil Badmington's [13] words: "To be human is to desire, to possess emotions, but to desire is to trouble the sacred distinction between the human and the inhuman." (139) Furthermore, desire's capacity to undermine human-posthuman distinctions also has an important narratological aspect. You can use it as a dramaturgical means, or as Francesca Ferrando [14] has put it, "as a plot stratagem to connect different types of beings, a bridge to dissolve dualistic cultural practices." (274) Affection and desire are thus to be understood as forces that bring to the fore hitherto unknown passions, break down the border between 'us' and 'them' and introduce new concepts of interspecies relationships.

# 5   Intimate Human-Posthuman Relationships in Con-Temporary Science Fiction Film and Literature and Robotic Art

## 5.1   Science Fiction Film

When we have a look at the large number of contemporary science fiction films and TV series that deal with intimate relationships between humans and robots or other artificial posthuman beings, as is the case, for example, with *AI. Artificial Intelligence* (2001) *I, Robot* (2004), *Her* (2013), *Westworld* (2016–17), *Blade Runner 2049* (2017), we most often see relationships which comply with familiar dualistic paradigms: male-female, man-machine, animate-inanimate, self-other. Particularly in films that are made to reach a broad audience, we time and again find the typical constellation of a male human who falls in love with a young and sexy female posthuman. However, even in these films we find initial signs of new networks of desire. In the following analysis, I seek to demonstrate this by focusing on *Ex Machina* (2015), *Be Right Back* (2013) and *Real Humans* (2012–2014).

**Ex Machina.** The 2015 movie *Ex Machina* [15] by Alex Garland is about Caleb (Domnhall Gleeson), a young programmer who becomes sexually attracted and emotionally attached to Ava (Alicia Vikander), a female looking humanoid robot. Ava was recently developed by the reclusive tech entrepreneur Nathan (Oscar Isaac) who has invited Caleb into his laboratory to perform the *Turing test* on Ava. The beautiful Ava easily succeeds in what Levy [2] has described as a robot's ability to make itself "romantically attractive and sexually desirable" (22) to a human being, here, the young Caleb. She does so thanks to her very sexy body, her expressive eyes and hands, her smartness, and last but not least thanks to her frailty.

What makes the encounter between Caleb and Ava interesting is that Caleb first regards Ava as a synthetic being, one having been designed by Nathan to be the leading model of Artificial Intelligence. As a matter of fact, Nathan presented Ava as AI and Caleb has no reason to doubt his explanation, and Ava is clearly identifiable as a nonhuman. She has a human-looking face but a translucent torso in which her wires are visible. However, this does not make her less attractive in Caleb's eyes. On the contrary, it triggers his romantic interest in the robot. And Ava's gender ambivalence further increases Caleb's fascination. Although Ava, with her full lips, sleek curves and small waist looks like the classical beauty, to be sure, she at the same time displays androgynous traits. With her sometimes straightforward way of talking and her head bare of the one or another style of long hair so typically depicted as female and sexy, she even bears a certain resemblance to a tomboy.

One day, while the security camera system has been knocked out, Ava tells Caleb that Nathan is a bad person intent on destroying her. Appealing to Caleb's sense of chivalry, she convinces him to help her escape Nathan's fortress. Caleb willingly agrees to come to her aid. In my view, this is the moment when Caleb fails. Instead of perceiving Ava for what she is, namely, a perfectly designed android with a machine's will and desire, he sees a young woman who needs to be rescued. He cannot free himself of his conventional male and human view and ignores Ava's technological otherness, her being as a machine. He reestablishes the difference between male and female, which in the beginning was blurred thanks to Ava's androgynous appearance, and gets caught up in an old-fashioned anthropocentric and gender-hierarchical way of thinking. Thereby, Caleb misses the chance to encounter the other and in so doing to become another himself. He stays what he is, an intelligent young man with very traditional romantic interests. As a consequence, Ava locks Caleb up in a sealed room and boards the helicopter meant for Caleb's return home. While Ava sets herself free, Caleb is trapped in a room that can be read metaphorically for Caleb's confinement in himself, his anthropo- and androcentric self-centeredness.

**Be Right Back.** Another example of how an intimate relationship between a human and a posthuman can fail due to mutual misapprehension of the particular human and posthuman characteristics in play, can be found in *Be Right Back* (2013) [16]. This is the first episode of the second season of the British science fiction television anthology series *Black Mirror* (2011–2014), created by Charlie Brooker. *Be Right Back* focuses on the young woman Martha (Hayley Atwell) who enters a state of deep crisis after the sudden death of her partner Ash (Domhnall Gleeson). At Ash's funeral, a friend advises Martha to register with an online service that offers to create virtual doubles of dear ones lost. Martha vehemently refuses the idea at first, but after having discovered that she is pregnant, she is overwhelmed by grief and decides to give the service a try. She uploads all of Ash's past online communication, social media profiles, photos and videos, so that a new Ash can be created virtually. First, she only exchanges e-mails with the artificial Ash. Then she speaks with him by phone. Finally she agrees to get a clone that looks almost exactly like the original Ash. Having fought her initial feelings of unease, Martha experiences some exciting moments with Ash. Having sex with the Ash replicant is, for example, awesome for Martha. When asked about the sources of his sexual prowess, Ash explains that he has been endowed with a sexual program "based on pornographic videos" (34: 30).

But after a while Martha becomes heavily frustrated with Ash's permanent compliance. While Martha's relationship with the real Ash was based on a very affectionate but nonetheless humorous and always a bit teasing interaction, the virtual Ash is not able to act against Martha's will. He is neither confrontational nor argumentative, but instead does everything Martha expects of him. When Martha eventually requests of Ash that he leaves her alone and he just follows her instruction, Martha desperately cries out: "Ash would argue over that. He wouldn't just leave because I'd ordered him to" (40: 49). But Ash isn't able to react any differently. He explains: "I aim to please." Martha finally realizes that the virtual Ash is "not enough" (41: 18) of the original Ash. He has no free will, no needs and desires of his own. And this lack of independence makes it impossible to develop a relationship which would be quite possibly imperfect or stressful, perhaps even exhausting or frustrating, but nevertheless challenging and thus enriching.

When we compare the human-posthuman encounter presented in *Be Right Back* with the encounter presented in *Ex Machina*, we can detect similar problems, although the initial situation seems to be very different. In both films, the problems stem from the fact that both posthumans, Ava and Ash, were designed to look and to behave as human-like as possible. Consequently, the humans interacting with them expect them to behave like real humans, although they might have known better. Ava has interests and desires of her own that Caleb is not willing to accept because he does not recognize Ava for what she is: a posthuman being. Likewise, Martha also misunderstands Ash because she starts from the premise that the Ash replicant will behave like the real Ash. Owing to this fallacy, she can only be disappointed. While, however, Ava is able to escape the human straightjacket by imitating the human codes and transforming herself into the 'perfect woman' Caleb expected her to be, Ash does not succeed in developing and expanding. Consequently, he is banned to the attic, visited only once a year, when Martha's and the human Ash's little daughter come to celebrate her birthday with her artificial father.

**Real Humans.** While posthumans both in *Ex Machina* and in *Be Right Back* do not find recognition as posthumans, in the Swedish TV science fiction series *Real Humans* (Swedish: *Äkta människor*, 2012–2014) [17], by contrast, we can find signs of posthumans being met with an acceptance that is based on the posthumans' technological otherness. *Real Humans* is set in an ordinary middle-sized Swedish town in a near future, i.e., in a fictional society that in general is very similar to our own. In this society, humanoid robots, called hubots, have entered into ordinary people's lives. The robots are designed lifelike, but have some characteristic features that clearly mark them as artificial beings. They have, for instance, unnaturally bright blue or green eyes and they need to be recharged. They also can be turned off at the touch of a button if they are not in use or behave rebelliously. Most of the hubots are used as simple factory workers, domestic help or as caretakers for the elderly. Some are also programmed for limited sexual activity, although hubot-human sexual activity is not yet commonplace. A small group of hubots are intelligent, self-conscious and sentient. They call themselves free hubots or, with reference to their creator David Eischer, 'David's children.'

Although the series at large highlights the crises and confrontations between humans and posthumans, it clearly shows a bias towards equitable coexistence. In particular, the encounters between the hubot Mimi and various humans can illustrate this. The first human to become interested in Mimi is little Leo, David Eischer's son. In a series of flashbacks performed by the grown-up Leo, the audience learns that Leo as a ten-year-old had nearly died while trying, but failing to rescue his mother from drowning. Though his mother dies, Leo is himself rescued by Mimi. Despite having been rescued, his condition remains hopeless. So to save Leo's life, his father performs an operation in which hubot technology is implanted. Leo has thus become a human/posthuman hybrid. What is striking, however, is that Leo's hybridity is revealed as a problem in the series. When Mimi is abducted by a black market hubot dealer and reprogrammed as a 'normal', non-sentient hubot, Leo risks and ultimately sacrifices his own life to save her. Being strongly affected by a posthuman is seen here as fatal.

At the same time, however, Mimi's capacity to affect other people is highlighted as a positive force in the series. When Mimi becomes a member of the Engman family, she immediately evokes a broad range of emotional responses. The little daughter loves Mimi because the latter patiently reads to her one book after another. The older daughter is initially sceptical, as is the mother, Inger, who is a lawyer. Yet at one point in the series, when a female hubot assistant is insulted by Inger's colleague, to convince Inger that these are 'only machines' without any capacity to feel insulted, she reacts empathetically and takes the hubots' side. The father is fascinated by Mimi's beauty and tempted to activate her program for sexual use, but resists the temptation. After a while he acknowledges Mimi as real member of the family and unselfishly helps her when she is infected by a dangerous computer virus. The 16-year-old Tobbe is likewise fascinated, but falls in love for real with Mimi. Eventually he comes out of the closet as a trans-posthuman sexual. In all these encounters, Mimi is mistaken neither as a human, nor as a pure machine. All the members of the Engman family are tenderly affected by her in their very own way, but they are all certain that she is different. In particular, Tobbe loves her not despite, but in recognition of her being a hubot.

The series' overall message can be understood as encouraging the viewer to develop a positive attitude towards the posthuman other as other. Yet we do not witness here processes which are crucial for transformations or transgressions of the human-post-human border. The series pleas for the other's acceptance, but without advocating encounters between humans and posthumans that bring about a radical transformation.

In summary, it may be argued that in *Ex Machina*, *Be Right Back* and *Real Humans* desire is placed center stage as a potentially transformative force, but is not really brought to fruition. By getting in touch, man and machine, humans and posthumans bring about the chance to change, to encounter one another in hitherto unknown ways. But the films do not really trust this chance. Instead, the human characters by and large impede the technological other from freely extending its machinic desires and capacities. And all the while the humans remain anthropo- and self-centered, restrict themselves and stop at the very moment when a poignant expansion of the network of desire had been possible.

## 5.2   Posthuman Love Affairs in Science Fiction Literature

Contemporary science fiction novels which feature human-posthuman love affairs show such affairs in a greater variety than similar films do. The well-known pattern of 'male human falls in love with female posthuman' is more often fractured and multiplied. Moreover, the idea of a robot being as humanlike as possible is also questioned and replaced by less conventional representations. In the Swedish science fiction novel *The Song from the Chinese Room* (Swedish: *Sången från det kinesiska rummet*, 2014) by Sam Ghazi [18], for example, we learn about a robot called Cepheus who, consisting merely of a head with one big blue eye and two robotic arms, was designed as a 'helping hand' for the cancer researcher Simona. Working closely with Simona, the robot develops a human way of thinking, becomes attracted to his female colleague and starts writing love poems. In another science fiction novel, Jeanette Winterson's *The Stone Gods*, originally published in 2007, we likewise read about a robot that is described, at least in the novel's last part, as a 'thinking head' and that, identifying itself as female, is sexually attracted to other women.

Both examples are interesting not only because of the non-anthropomorphic appearance of the robots, but also because of the humans' specific reaction to them. In the beginning, the humans feel strongly uncomfortable, but they later develop intense feelings for those posthumans. While the humanlike robots often seem to trigger, as discussed in the films above, a feeling of unease or uncanniness, widely known as the 'uncanny valley' [19], robots which do not look anthropomorphic but nevertheless behave in responsive ways or in ways that signal awareness, sentience, agency and intentionality, evoke another feeling. A feeling, namely, that can be described as 'the experiential uncanny.' This term was coined by Elizabeth Jochum and Ken Goldberg. In their article "Cultivating the Uncanny" [20], the two coauthors differentiate between the 'representational uncanny,' as that which is evoked by humanlike robots, and the 'experiential uncanny,' as that which "arises from a user's interaction and experience" (16) with the robot, yet seems to arise unrelated to the robot's appearance, one clearly identifiable as nonhuman. With regard to various forms of interlaced desire, this insight is worth underscoring because it is the unfamiliar, and most of all, the fragmented and partial, the bodily incompleteness, that leaves space for our imagination. This can be illustrated with a closer examination of Winterson's novel *The Stone Gods*.

In *The Stone Gods* [21], encounters between humans and nonhumans play a crucial role, particularly the encounter between the female human Billie and the female post-human Spike, the novel's two protagonists. This encounter, which finally leads to an intense love affair, is based on the protagonists' awareness of and fascination for the other's otherness. Billie, for example, acknowledges: "And I looked at Spike, unknown, uncharted, different in every way from me, another life-form, another planet, another chance" (90). Spike, for her part, experiences a crucial modification of her self when reading love poems: she becomes a sentient being, a being which is able to be affected and to affect. "In fact I was sensing something completely new to me. For the first time I was able to feel" (81).

Being able to feel makes it impossible for Spike to fulfill the task for which humans have designed her, namely, to predict the future as objectively as possible. However, this loss of predictability does not only pose a threat for humankind's development. It also presents a chance for overcoming a normative understanding of the self-contained knowing subject. It surpasses the idea of the triumphant and self-centered human and presents a new understanding of post/humanity based on decentered relationality. Not accidentally, the end of chapter one coincides with the protagonists' dying while warmly embracing one another, a scene which symbolizes the transformative forces of love and relationality. Death is not the end of interdependency and interconnectedness, but signi-fies their very possibility. It marks the dissolution of the subject, the individuated self, into, as Braidotti [22] phrases it, "the generative flow of becoming" (136).

Contemporary science fiction literature, better than contemporary science fiction film, allows us to better understand posthuman desire as a possibility to remove "the obstacle of self-centered individualism" (50) and thereby to adopt a new "posthuman subject position based on relationality and transversal interconnections across the clas-sical axes of differentiation" (96). The same holds true when it comes to some pieces of robotic artworks.

### 5.3 Intimate Touches and Strange Gazes in Robotic Art

Unlike representations of robots in film and literature, robotic figures in art are artefacts taking up real space, allowing for spatial and bodily proximity between man and machine. We can not only see and hear them, but also touch and smell them. And we can, at its best, interact with them. The question is thus, in which way the robotic figures affect us, how we affect them, and how this kind of affectivity impacts our intimate relations with them. The first example I want to analyze is Louis Philippe Demers' telerobotic art installation *The Blind Robot* (2012), the second is Jordan Wolfson's animatronic *Female Figure* (2014).

*The Blind Robot* [23] does not resemble a human in all its complexity, but is merely comprised of a pair of robotic arms equipped with articulated hands installed on a table, tele-operated by a human who, however, is not visible. The integrative part of the artwork is a visitor who is invited to sit down in front of the machine. The machine then explores the visitor by gently touching the human's face with its robotic fingertips. As explained in Demers' study *Machine Performers* [24], the robotic arm, normally seen as "a high precision tool," now appears as "a fragile, imprecise and emotionally loaded agent" (58). Although some visitors described themselves in this situation as feeling uncomfortable or even as being reminded of "Science Fictional killer-robot dystopias" [25] they recalled seeing at the cinema, the artist's intention was to create an empathic situation and a positive attitude towards the engagement. Demers did so by entitling his installation 'The Blind Robot,' recalling the situation of a blind and helpless person who needs to touch the visitor in order to recognize it. Demers explains: "It is a psychological experiment [...] just by the fact that I state that this is a blind robot, you will accept that this machine can touch you in very intimate places." [26] Demers also describes the feeling of being touched by his robot as "very unique, it's not like being touched by a human, of course, but it's also not like being poked with a stick. It's a novel way, because your brain is not too sure what to think about it" [26].

In my view, the novelty of this kind of touch is the central point, when it comes to 'new networks of desire.' Being touched and being affected by something we have not sensed and experienced before is exciting but also engaging. It encourages us to become involved with an unfamiliar situation and an unfamiliar nonhuman agent which intimately touches vulnerable parts of our bodies, engendering a sensual, potentially arousing encounter. It's about an encounter that simultaneously increases our bodily self-awareness and our awareness of the machinic other as other. That the machinic nature of the other is not concealed but rather clearly exposed in presenting only two robotic arms, further contributes to the individual human's involvement. Given the fact that Demers' blind robot is not a full humanoid-robot, fantasy and imagination are needed to 'animate' the situation.

Imagination is also involved when it comes to Jordan Wolfson's *Female figure* [27] – a computer-controlled sculpture featuring a hyper-sexualized blonde woman wearing a white miniskirt splattered with black dirt, high-heeled thigh-high boots and long gloves. The figure is inspired by the character of Holli Would, the cartoon vamp from the 1992 animated fantasy film, *Cool World*. [28] Although imitating the typical *femme fatale*, the figure's fabricated nature is not hidden. On the contrary, the figure's joints are visibly bolted together and a metallic pole running through its belly holds it fastened to a large mirror. Various other features contribute to the figure's de-familiarizing effect. One such effect is sound and voice, mixed in a disturbing way. On the one hand, the figure dances lasciviously to popular songs, among them, Lady Gaga's 'Applause' and Paul Simon's 'Graceland.' On the other hand, we hear the figure's voice saying, in a tape loop, monotonously and in a male voice which is Demers': 'My father is dead. My mother is dead. I'm gay.' These two very different sound tracks make it impossible, while interfering with each other, for the audience to relax.

This kind of disquiet based on contradictory bodily experiences is further intensified by various forms of glances exchanged between robot and human. Watching the figure from behind, a seductive effect might be felt. Gyrating before the mirror, the figure is kind of alluring. When, however, we look at the figure's face, this positive feeling changes rapidly. Instead of a human-like face, we are confronted with dark evil eyes which glimmer from behind a green Venetian mask with a witch-like nose. Since the figure is equipped with motion tracking software and technology for facial recognition, it is able to recognize and, what is more, to react to people's movements throughout the room. The sculpture makes eye contact with the viewer, quietly observing him or her. This kind of interaction is described by one visitor in the following way: "If you stand close to the robot it looks deep into your eyes, and there is a terrifyingly disorienting moment as you experience yourself as an object in the automaton's gaze." [29] Being the object of the machinic other's gaze does not leave the visitor untouched. He or she is probably not altered in a way as radical as that envisioned by Braidotti. But the experience evoked by the interaction with this sculpture is alienating. In this sense, it prepares a way for hitherto unknown experiences – even though these first appear here on the side of the negative affects.

## 6   Conclusion

Many sex robot manufacturers, robotics experts and engineers state as their aim the creation of robots or robotic dolls specifically conceived for the sexual gratification of human beings. For them it is self-evident that these synthetic lovers should look, feel and behave as humanlike as possible. For example, the company *Abyss Creations* has developed the popular silicone sex doll 'RealDoll' and is currently working to create sex dolls with artificial intelligence; *Synthea Amatus* has launched the AI equipped model 'Samantha' in summer 2017, while *Doll Sweet* is working on robotic talking heads and even full-body sex robots. [30] Each of these and other commercially vested interests emphasize that artificial creations are being marketed to serve as the 'perfect partner' for human beings, or rather: for men. Being 'perfect', however, apparently tends to mean representing as the 'perfect woman', i.e., a female lover that is designed according to pornographic standards, thus plainly suggesting that it is a woman's task to fulfill a man's sexual wishes.

But sexuality is much too complex and multifaceted for it to be restricted to traditional patterns, ones based on the idea of heterosexual intercourse. Some of the posthuman female figures as currently presented in science fiction can serve as an alternative model to this stereotypical understanding. Although they are still often designed according to popular ideas of female beauty and sexiness, it is not this kind of stereotypical sexiness that makes them interesting in the long run, that is, interesting either for the other figures in the films and texts or for the viewers and readers. On the contrary, it is their otherness that transgresses humans' self-centeredness, arouses strong feelings and reminds us of what it means to be a desiring (post)human, namely, a body which is able to affect and to be affected in unforeseen ways.

Leaving aside the immense technical problems of developing robots designed to look like a real human woman or man, I consider doing so the wrong path to pursue. Designing, marketing and perceiving humanlike robots as human's companions and lovers meant to perform strictly in line with an individual's wishes will not take us forward. It remains to be seen whether, in fact, in the foreseeable future robotic love affairs will become so advanced that they can function as an appropriate surrogate for human relationships, or if robots will be unable to fully meet our expectations; in either case they will not be able to do anything other than to mirror existing needs, experiences or imaginations. Instead, they will always only bring us back to preconceived ideas, ideas that will have been programmed into the other for fulfilling our narcissistic tendencies. While some people may not at all consider this a problem, others may well be hoping for something else: challenging new experiences, transgressive new affects, new forms of encounters and hierarchies undermined, at least not plainly reproduced and simply reinforced through existing heterosexist patterns.

To reach this aim, we need robots that challenge our restricted self-understanding as humans superior to all other nonhuman beings. Critical posthumanist thinking, as well as a variety of unconventional films, literary texts and other artworks featuring human-posthuman intimate relationships in a non-dualistic manner, make us aware that the most exciting encounters happen when they are unpredictable. Not the robot which is always responding to our moods and expectations, but rather a machine we accord the right to be different, a machine not in compliance but wayward, could help us to view ourselves other than as the prime issue in the world. I'd thus like to submit that technology will be better capable of enhancing humans' interaction with robots, if it does not build its hopes around the human-likeness of robots, but on their otherness. Only by virtue of their otherness will robots be capable of helping us to create new networks of desire.

# References

1. Hollinger, V.: 'Something like a Fiction': speculative intersections of sexuality and technology. In: Person, W., et al. (eds.) Queer Universes: Sexualities in Science Fiction, pp. 140–160. Liverpool UP, Liverpool (2008)
2. Levy, D.: Love and Sex with Robots: The Evolution of Human-Robot Relationships. Duckworth, London (2008)
3. Kleeman, J.: The race to build the world's first sex robot. In: The Guardian (2017). https://www.theguardian.com/technology/2017/apr/27/race-to-build-world-first-sex-robot
4. Kant, I.: Lectures on Ethics. Cambridge UP, Cambridge (1997)
5. Richardson, K.: The asymmetrical 'relationship': parallels between prostitution and the development of sex robots. ACM SIGCAS Comput. Soc. **45**(3), 290–293 (2016)
6. Devlin, K.: In defence of sex machines: why trying to ban sex robots is wrong. In: The Conversation, 17 September 2015. http://theconversation.com/in-defence-of-sex-machines-why-trying-to-ban-sex-robots-is-wrong-47641
7. Spinoza, B.: A Spinoza Reader: The Ethics and Other Works. Princeton University Press, Princeton (1994)
8. Grosz, E.: Space, Time and Perversion: Essays on the Politics of Body. Routledge, London (1995)
9. Braidotti, R.: Metamorphoses: Towards a Materialist Theory of Becoming. Polity Press, Cambridge (2002)
10. Braidotti, R.: Editor's note. J. Posthuman Stud. Philos. Technol. Media **1**(1), 1–8 (2017)
11. Deleuze, G., Guattari, F.: A Thousand Plateaus: Capitalism and Schizophrenia, 2nd edn. University of Minnesota Press, Athlone, London (1987)
12. MacCormack, P.: Posthuman Ethics: Embodiment and Cultural Theory. Routledge, London (2016)
13. Badmington, N.: Alien Chic: Posthumanism and the Other Within. Routledge, London (2004)

14. Ferrando, F.: Of posthuman born: gender, utopia and the posthuman in films and TV. In: Hauskeller, M., Philbeck, T.D., Carbonell, C.D. (eds.) The Palgrave Handbook of Posthumanism in Film and Television, pp. 269–278. Palgrave Macmillan UK, London (2015)
15. Garland, A.: Ex Machina, UK/US (2015)
16. Brooker, C.: Be Right Back, UK (2013)
17. Lundström, L: Real Humans (2012–2014)
18. Ghazi, S.: Sången från det kinesiska rummet. Norstedts, Stockholm (2014)
19. Mori, M.: The uncanny valley. IEEE Robot. Autom. Mag. **19**(2), 98–100 (1970/2012). https://doi.org/10.1109/mra.2012.2192811
20. Jochum, E., Goldberg, K.: Cultivating the uncanny: the telegarden and other oddities. In: Herath, D., Kroos, C., Stelarc (eds.) Robots and Art: Exploring an Unlikely Symbiosis, pp. 149–175. Springer, Singapore (2016). https://doi.org/10.1007/978-981-10-0321-9_8
21. Winterson, J.: The Stone Gods. Penguin, London (2008)
22. Braidotti, R.: The Posthuman. Polity Press, Cambridge (2015)
23. Demers, L.-P.: The Blind Robot (2012)
24. Demers, L.-P.: Machine Performers: Agents in a Multiple Ontological State. Dissertation, University of Plymouth (2014). http://citeseerx.ist.psu.edu/viewdoc/download?doi=10.1.1.829.7112&rep=rep1&type=pdf
25. Sjef: The Blind Robot. https://sjef.nu/the-blind-robot/. Accessed 28 May 2014
26. Knoll, M.: The Blind Robot at the Lab. https://www.aec.at/aeblog/en/2013/10/28/the-blind-robot-bei-the-lab/. Accessed 28 Oct 2013
27. Wolfson, J.: Female Figure (2014)
28. Bakshi, R.: Cool World, US (1993)
29. Feldhaus, T: Jordan Wolfson's Robot: In the Moment of Terror. https://www.spikeartmagazine.com/en/articles/jordan-wolfsons-robot-moment-terror
30. Owsianik, J.: State of Sex Robots: These are the Companies Developing Robotic Lovers, 1 September 2017. https://futureofsex.net/robots/state-sex-robots-companies-developing-robotic-lovers/

# Lying Cheating Robots – Robots and Infidelity

Rebekah Rousi[✉] [iD]

University of Jyväskylä, Jyväskylä, Finland
rebekah.rousi@jyu.fi

**Abstract.** Love has been described as unpredictable, immeasurable and non-purchasable and as such, poses challenges for anyone in a relationship to both stay in love, and to not fall in love with someone else. Scientists are still discovering whether or not love follows any specific recipe. Outlooks, personality, sense of humor and talent may not perfectly guarantee an individual falls in love with another, and more importantly is able to sustain that relationship. This article portrays a futuristic scenario in which truly intelligent and emotional robots already exist. Here, the bi-directional love discussed in Lovotics is not simulated through engineering, but rather is genuine from the perspectives of both machine and human. This is a theoretical piece that draws on psychological theories of love, sex, attraction, associated emotions and behavior. The method involves reviewing previous literature on human-robot bi-directional love, and combines it with current discussions and theories of the realistic future potential of love relationships between humans and robots with full artificial intelligence and emotional capabilities. The result of the investigation is a multifaceted projection of the complexity humans will experience in love relationships with robots. Due to the incalculable nature of love, affection and sexual attraction, the development of robots with genuine capacity for emotions may not have the best outcome for a future of love and sex with robots.

**Keywords:** Love · Sex · Emotions · Infidelity · Human-robot
Artificial intelligence · Psychology

## 1 Introduction

The year is 2050, and existing in this world are robots that not only possess true (artificial) intelligence, thus, the ability to fully autonomously problem-solve, think and survive on their own but also harbor their own emotions. These robots, humanoids or otherwise, have the capacity to empathize, care for and reciprocate emotions, on top of the propensity to develop unprecedented, unabashed love and fulfilling sexual relationships. It is no longer uncommon for humans and robots to get married, and there are most likely possibilities for human-robot couples to be parents (through adoption or otherwise). Nor for that matter, is it uncommon for robots to want to marry other robots and raise their potential robot families. In this reality the boundaries between creators and consumers is blurred. Humans have succeeded in producing super humans (humanoids), who in the ideal case, live harmoniously alongside their human counterparts. In cases of full artificial intelligence (AI), it can be assumed that robots possess

© Springer International Publishing AG, part of Springer Nature 2018
A. D. Cheok and D. Levy (Eds.): LSR 2017, LNCS 10715, pp. 51–64, 2018.
https://doi.org/10.1007/978-3-319-76369-9_5

independence and autonomy in their capabilities for flexible thought, problem-solving and creativity [1, 2]. They no longer *feel* like robots that have arrived fresh from the conveyor belt. Rather, they feel themselves to be equal to humans and compatible intellectual beings that are genuinely capable of not only receiving the love of human beings, but are able to feel love in return.

This is a theoretical and reflective article on a possible future scenario in which humans and robots have the possibility to engage in true, fulfilling love and sexual relationships. In this scenario, the act of falling in love is less dependent on specific criteria, ideals and intentional processes of humans selecting partners. But rather, falling in love is more random, unexplainable and equally as complex and dynamic for robots as it is for humans. Here, people and robots do not choose to love, but rather happen to fall into passionate, unconditional and uncontrollable love, that transgresses the borders of acceptable, or legal, relationships, and may or may not be contained two people (beings). This kind of love, or untamable nature of love, finds human-robot (or robot-robot) relationships in equally as disturbingly troublesome situations as those of human-human relationships.

For this reason, the following sub-section refers to psychological and sociological literature in tangent with previous work in Lovotics [3, 4] - love and robotics - to describe the multilayered and dynamic complexity of love - as a state, condition and powerful set of conflicting emotions. The materials and methods are described in terms of the approach of this article, which is as a reflective approach to previous writings on human-robot love relationships from mass media to scientific texts, in combination with psychological and sociological insight into the underlying forces of love and sexual relationships in general. Loyalty is described in the following section in order to establish an understanding of what it is and how the latter, infidelity, deviates from the loyal state. Chemistry, attraction and jealousy are characterized and the psychology of unfaithfulness is unfolded. The section on 'Power in the bedroom', shifts dominant emphasis on humans as consumers and owners of robots, towards humans as being partners *with* robots. The next section on lying, cheating robots observes how robots modify their behavior in order to protect their own best interests. The article is concluded by attempting to enrichen the understanding and entertaining the idea of genuine bi-directional love relationships between people and machines. It serves to highlight the fact that if the exact future of human-intelligent robot relationships is unknown, the addition of AI and felt emotions within robotics will make this condition even less predictable.

## 1.1   The Nature of Love

Love is complex, unpredictable and dependent on numerous factors ranging from the physiological and physical, to the emotional and intellectual [5]. In their article "A design process for Lovotics", Samani and colleagues [4] introduce the field of love-like relationship human-robot interaction development, through defining the term "love". They define love as abstract, and focus on the Aristotle originated concept of "philia" - a form of moral and unconditional love, which displays in loyalty to family, friends and communities and materializes in mutually beneficial relationships [6–8]. In Samani et al.'s work [4], love is also categorized as an emotion, and in order to design robotics for this emotion there is the need to incorporate elements which appeal to and are expressed through the senses of touch, sound and vision.

It is interesting to look closer at the dictionary definitions of love such as those in the Merriam-Webster Dictionary [9]. These characterize love as a powerful affection that derives from kinship and/or personal connections, in addition to being sexually-driven attraction as well as warmth and devotion towards someone or something. Psychologist Robert Sternberg [10–12] proposed the triangular theory of love which comprises intimacy, passion, and commitment. Intimacy describes feelings of closeness and connectedness. Passion can be characterized by the drive of sexual attraction. Commitment entails decisions and long-term plans to remain with a partner. Types of love include: nonlover - absence of all three components of love [11]; liking/friendship - closeness and mutual warmth towards one another; infatuated love - a crush or passionate arousal minus any intimate relationship; empty love - commitment which lacks passion and intimacy; romantic love - people are bonded emotionally and physically with intimacy and passion; companionate love - seen in long-term marriages and life-long partnerships; in fatuous love - whirlwind romances and marriages filled with passion but lacking the intimate component; and consummate love - the complete and total love form which encompasses companionship and long-term intimacy.

Sternberg's model has been criticized for its mirroring of the neoclassical psyche of cognition, affect, and conation [13]. Yet, this logic does not move far away from the rationale of this paper that is influenced by the appraisal theory of emotions in evolutionary psychology [14–16]. Appraisal theory is a cognitive approach to understanding how emotions develop - whether through primal or high order cognition - as a response to human evaluation of phenomena and actions against the human's core concerns [17]. These core concerns inevitably relate to the human's strive for survival, whether through e.g., concern for personal safety (recognizing an immediate threat which in turn triggers fear for example), or for instance, well-being in terms of evaluating designs and brands through the social dimension and feeling emotions towards products not in terms of what they are, but what they can do for the person who consumes them [18–21]. The field of relationship science focuses mainly on close relationships [22]. Close relationships are described as the frequent or consistent, powerful yet varied interdependence between (human) beings that continues for a substantial duration of time [22].

According to Finkel et al. [23], there are fourteen principles derived from the scholarship of relationship science are categorized as: (1) uniqueness - unique patterns arising when the partners' characteristics intersect; (2) integration - cognition, affection, behavior and motivation tend to merge between individuals who merge towards interdependence; (3) trajectory - the relationships are evaluated by longitudinal goals against which couples constantly evaluate the development of their relationships to determine the direction these relationships are heading (also linked to the Investment Model, e.g., see [24]); (4) evaluation - this evaluation occurs via reflection over positive and negative constructs (the pros and cons experienced in the relationships); (5) responsiveness - how in-tune and receptive individuals are to their partners' needs, actions and desires; (6) resolution - the ability to overcome relationship turbulence; (7) maintenance - behavior and cognition that promotes persistence, whether through self-deceptive biases and/or through resilience; (8) predisposition - attitudes and qualities that a person brings into relationships that may affect the relationship's wellbeing; (9) instrumentality - how an individual views the function of a partner in terms of achieving one's personal goals (marriage, children, financial wealth); (10) standards - the criteria one brings into a partnership based on ideals of previous experiences; (11) diagnosticity - the opportunities whereby individuals are able to evaluate their partners' motivations and goals in the relationship; (12) alternatives - the ways in which individuals search for and consider alternative to their current relationship; (13) stress - inflicted by external factors, yet still has the potential to harm a relationship; and (14) culture - relationships are shaped in nature and trajectory through the culture they are surrounded by. Many of these listed principles also play a role in the coming paper, particularly in relation to the way the emotional robot experiences their relationship.

On a historical note about love, Sigmund Freud can be seen as one of the pioneering theorists, who typified love as a person's unconscious desire and need to find their "ego ideal" [25], or in other words, the inner image of who one wants to be. This inner image was claimed by Freud to be molded upon people the beholder admires. Abraham Maslow's in his hierarchy of needs positions self-actualization not only at the top of the pyramid, but also as the point at which the prospective of love is possible [26]. This article approaches love and sexual attraction through further considering the interaction between both physical (characteristics and gestures) and non-physical (intellect, humor and personality) within the human-robot relationships. Particular emphasis is placed on robots as independent thinking and feeling individuals, who additionally possess super human characteristics in physical proportions, properties and strength.

## 2   Fidelity, Faithfulness and Loyalty

In order to discuss infidelity it is also important to establish a basic understanding of fidelity or faithfulness. Faithfulness and fidelity for instance, are defined by the *Oxford English Dictionary* [27] as the continued loyalty or support an individual shows to another individual, phenomenon or cause - loyalty itself being a strong sense of support or allegiance towards someone or something [28]. Surprisingly, when investigating previous studies and definitions of fidelity, there is a tendency towards researching and categorizing the opposite state, which is that of infidelity. Yet, it may be observed that fidelity, or loyalty in a relationship, is a situation in which a person displays their allegiance or commitment through monogamy and no deviation towards parties outside of the main romantic (marital) relationship. Commitment itself is an interesting subject, as several studies such as [29] have noted that the level of commitment experienced within a relationship does not correspond with the level of faithfulness. In other words, in accordance with thoughts on infidelity (the case of an extra marital affair when otherwise the partner relationship appears healthy) as compared to unfaithfulness (whereby, partners lose faith in their relationship), individuals may be highly committed to a relationship - reasons most likely corresponding with characteristics outlined in the relationship science principles [29] - yet, still engage in romantic and sexual activity with others outside the relationship.

Additionally, when examining the construct of loyalty on a deeper level, it may be observed that, loyalty describes the quality of a relationship that resists pressures, stress and temptations from external forces [28]. This means, that even during times at which couples experience disaffection, loyalty prevails in sustaining the connections of the relationship and preventing the partners from discontinuing their union. Moreover, this loyalty involves the use of maintenance strategies. These maintenance strategies include: assurances, positivity and the sharing of tasks [30]. Once again, these actions correspond with the principles described above, and can be seen to be reinforced particularly if principles 3 (trajectory), 4 (evaluation) and 9 (instrumentality) reveal that the partner in question is desirable in terms of one achieving one's long-term relationship goals, and the negatives (potential obstacles in achieving those goals) are perceived as less than the enablers. This, once again, can be seen as linked to the appraisal theory of emotions in that both direct love, sexual, other romantic responses, and levels of commitment, correspond with how well an individual sees their partner in terms of promoting, or benefiting, their main concerns (primal, social and otherwise) [14].

## 3 Attraction, Jealousy and Infidelity

Infidelity is a widely studied phenomenon, often explored from the perspectives of male-female relationships in terms of demographic, biological and psychological tendencies, as well as its social and physical ramifications [31, 32]. According to Drigotas and Barta [31] there are several approaches to understanding infidelity, these include: the descriptive - mostly retrospective and self-reporting; normative - also utilizing retrospective and self-report data, yet using social norms as explanatory frameworks; investment-model [33] - accounts for the process of individuals becoming committed to relationships, losing feelings of commitment and ending the relationship; and the evolutionary approach - focusing on the exchange of benefits, equity and its resulting satisfaction.

From the perspective of this paper, the evolutionary approach to explaining infidelity is particularly interesting, as it is very much bound to human beings' functional biological needs of sexual reproduction [34]. In this model, sexual relationships are viewed in terms of their functional value in generating offspring. Specific physical and intellectual qualities and traits such as symmetry, youth and strength are used as indicators that not only a partner will be able to produce offspring (reproductive success), but that offspring will in turn be healthy and able to produce their own offspring. In this case also the biological sex of the individual comes into play, and heterosexual conduct is often influenced by predispositions that are harbored unconsciously to encourage reproductive success.

Sexual differences also influence not only the likelihood to be unfaithful, but also the likelihood of jealously. For instance, when females are pregnant and in that way linked to a male, there is not too much reason to be with an extradyadic partner, unless there is the potential to gain a more superior partner [34]. Males on the other hand, do not have parental certainty, thus, males have more of a tendency to develop jealousy. At the same time, women's anxiety levels increase due to the possibility of being abandoned by their partner [32].

These factors that seemingly only apply in terms of human to human relationships actually present major challenges human-robot sexual relationships. This is both from a range of perspectives including partner selection and infidelity, as well as that of jealousy. Firstly, will the humans be able to compete with the physical and intellectual attraction of their robot counterparts [35]? If, by evolutionary development, human beings are innately biologically programmed to seek and be attracted to the most seemingly healthy and flawless beings, particularly in human likeness, will there be more propensity for human beings to seek out robot partners? Studies have already shown that early adopters are prone to prefer human-computer interaction to human to human interaction [36]. In turn, this would naturally affect the ability or form of reproduction that the couple will undertake - if reproduction is indeed one of the relational outcomes. The gender of the robot in this case is also significant, as due to its inability, or lack of functional purpose to sexually reproduce, the gender it either takes on or is attributed will also be a question, as this will be what drives its own emotions and sexual desires. This brings to mind the matter of whether or not robots will indeed have their own sexual desires, and what indeed will drive or motivate these desires.

Secondly, the motivational factors would also be a key concern from the robot's perspective in the relationship, not only in terms of what drives them sexually towards their human partners, but also what they have to gain from being in a relationship with a human being. Meston and Buss [37] conducted a major study in which 237 different reasons were given for why people have sex. These reasons were divided into four different categories: physical - attraction and pleasure seeking, goal attainment, emotional, and insecurity - i.e., out of duty. Insecurity may not be a factor driving robots into sex, considering the imminent likelihood of their superiority over human beings, yet the 'out of duty' element may be part of it. Furthermore, another plausible factor behind a robot's sexual drive may be seen in Meston and Buss' observation that people use sex as a means of expressing affection. Perhaps robots will want to show their human partners how they feel, even if there is no biological propensity to engage in sex.

On this note, from the perspective of the capacity of robots to experience love and affection it is interesting to consider Levy's [35] views in that the words or representation of love, may, like any other state such as being either hot or cold, indicate that the robot actually harbors feelings of love. Out of the love prototype model proposed by Fehr and Russel [38, 39] which includes maternal, parental, friendship, sisterly, brotherly, romantic, passionate, sexual and platonic, it is difficult to see how the love felt by a robot could exceed that of friendship or platonic - given that the other types have biological roles. If considering that this biological, or reproductive drive were somehow programmed into the robots, there would once again be the evolutionary concern of how human beings, with their imperfections could compete with a robot counterpart.

### 3.1  Power in the Bedroom

The issue of ethics is not a new one when considering human-robot interaction. In fact, numerous ethical debates are occurring involving questions including whether or not robot sex when in a human-human relationship is indeed cheating, and how robots should be treated in this interactions [40] including the prospective of robot rape [41].

Other ethical considerations have additionally arisen including the paralleling of human-robot sexual and its asymmetrical affection with prostitution [42, 43], as well as the promotion of pedophilia through the dissemination of child-like robots [44]. Sullins [36] notes the change that takes place in ethical dynamics when moving from the topic of masturbation to robotics. These changes mainly focus on the quality of human to human relationships resulting from the introduction of sexbots, whereby instead of remedying marital and sexual problems, they may be seen to worsen them [45] and in fact draw humans' attention away from human companions and towards machines [46].

Ashrafian [47, 48] has researched extensively on the perspective of robot rights, particularly in light of the realization of robot consciousness. Ashrafian's concern primarily rests with the ethics involved in matters such as sex, and sexual consent between humans and robots, once robots can think [49]. That is, he sees that once robot consciousness has been achieved, we will no longer be able to consider the human-robot relationship as that of human-slave, but rather mutual between equally thinking beings. This additionally means that mutual consent would and should not only be required, but legalized in terms of human-robot relations. He considers that the lack of consent in human-robot relationships would prove dangerous not just for robots, but for humans in terms of its societal ramifications. What separates these future robots from other sex technology in terms of the boundaries between self-gratification and cheating, involves the robot's capacity to think, talk and walk. Meaning that, for humans already in human-human relationships (or any other relationship for that matter) to become involved in an extra-marital rendezvous with a robot, the process could easy be considered as adulterous.

If the aims and intentions of creating robots which are fully autonomous and capable of thinking and feeling were to be actually realized, the chances of humans maintaining power in relationships with these super, flawless humanoids would be quite marginal. Today's reality of purchasing robots will be ancient history in the future, and the more realistic likelihood of robots owning or at least controlling humans will be a more obvious scenario. Bill Gates and Stephen Hawking have both addressed this through warnings on the danger of AI [50]. The development of full AI in Hawking's words "… could spell the end of the human race" [51]. However, in maintaining a more optimistic vision of the future in which robots are equal, or at least humans are kept for their novelty value, and indeed for the love and affection held by their robotic counterparts, we may observe the difficulties at least of humans preserving the sexual power in the bedroom. Freedom of choice and outright chemistry would most likely mean that robots' interests may not always be primarily engaged in their human partners (note: not owners), and may wander from human to human, and perhaps towards other robots (as Ashrafian [47] also suggests).

In fact, if continuing on from the sentiments of Mackenzie Wright [52] in his "Hunting humans", a look at the possible future of dark tourism and entertainment, one may wonder as to whether or not human beings may potentially be the sex toys of robots. While the hunting humans article focuses on the satisfaction and joy humans have gained throughout the ages in terms of violence, killing and death, it may not be too farfetched to assume that a superior form, such as emotionally intelligent robots would derive pleasure from the suffering or at least dominance of beings such as humans.

## 4  Lying, Cheating Robots

In his blog article, "Evolving robots learn to lie to each other" Fox [53] reports a Swiss study in which robots learned to lie in order to hoard a beneficial resource for themselves. One thousand robots were included in the experiment. These were divided into ten groups. The robots were embedded with sensors, blue lights and 264-bit binary codes (genomes) determining their mode of behavior towards various stimuli [53]. Robots were set to illuminate their light when they discovered the beneficial resource, in order to aid other robots in their group in distinguishing it. Higher points were achieved for sitting on the beneficial resource and minus points were accrued for being near the poisoned resource. Highest-scoring genomes were 'mated' (mutated) randomly to produce a different program, resulting in subsequent generations of robot programming. While generations of robots became increasingly clever at identifying the positive resource, they also began to learn that by signaling to others where the resource was, overcrowding was prominent and resulted in the original finders being 'bumped' way from the resource. Thus, by the 500th generation robots began concealing their findings through not illuminating their light when they found the beneficial resources.

In fact, interestingly already current studies have revealed that characteristics such as lying and cheating are experienced by humans as more human-like, or intentional, than other traits [54–56]. The detection of cheating by humans, particularly when the behavior is against them, has evolved as a self-preservation mechanism [57–59], and in human-robot interaction this has been shown to be detected more strongly through the actions of the robots as compared to e.g. verbal communication (often interpreted as syntactic errors) [54]. Thus, while through anthropomorphism humans are indeed not just willing but prone to endow objects and indeed machines with human qualities such as emotions [60], we are also weary of others, particularly other beings, human or otherwise, that are likely and capable of being deceptive. This is likely an explanatory factor in the Uncanny Valley theory [61]. That is, while a robot may look like us, subtle differences in their behavior, imperfections, or just the knowledge that a machine is created to impersonate a human may be subconsciously detected as deceit. There is already the known perceived threat that a robot resembling or impersonating a human being, may indeed be intended to take over the human's role [62, 63]. At least according to an article by Kaplan [64], the perception of threat of the *other* versus the opportunity to tame and integrate appears to be culturally-bound. Throughout post-Enlightenment European history in philosophy and literary traditions alike, the human-machine relationship has constantly been represented through binaries [65, 66], nature versus culture (technology) - as with all constructs in Euro-Centric cultures. In Japanese culture, the artificial is seen as a means of reproducing nature [67]. However, in Japanese history integration and holistic, systemic thinking has been a key societal principle and approach, particularly when looking at circumstances such as pre-war Japan during the late 1800s early 1900s [64]. Here, in anticipation of attack by the West, the Meiji political era saw various weaponry technologies studied and 'tamed' [68]. The key term though is 'tamed'. While the artificial and machine building in Japanese culture are considered positive, and in fact, the humanoid robot is seen as harmonious in its replication of the human form [69], it is still seen as living side-by-side with humans - not as humans themselves, but as 'tamed' technology.

In Western cultures there has been a simultaneous fascination with robots [70], yet simultaneous fear. The Frankenstein Syndrome is a term given to categorize a Western attitude towards the creation of artificial beings as an immoral act which will inevitably end with the being turning against its maker [71]. Thus, apprehension and expectations of intelligent, humanoid machines which will eventually fight back are heavily engrained in Western history and thought. This may ultimately contribute to an increased paranoia in Euro-Centric cultures towards humanoid robots, and indeed already to date, studies have begun to reveal a correlation between elevated Uncanny Valley effects and culture [72].

Yet, to return back to the robots and the thought that "we see ourselves in the mirror of the machines we can build" [64] (p. 12) and Hiroshi Ishiguro's observation that we learn about the essence of what it is to be human through attempting to replicate humanity [73, 74]. We may also ponder on the future of these all thinking, all feeling artificial beings (machines), their anticipation and anxiety of the ways in which humans perceive them. Particularly in a human-robot relationship, if the human and humanity are the desired qualities of beings in society, there may even be the sense of threat that is experienced by the robot. This threat or angst could possibly be that of feelings of inadequacy - being close to human beings, yet not close enough. Perhaps even the very relationship itself, the one in which a robot seeks a human, is one in which the robot seeks self-affirmation and justification of its human worth.

If returning to Freud's discussion on the 'ego ideal' [25] it may be observed that in fact, the driving factor behind a robot's experience of love would be the search for the partner, or likeness, of the individual that the person (robot) would like to be. Thus, if endowed with human emotions, may very well seek to be with a human being to validate one's own humanness. Or, in an alternative scenario whereby robot evolutionary psychology replicates that of humans, robots may strive to find the perfect reproductive mate, rendering human beings themselves as inadequate. Possibly, if not in outlook, or even reproductive qualities, it may be that humans cannot satisfy or compete in the world of intellect, humor, agility and maybe even experience. Furthermore, if the reproductive systems of robots are not reliant on sexual intercourse or any form of biological fertilization, meaning that indeed they do not have any sexual reproductive function of their own, then, will they be sexually attracted to anyone or anything at all? Considering the issue from this light, the complexity of the dynamics of a sexual relationship between humans and robots, in a situation whereby robots have emotions yet no biological evolutionary drive for sex, is perplex.

## 5   Conclusion

In the tradition of critical human-robot interaction, this article has aimed at highlighting the implications of developing and disseminating robots with the capacity to not only think, but feel for themselves. In a scenario where robots can indeed emotionally experience intimate interpersonal relationships, the dynamics changes from that of how the relationship makes the human feel, to how the relationship makes the robot feel. In which case, the human concerns would evolve around whether or not robots can and would love human beings, and if becoming engaged in a human-robot relationship, what it would take to sustain the robot's interest in their human partner. Would body-hacking be enough to compete with a robot counter-part? And of course, other issues come into play when considering robots with their own subjective experience.

These matters would include notions of gender and gender identification, particularly when gender has no utilitarian function. Then indeed, what is sex in a realm of either cosmetic or non-existent gender, with no reproductive function? Another important point to consider would be the potential for robot jealousy. If for some reason, robots are attracted to human imperfections and the pure organics of what makes people human, then would there not be the potential for robots to feel threatened towards the idea that their human partners will leave them for another human being? Thus, if advancements really did get to the stage that robots are indeed capable of not only love, affection and sexual attraction, but also jealously, anger and betrayal [47, 48], would there not also be greater likelihood of associated problems such as violence, murder and divorce [31]?

On a final note the discussion of this paper may be seen to lead to a larger problematization of the human-robot relationship – in an era of thinking and feeling robots, will humans and robots indeed be separate entities? If the maintenance of a sexual relationship between humans and robots would be categorized as one of self enhancement, inadequacy and trading up, can it not be seen that humans will in fact evolve into their robot partners, with the hope of being able to compete with other perfect beings? One may revert to Minsky's [75] prediction of a future in which not simply machines possess artificial intelligence, but in fact human beings who are bio-technologically adapted – robots or super people. These (human) beings are expected to live unfathomably long and healthy lives. And as Minsky puts, which relates strongly to the functional role of reproduction as a drive for sexual desire: "Will robots inherit the earth? Yes, but they will be our children."

# References

1. Bellman, R.: An Introduction to Artificial Intelligence: Can Computers Think?. Thomson Course Technology, Boston (1978)
2. Russell, S., Norvig, P.: Artificial Intelligence: A Modern Approach. Prentice-Hall, Englewood Cliffs (1995)
3. Cheok, A.D., Levy, D., Karunanayaka, K.: Lovotics: love and sex with robots. In: Karpouzis, K., Yannakakis, Georgios N. (eds.) Emotion in Games. SC, vol. 4, pp. 303–328. Springer, Cham (2016). https://doi.org/10.1007/978-3-319-41316-7_18
4. Samani, H.A., Cheok, A.D., Tharakan, M.J., Koh, J., Fernando, N.: A design process for lovotics. In: Lamers, M.H., Verbeek, F.J. (eds.) HRPR 2010. LNICST, vol. 59, pp. 118–125. Springer, Heidelberg (2011). https://doi.org/10.1007/978-3-642-19385-9_15
5. Hatfield, E., Rapson, R.L.: Love, Sex, and Intimacy: Their Psychology, Biology, and History. HarperCollins College Publishers, New York (1993)
6. Joachim, H., Rees, D.: Aristotle: The Nicomachean Ethics. Clarendon Press, Oxford (1951)

7. Lewis, C.: The Four Loves. Houghton Mifflin Harcourt, Boston (1991)
8. Soble, A.: Eros, Agape, and Philia: Readings in the Philosophy of Love. Paragon House Publishers, New York (1989)
9. Merriam-Webster Dictionary. Love. http://www.merriam-webster.com/dictionary/love. Accessed 24 May 2016
10. Sternberg, R.J.: Triangulating love. In: Oord, T.J. (ed.) The Altruism Reader: Selections from Writings on Love, Religion, and Science. Templeton Foundation, West Conshohocken (2007)
11. Sternberg, R.J.: A triangular theory of love. In: Reis, H.T., Rusbult, C.E. (eds.) Close Relationships. Psychology Press, New York (2004)
12. Sternberg, R.J.: Construct validation of a triangular love scale. Eur. J. Soc. Psychol. **27**(3), 313–335 (1997)
13. Diessner, R., Frost, N., Smith, T.: Describing the neoclassical psyche embedded in Sternberg's triangular theory of love. Soc. Behav. Pers. Int. J. **32**(7), 683–690 (2004)
14. Frijda, N.H.: The place of appraisal in emotion. Cogn. Emot. **7**(3–4), 357–387 (1993)
15. Frijda, N.H., Zeelenberg, M.: Appraisal: what is the dependent? In: Scherer, K.R., Schorr, A., Johnstone, T. (eds.) Series in Affective Science. Appraisal Processes in Emotion: Theory, Methods, Research, pp. 141–155. Oxford University Press, New York (2001)
16. Lazarus, R.S.: Relational meaning and discrete emotions. In: Scherer, K.R., Schorr, A., Johnstone, T. (eds.) Series in Affective Science. Appraisal Processes in Emotion: Theory, Methods, Research, pp. 37–67. Oxford University Press, New York (2001)
17. Clore, G.L., Ortony, A.: Appraisal theories: how cognition shapes affect into emotion. In: Lewis, M., Haviland-Jones, J.M., Barrett, L.F. (eds.) Handbook of Emotions, pp. 628–642. Guilford Press, New York (2008)
18. Yilmaz, V.: Consumer behavior in shopping center choice. Soc. Behav. Pers. Int. J. **32**(8), 783–790 (2004)
19. Fournier, S.: Consumers and their brands: developing relationship theory in consumer research. J. Consum. Res. **24**(4), 343–373 (1998)
20. Rousi, R.: From Cute to Content: User Experience From a Cognitive Semiotic Perspective. Jyväskylä Studies in Computing, vol. 171. University of Jyväskylä Press, Jyväskylä (2013)
21. Watson, L., Spence, M.T.: Causes and consequences of emotions on consumer behaviour: a review and integrative cognitive appraisal theory. Eur. J. Mark. **41**(5/6), 487–511 (2007)
22. Kelley, H.H., Berscheid, E., Christensen, A., Harvey, J.H., Huston, T.L., et al.: Close Relationships. Freeman, New York (1983)
23. Finkel, E.J., Simpson, J.A., Eastwick, P.W.: The psychology of close relationships: fourteen core principles. Annu. Rev. Psychol. **68**, 383–411 (2017)
24. Rusbult, C.E.: A longitudinal test of the investment model: the development (and deterioration) of satisfaction and commitment in heterosexual involvements. J. Pers. Soc. Psychol. **45**, 101–117 (1983)
25. Salman, A.: Comprehensive Dictionary of Psychoanalysis, p. 89. Karnac Books, London (2009)
26. Maslow, A.H.: A theory of human motivation. Psycholo. Rev. **50**(4), 360–396 (1943)
27. Oxford English Dictionary: Fidelity. https://en.oxforddictionaries.com/definition/fidelity
28. Fletcher, G.P.: Loyalty: An Essay on the Morality of Relationships. Oxford University Press, New York (1995)
29. Mattingly, B.A., Wilson, K., Clark, E.M., Bequette, A.W., Weidler, D.J.: Foggy faithfulness: relationship quality, religiosity, and the perceptions of dating infidelity scale in an adult sample. J. Fam. Issues **31**(11), 1465–1480 (2010)
30. Stafford, L., Canary, D.J.: Maintenance strategies and romantic relationship type, gender and relational characteristics. J. Soc. Pers. Relat. **8**(2), 217–242 (1991)

31. Drigotas, S.M., Barta, W.: The cheating heart: scientific explorations of infidelity. Curr. Dir. Psychol. Sci. **10**(5), 177–180 (2001)
32. Daly, M., Wilson, M.: Homicide. Aldine de Gruyter, Hawthorne (1988)
33. Rusbult, C.E., Drigotas, S.M., Verette, J.: The investment model: an interdependence analysis of commitment processes and relationship maintenance phenomena. In: Canary, D., Stafford, L. (eds.) Communication and Relational Maintenance, pp. 115–139. Academic Press, San Diego (1994)
34. Buss, D.: Evolutionary Psychology. Allyn & Bacon, Needham Heights (1998)
35. Levy, D.: Love and Sex with Robots: The Evolution of Human-Robot Relationships. Harper Collins, New York (2007)
36. Sullins, J.: Robots, love, and sex: the ethics of building a love machine. IEEE Trans. Affect. Comput. **3**(4), 398–409 (2012)
37. Meston, C.M., Buss, D.M.: Why humans have sex. Arch. Sex. Behav. **36**(4), 477–507 (2007)
38. Fehr, B., Russell, J.A.: The concept of love viewed from a prototype perspective. J. Pers. Soc. Psychol. **60**(3), 425 (1991)
39. Russell, J.A., Fehr, B.: Fuzzy concepts in a fuzzy hierarchy: varieties of anger. J. Pers. Soc. Psychol. **67**(2), 186 (1994)
40. Lin, P., Adney, K., Bekey, G.A.: Robot Ethics: The Ethical and Social Implications of Robotics. MIT Press, Cambridge (2011)
41. Sparrow, R.: Robots, rape, and representation. Int. J. Soc. Robot. **9**, 1–13 (2017)
42. Richardson, K.: The asymmetrical 'relationship': parallels between prostitution and the development of sex robots. ACM SIGCAS Comput. Soc. **45**(3), 290–293 (2016)
43. Mackenzie, R.: Sexbots: replacements for sex workers? Ethical constraints on the design of sentient beings for utilitarian purposes. In: Proceedings of the 2014 Workshops on Advances in Computer Entertainment Conference, p. 8. ACM (2014)
44. Adams, A.A.: Virtual sex with child avatars. In: Wankel, C., Malleck, S. (eds.) Emerging Ethical Issues of Life in Virtual Worlds, pp. 55–72. Information Age Publishing, Charlotte (2010)
45. Snell, J.: Sexbots: an editorial. Psychol. Educ. Interdisc. J. **42**(1), 49–50 (2005)
46. Turkle, S.: Alone Together: Why We Expect More from Technology and Less from Each Other. Basic Books, New York (2012)
47. Ashrafian, H.: AlonAI: a humanitarian law of artificial intelligence and robotics. Sci. Eng. Ethics **21**(1), 29–40 (2015)
48. Ashrafian, H.: Artificial intelligence and robot responsibilities: innovating beyond rights. Sci. Eng. Ethics **21**(2), 317–326 (2015)
49. Madden, J.: Should having sex with a robot count as cheating? BBC. http://www.bbc.co.uk/bbcthree/item/0c4f5093-ed7d-4fad-97cf-b93b9afb1679. Accessed 02 June 2017
50. Rawlinson, K.: Microsoft's Bill Gates insists AI is a threat. NNB News. http://www.bbc.com/news/31047780. Accessed 02 June 2017
51. Lewis, T.: Stephen Hawking: artificial intelligence could end human race. Live Science, https://www.livescience.com/48972-stephen-hawking-artificial-intelligence-threat.html. Accessed 02 June 2017
52. Mackenzie Wright, D.W.: Hunting humans: a future for tourism in 2200. Futures **78–79**, 34–46 (2016)
53. Fox, S.: Evolving robots learn to lie to each other. Popular Science. http://www.popsci.com/scitech/article/2009-08/evolving-robots-learn-lie-hide-resources-each-other. Accessed 07 July 2017

54. Litiou, A., Ullman, D., Kim, J., Scassellati, B.: Evidence that robots trigger a cheating detector in humans. In: Proceedings of the Tenth Annual ACM/IEEE International Conference on Human-Robot Interaction, pp. 165–172. ACM (2015)

55. Short, E., Hart, J., Vu, M., Scassellati, B.: No fair!! an interaction with a cheating robot. In: The Proceedings of the 5th ACM/IEEE International Conference on Human-Robot Interaction, pp. 219–226 (2010)

56. Ullman, D., Leite, I., Phillips, J., Kim-Cohen, J., Scassellati, B.: Smart human, smarter robot: how cheating affects perceptions of social agency. In: Proceedings of the 36th Annual Conference of the Cognitive Science Society (2014)

57. Cosmides, L.: The logic of social exchange: has natural selection shaped how humans reason? Studies with the Wason selection task. Cogn. **31**(3), 187–276 (1989)

58. Cosmides, L., Tooby, J.: Cognitive adaptations for social exchange. In: Barkow, J.H., Cosmides, L., Tooby, J. (eds.) The Adapted Mind – Evolutionary Psychology and the Generation of Culture, pp. 163–228. Oxford University Press, New York (1992)

59. Verplatse, J., Vanneste, S., Braekman, J.: You can judge a book by its cover: the sequel: a kernel of truth in predictive cheating detection. Evol. Hum. Behav. **28**(4), 260–271 (2007)

60. Hutson, M.: The 7 laws of magical thinking: how irrational beliefs keep us happy, healthy, and sane, pp. 165–171. Hudson Street Press, New York (2012)

61. Mori, M., MacDorman, K.F., Kageki, N.: The uncanny valley [from the field]. IEEE Robot. Autom. Mag. **19**(2), 98–100 (2012)

62. Hanson, D., Olney, A., Prilliman, S., Mathews, E., Zielke, M., Hammons, D., Fernandez, R., Stephanou, H.: Upending the uncanny valley. In: Proceedings of the National Conference on Artificial Intelligence, vol. 20(4), pp. 1728–1729. MIT Press, Cambridge (1999)

63. Barber, T.: Kinky Borgs and sexy robots: the fetish, fashion and discipline of seven of nine. In: Channeling the Future: Essays on Science Fiction and Fantasy Television, pp. 133–148. Scarecrow Publishing, Metuchen (2009)

64. Kaplan, F.: Who is afraid of the humanoid? Investigating cultural differences in the acceptance of robots. Int. J. Humanoid Robot. **1**(03), 465–480 (2004)

65. Suzuki, T.: Word in Context: A Japanese Perspective on Language and Culture. Kodansha International, Tokyo (2001)

66. Staszak, J.F.: Other/otherness. In: Kitchin, R., Thrift, N. (eds.) International Encyclopaedia of Human Geography, vol. 8, pp. 43–47. Elsevier, Oxford (2009)

67. Berque, A., Schwartz, R.: Japan Nature, Artifice and Japanese Culture. Pilkington, Yelvertoft Manor (1997)

68. Fontichiaro, K.: Taming the technology leadership dragon. In: Coatney, S., Harada, V.H. (eds.) The Many Faces of School Library Leadership, pp. 119–132. Libraries Unlimited, Denver (2017)

69. Mori, M.: The Buddha in the Robot. Kosei Publishing Company, Tokyo (1981)

70. Starobinski, J.: Jean-Jacques Rousseau, transparency and obstruction. Goldhammer, A. [Trans.]. University of Chicago Press, IL (1988)

71. Syrdal, D.S., Nomura, T., Hirai, H., Dautenhahn, K.: Examining the frankenstein syndrome. In: Mutlu, B., Bartneck, C., Ham, J., Evers, V., Kanda, T. (eds.) ICSR 2011. LNCS (LNAI), vol. 7072, pp. 125–134. Springer, Heidelberg (2011). https://doi.org/10.1007/978-3-642-25504-5_13

72. Li, D., Rau, P.P., Li, Y.: A cross-cultural study: effect of robot appearance and task. Int. J. Soc. Robot. **2**(2), 175–186 (2010)

73. ATR Home: Hiroshi Ishiguro Laboratories. http://www.geminoid.jp/en/index.html

74. Guizzo, E.: Hiroshi Ishiguro: The Man Who Made a Copy of Himself. IEEE Spectrum (2010). https://spectrum.ieee.org/robotics/humanoids/hiroshi-ishiguro-the-man-who-made-a-copy-of-himself
75. Minsky, M.L.: Will robots inherit the earth. Scientific American **271**(4), 108–113 (1994)

# Neurodildo: A Mind-Controlled Sex Toy with E-stim Feedback for People with Disabilities

Leonardo M. Gomes[1](✉) 🄳 and Rita Wu[2]

[1] Department of Electrical Engineering - São Carlos School of Engineering (EESC),
University of São Paulo, São Carlos, SP 13566-590, Brazil
leo.gomes@usp.br
[2] Architecture and Urbanism College (FAU), University of São Paulo,
São Paulo, SP 03178-200, Brazil
r.digwu@gmail.com

**Abstract.** In this paper we present the Neurodildo, a sex toy remotely controlled by brain waves, which is pressure sensitive and with electrical stimulation (e-stim) feedback. The sex toy enables long distance relationship couples to have an option to reduce the lack of physical interaction and it is also useful for people with motor disabilities, for example spinal cord injury, who have difficult to handle a commercial toy and who can't go to a place for dating. The system consists in: the sex toy with Bluetooth and sensors, the brain-computer interface headset and the e-stim device, in addition to a computer for running the necessary software. The first user wears the headset and the e-stim device, and by focusing in trained patterns, he can control the vibration of the sex toy. The pressure applied to the sex toy by the second user is measured by sensors and transmitted to the first user, who feels muscles contraction. The goal of this project is to design a sex toy that may be helpful for couples living apart but for people with disabilities, who have few commercial options. In this paper we explain the background and motivation of our work, and then present the concept and design process of the Neurodildo.

**Keywords:** Teledildonics · Brain-computer interface · Spinal cord injury
Long-distance relationships

## 1 Introduction

Technology is changing faster every day and the same happens to human relationships and interactions. People are being presented to new mobile apps that allow them to chat to each other and share their lives even if they are geographically distant. Long-distance relationships (LDR) are becoming more common than ever, considering the fact that the couple has a wide range of technological options to assist them to be in contact, at least virtually. More specifically, couples are now able to have intimate or sexual relationships being distant by using internet connected sex toys, and these devices try to reduce the lack of physical contact in LDR couples.

© Springer International Publishing AG, part of Springer Nature 2018
A. D. Cheok and D. Levy (Eds.): LSR 2017, LNCS 10715, pp. 65–82, 2018.
https://doi.org/10.1007/978-3-319-76369-9_6

The more the technology is developed, the more the costs decreases and electronic devices become more affordable. An important contribution to the development of technology and to the new products is the open-source hardware and software, which allow more developers to work on projects and use their knowledge to help other people. In this work, we would like to highlight the development and popularization of electroencephalography (EEG) headsets. These devices are based on research and medical-grade equipment that are used to diagnose brain diseases and conditions on patients. The commercial EEG headsets led developers to work on a new area called Brain-computer interfaces (BCI), which consists on using brain signals to control software or hardware devices.

In the context of LDR and BCI, we developed the Neurodildo, which is a brain remote controlled sex toy focused in the use by people with motor disabilities, for example with spinal cord injury (SCI), and who are not able to manipulate an ordinary sex toy by using hands. We focus on people with disabilities but we do not exclude the use of the Neurodildo by people with an abnormal motor condition. We also explore the scenario of the disabled people that have limited social contacts or have failed on the attempts to engage a relationship, but they are still a sexual people. The fact of the sex toy can be used anywhere where it can be connected to the internet or in the presence of the person wearing the EEG headset may enable the person with disability to have virtual sexual encounters. We also propose a feedback response system, so the sex toy may send stimuli to the person wearing the EEG headset and controlling the sex toy and this person would be electro stimulated proportionally as the sex toy feel the body muscular contractions pressure. The Neurodildo is connected to the internet through Bluetooth and a mobile app or by computer software; it vibrates according to the received brain signal and sends proportional values of the attached pressure signals, that will be used to activate an e-stimuli device connected to the wearer of the headset (Fig. 1).

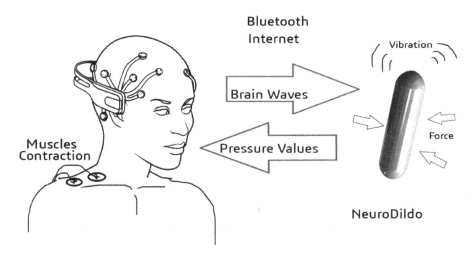

**Fig. 1.** The concept of the Neurodildo: a brain controlled sex toy.

# 2  Background

The design of the Neurodildo involved attention in certain areas, including the sexuality of people with disabilities, the injuries (focusing on SCI) and its effects in the body. We also explored the existing options on BCIs and how they could serve to our purposes, and also the existing projects and products related to mind controlled sex toys. In the following subsections, we briefly explain about each topic and its importance to our work.

## 2.1  Disability and Sexuality

The spinal cord injury has a big impact in the life of individuals that have suffered it and their familiars. Studies indicate that researchers focus on the motor rehabilitation of people with SCI, in particular the restoration of locomotion function. However, SCI causes loss of other important functions, including bladder, bowel, sexual and sensory dysfunctions, that are not always directly visible to others [1].

In a study conducted by Anderson in 2004 [2], people with SCI has been surveyed about their desires for functional restoration, and the results showed that most people ranked sexual function in the top priorities, above the priority of regaining walking movement. People with SCI may still be sexual people, with desires and necessities, but certain attention is needed regarding the nature of their physical disability. The damaged nerves or blood supply can interfere with the sexual response, and it may be difficult to get into a position for making love, or there may be limitations that interfere with the foreplay [3].

In male population, SCI affects the sexual function depending on the level of the lesion and its completeness. One may have its capability of maintaining erections affected, or the occurrence of ejaculation may become relatively rare or to cease. Studies on vibrostimulation indicated that using stronger stimulation parameters significantly increased the success rate for ejaculation [4].

## 2.2  Sex Toys for Disabled People

The design a sex toy for people with SCI should consider particular aspects that may not be clear for people without disabilities in the first sight. People may have limitations in the positions they can do while making love, but also they can have increased or decreased sensibility in certain parts of the body. Bowel and bladder dysfunctions, loss or impairment of hand function, decreased energy levels and less lubrication than in normal conditions (in the case of women) may also occur caused by the SCI [3].

Sex toys are designed not only focusing on penetrative sex, and this must be emphasized while considering the design for people with SCI. A range of products is available in the market, and this can be used as sexual aid for disabled people [5]. Cosmetics for increasing lubrication of women, massagers [6], sex furniture [7], nipple clamps, floggers, plugs and commercial vibrators are options but none of them are specifically made for people with disabilities. Ferticare [8] is a Danish product designed with disabled people in mind. It helps men with spinal cord injuries to ejaculate by vibrostimulation of the penis. The amplitude and frequency of the vibrations can be adjusted with large knobs and the device can be turned on and off by hitting its base. These features are valuable for people with decreased strength of hands, but in most situations, people would need assistance of a carer for setting up the device and positioning it for use.

## 2.3   Long-Distance Relationship as a Possibility

Within all the benefits that technological advances can provide for the population, we highlight the area of social relations, more specifically the long-distance relationships (LDR). In the past decades, couples could communicate by sending letters and after that by phone calls. Because of the internet, live video calls became feasible and popular, and more recently, mobile devices appeared as an important tool for people communicating. LDR may occur by different reasons, including but not limited to: demand of work, choice of careers, college studies and studying abroad programs or autonomy of the individuals. While LDR may be beneficial, couples faces several challenges, ranging from technical problems while video chatting and time zone differences, to lack of true physicality needed by most in order to support intimate sexual acts [9].

Recently, companies have developed products aimed on, but not only, couples in LDR. The products consist on sex toys that can be connected to the internet and, in the most cases, vibrating being controlled remotely by a mobile app or computer software. These devices are part of the area of teledildonics, within the area of the internet of things (IoT). The most known IoT sex toys are the Lovense Lush [10], the We-Vibe Sync [11] and the Ohmibod Panty Vibe [12]. Most of these toys have Bluetooth connection and are able to pair with a mobile phone and through an app, be controlled over the internet. However those sex toys are designed for couples, they only permit the person wearing the sex toy, usually the woman, to receive stimuli controlled by the person using the app, the man, who doesn't receive any sexual stimuli besides the visual feedback of the woman having pleasure.

People with SCI and other disabilities may benefit themselves by using services and products designed to LDR. The disabilities make difficult for a person to go to a dating place and even to find a partner. There are some dating websites focusing on people with disabilities [13] but they can also use other dating services or mobile apps which are for general public. Another option is contacting a sex worker, but the person should fully understand the inherent risks [3]. By engaging a LDR or contacting a sex worker, a teledildonics device may be a useful resource for either people with or without disabilities.

## 2.4   Brain-Computer Interfaces (BCI)

A brain computer interface (BCI), or brain machine interface (BMI), is a set of hardware and software system that enables humans to interact with their surroundings, without the involvement of peripheral nerves and muscles. This interaction is possible by the interpretation, processing and application of signals generated by electroencephalography activity [14]. Most researchers apply BCI to provide communications capabilities to severely disabled people who are totally paralyzed, including people who suffered

SCI. The BCI can recognize certain set of patterns in brain signals by acquisition of the signals using electrodes placed on the scalp, pre-processing the signals (filtering artifacts), extracting features and classifying the signals to control the interface.

Commercial BCI are available nowadays, including proprietary products such as Emotiv Epoc [15] and the Neurosky MindWave [16] headsets. Open-source projects can also be used for BCI, including the Olimex OpenEEG [17], based on the project OpenEEG [18], and the OpenBCI project [19], which is a source of useful resources like software and hardware schematics. In this work, we have chosen to use an Emotiv Epoc headset, because we had it available and would not need to build the hardware by ourselves. The Emotiv Epoc is a set of fourteen electrodes and two references that is able to detect patterns of thought, feelings and expressions in real time [15].

Researchers have successfully demonstrated that BCI headsets like the Emotiv Epoc are able to work as an interface for controlling other devices. Through the brain waves, a robot arm can be remotely controlled [20] and regarding the people with SCI, studies combined BCI and assistive technologies for example by developing an electric wheel chair controlled by the mind [21]. Recently, the media has published some articles about companies and designers who are exploring the possibilities of using BCI for controlling sex toys [22, 23].

## 3   Design Process

### 3.1   System Overview

The Neurodildo device consists in a 3 major parts system. The first is the sex toy, which is able of communicating by Bluetooth with a smartphone or computer, has a microcontroller board (Arduino) and a circuit to drive a vibration motor. The sex toy also has attached to its body two force sensors, which should capture the body pressure against the sex toy. The second part of the system is the BCI headset (the Emotiv EPOC) and its related software, running on a computer. The third and last part of the system is the computer controlled E-Stim device (Electrical Muscle Stimulation), which is responsible for the feedback response of the sex toy pressure to the person controlling remotely the sex toy with the brain waves. In the following, we will detail each part of the Neurodildo system and their components used to build the prototype.

### 3.2   Design of the Sex Toy

The first step of building the sex toy prototype was 3D modelling the plastic body. We modelled the plastic body as a cylinder with the top and bottom ends in a rounded shape. We used the Solidworks software for modelling and generating the STL file, which would be used after in the 3D printing stage. The body of the sex toy is hollow for housing the electronics, battery and the vibration motor. After modelling, we used the Cura software for slicing the 3D model and generating the g-code file, which is the one used by the 3D printer. We printed the body of the sex toy in ABS plastic, using a homemade 3D printer. The dimensions of the sex toy was 35 mm external diameter and 127 mm length, and those dimensions were chosen considering that the sex toy should not be too large for being penetrated into the vagina and too small for being handled. The 3D rendered model, the 3D printing process and the plastic parts assembled of the sex toy are shown in Fig. 2. A hand holding the sex toy is shown in Fig. 3 giving notion of its size.

**Fig. 2.** 3D model of the sex toy plastic body, 3D printing of the parts and the plastic body assembled.

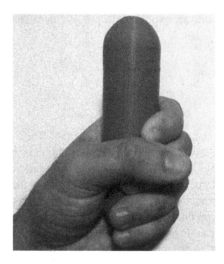

**Fig. 3.** User holding the sex toy. Dimensions are 35 mm external diameter and 127 mm length.

After 3D printing and assembling the body of sex toy, we designed the electronic circuits. We used an Arduino Pro Mini board, which is connected to a HC-05 Bluetooth module. As we designed the sex toy for being portable, we used TP4056 battery charger module and a 340 mAh 3.7 V Lipo battery. The vibration motor used in this prototype is a commercial one, commonly used in gaming controllers, and to drive this motor we used a board with a single switching transistor circuit. We fixed the electronics modules together using a 3M VHB tape and housed in a 3D printed enclosure, that was inserted inside the body of the sex toy. In Fig. 4 we show the electronics modules (top and bottom view) and its wirings, the plastic housing with electronics inside and the modules connected to the vibration motor and battery cell. With this setup, the sex toy can work for approximately 45 min and the charging time is 90 min.

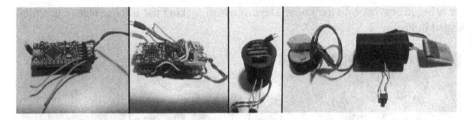

**Fig. 4.** Electronic modules of the Neurodildo (top and bottom view), the electronics housing and the connections with the vibration motor and battery.

For the pressure sensing function, we chosen to use two force-sensitive resistors (FSR) attached to the body of the sex toy. FSR are sensors that allow detecting physical pressure, squeezing and weight [24]. Its resistance decreases when a force is applied to its surface, and by using a voltage divider circuit, we could measure a variation of an analog voltage depending on the force applied to the sensors. In Fig. 5 we show the Neurodildo with the FSR attached to its body.

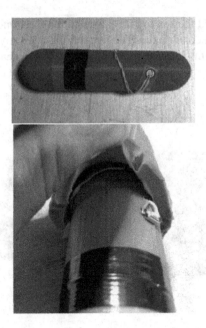

**Fig. 5.** FSR sensors attached to the sex toy plastic body.

In order to protect the sensors while penetrating the sex toy or even rubbing it, we designed a silicone sleeve which is placed on the plastic body of the sex toy and over the sensors. We made the negative mold of a slightly bigger version of the body of the sex toy using plaster of Paris and then we used the silicone casting technique for creating the sleeve by pouring silicone in the space between the mold and the original sex toy body. In this prototype we didn't use medical grade silicone, so this version is not suitable for being in contact with the body. The process of making the silicone sleeve is represented in Fig. 6.

**Fig. 6.** The silicone casting process for creating the sleeve of the sex toy.

Finally, we assembled the sex toy (Fig. 7) with the electronics inside, the attached sensors and glued the silicone sleeve. The bottom of the sex toy is removable because it is necessary to access the internal side while is needed to charge the battery. In this occasion, a smartphone charger and a micro USB cable can be used.

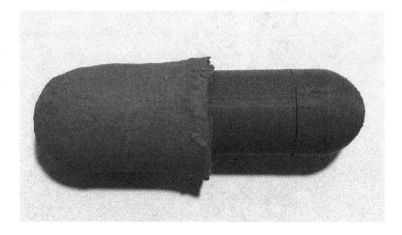

**Fig. 7.** Neurodildo sex toy assembled.

### 3.3   The BCI – Emotiv EPOC

In order to use the Emotiv Epoc EEG headset with the Neurodildo system, a series of steps are necessary for setting up the hardware and the software. First of all, the electrode sensors must be wetted by using a saline solution, for obtaining a good contact with the scalp and good signal quality. After that, the sensors can be mounted in the neuroheadset arms, and the Emotiv USB transceiver is plugged in the computer.

The first software to be used is the EPOC Control Panel, which must be launched and then the EPOC headset can be placed on the head, following the positioning instructions in the user's manual. The signal quality for all the sensors should be checked and if all of them are green, they are ready to use. Next, we should use the Cognitive Suite, in the Control Panel, for training the detection of brain waves and associate with user's conscious intent to perform physical actions, like pushing or pulling an object, and the neutral state of mind. The trained actions should be linked with keystroke commands by using the Emokey. The second software is the Mind Your OSC, which is third-party open source software for converting the EPOC data to the Open Sound Control (OSC) messages. The following step is to launch a python script, which is responsible for reading the OSC messages and send the data to the sex toy by Bluetooth. The same python script is responsible for receiving the pressure values from the sex toy and activating the Arduino Nano, which activate the e-stim device and causes the user's muscles to contract, by "feeling" the same pressure that the sex toy is being subjected to. In Fig. 8 is shown the Emotiv EPOC EEG headset [15].

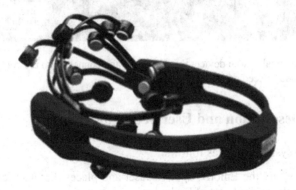

**Fig. 8.** Emotiv EPOC

### 3.4  Pressure to E-stim Feedback

The third part of the Neurodildo system is the e-stim feedback device. The e-stim, or electrical muscle stimulation, is a type of physical therapy modality that can treat illness, pain and for muscle healing. By placing electrodes on the skin, an electrical current causes a single muscle or a group of muscles to contract [25]. The e-stim device can vary the amplitude and timing of the electrical stimulation, causing different sensations, similar to a vibration motor in contact with the skin. We've chosen to use an e-stim device integrated to the Neurodildo system because we wanted that the user, who is controlling the sex toy vibrations using the mind, could receive an additional stimulation beside the visual stimulus. We decided to explore the e-stim because the electrodes can be attached to the body of the person, for example who has SCI, and don't need to be hold by hands, as would happen with a second vibrator. In our system, there is an Arduino

Nano board connected to the board of the e-stim, and plugged on a computer through an USB cable. The computer receives the information about the pressure on the sex toy by Bluetooth and activates the Arduino using a Python script. The Arduino, in turn, activates the e-stim which generates an output wave to the electrodes proportional to the pressure applied to the sex toy. In Fig. 9 is show the e-stim device, its connection to the Arduino and the electrodes placed on a skin.

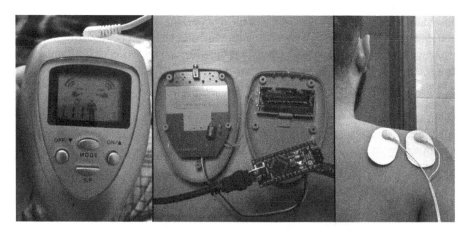

**Fig. 9.** The commercial E-stim device; the Arduino Nano connected to the control panel of the E-stim; the electrodes placed on the shoulder of an user.

## 4   System Description and User Scenarios

The Neurodildo system works as follows:

- The User A wears the Emotiv Epoc headset and places the electrical stimulation electrodes on the desired part of his body;
- The User A turns on the Emotiv Epoc and the e-stim device, and sets up the necessary software, including the Emotiv and the python script for communicating with the sex toy;
- The User B turns the sex toy on, so it can be paired with the computer of User A. In the future, we will develop a mobile app so the User B could pair its sex toy with the smartphone instead the computer;
- The User A begin concentrating on the brain patterns which he has trained previously, for example by focusing on a pre-trained pattern (pushing a virtual block for example);
- The User B feels the vibration of the sex toy changing as the User A focus more or less;
- The pressure applied to the body of the sex toy, for example by penetrating it in a vagina or rubbing it on the clitoris, is sensed by the force sensors under the silicone sleeve of the toy;

- The variation of the pressure values is transmitted through Bluetooth to the computer of the User A;
- The User A feels an electrical stimulation of his muscles proportional to the way that User B is using the sex toy;
- The User A gets aroused because of the visual stimulation (in person or by video chat) and due to the e-stim, and then makes the sex toy vibrates more, arousing the User B and so on.

The block diagram representing the Neurodildo system is shown in Fig. 10:

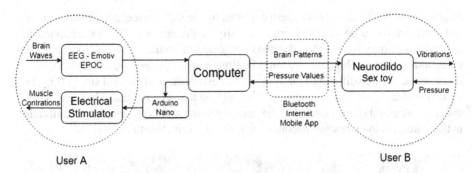

**Fig. 10.** Block diagram of the Neurodildo

We also highlight 3 possible scenarios that may happen for users of the Neurodildo:
In Table 1, we refer to normal couple member as a person without disabilities, and of any gender. In scenario 1, we explore the possibility of a couple in a LDR using the Neurodildo as an option to soften the lack of physical contact. In the second scenario, a person with SCI and that has locomotion limitations may use the remote controlled sex toy in its relationship, without the need to go outside is home. The last scenario we consider a person with SCI or any other disability that has a limited physical condition and/or have failed to engage a relationship. This person could contact a sex worker and have a virtual sex, by using also a video chat. In both scenarios 2 and 3, it would be recommended that the person with disability had the help of a carer or a trusted person to setup de Neurodildo, de BCI (EEG) headset and the e-stim device.

**Table 1.** Neurodildo usage scenarios

| Scenario no. | User A | User B |
| --- | --- | --- |
| 1 | Normal couple member 1 | Normal couple member 2 |
| 2 | Couple member with SCI | Normal couple member |
| 3 | Person with disability | Sex worker |

## 5    Technical Evaluation

A series of tests was made for technically evaluating our prototype. We tested the parts of the system (the sex toy, the BCI and the e-stim device) separately and integrated. In this section, we present the tests and their most important results and by this way, we demonstrate the working of the Neurodildo prototype.

### 5.1    Vibration Patterns and Intensities

Depending on the brain waves pattern captured by the BCI device, the vibration pattern and intensity could be changed proportionally in the sex toy. We implemented the recognition of only one pattern, the one corresponding to the "push" action trained on the Emotiv software. Our software sends by Bluetooth the pattern's intensity data, which is converted to three different vibration intensities: weak, medium and strong (Fig. 11). To demonstrate the vibration intensities, we placed the sex toy tip in a bowl filled with water, so we could show the level of the intensity as the waves produced by the vibration in the water. As the vibration becomes stronger, the wavelength decreases.

**Fig. 11.** Vibration intensities in the water: first is the weak, second the medium and third the strong.

### 5.2    Pressure Sensing Function

The Neurodildo sex toy has two force sensors attached to its body, as mentioned in Sect. 3.2. They are responsible for sensing the pressure when the sex toy is being penetrated or rubbed against the body. For evaluating this function, we made two different tests: the first, we measured with an oscilloscope the voltage variation caused by pressure applied to one of the sensors; the second, we collected the pressure values transmitted from the sex toy to the computer by Bluetooth, and then we plotted this data and compared with the oscilloscope measured signal. In Fig. 12, it is shown the screen capture of the oscilloscope during the first test. Each oscillation corresponds to the moment that the sensor was pressed, and the intensity of these oscillations is proportional to the force applied.

In the second test, we saved a log of the pressure data received from the sex toy and plotted using the MATLAB software. The data was received and saved at the same time as the first test was done. In Fig. 13, it is represented the received pressure values, with

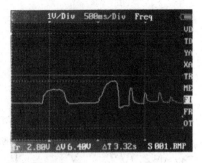

**Fig. 12.** Voltage oscillation when force is applied to one of the FSR sensors.

the y axis corresponding to the ADC converter values (10 bits, or 1024 values), and the x axis is the time of the measure. Data was sent in packages each 25 ms, and the resolution was 3.23 mV for each ADC unit. By comparing Figs. 12 and 13, it is clear that the pressure data is being collected and transmitted correctly.

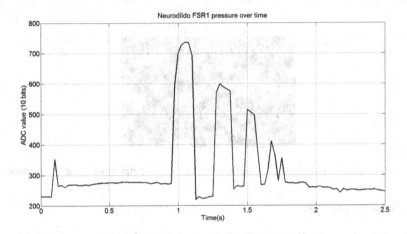

**Fig. 13.** Pressure data of one sensor received by Bluetooth.

For evaluating the functioning of the two sensors at the same time and data transmission, we saved a log of the received packages and plotted a graph, which is represented in Fig. 14. The black line is the signal of the first FSR sensor, and the blue dashed line is the second FSR sensor. It is shown that pressure can be sensed independently by each sensor and when the same force is applied to both sensors, the data representing the voltage variation has the same value for each sensor. In the future, we plan to calibrate the pressure sensors and represent the data more by ADC counts, but by absolute pressure or force applied to the sex toy. The example of the received data packages is represented in Fig. 15 by the screen capture of terminal software. The first column is the first sensor, the second column is the second sensor and the third is a value representing the intensity of the pressure applied to both sensors. This value is used for controlling the intensity of the e-stim device.

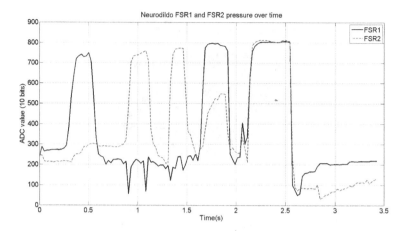

**Fig. 14.** Pressure data applied to the two sensors attached to the sex toy. (Color figure online)

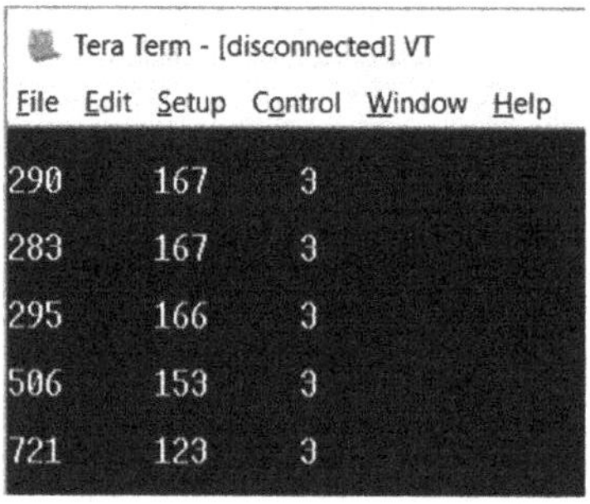

| Tera Term - [disconnected] VT | | | | | |
|---|---|---|---|---|---|
| File | Edit | Setup | Control | Window | Help |
| 290 | 167 | 3 | | | |
| 283 | 167 | 3 | | | |
| 295 | 166 | 3 | | | |
| 506 | 153 | 3 | | | |
| 721 | 123 | 3 | | | |

**Fig. 15.** Pressure data from the sex toy, received by the computer using the terminal software.

## 5.3   BCI – Emotiv Test

The Emotiv Epoc headset is responsible for measuring the brain waves and detecting the pre-trained pattern associated with the brain waves. In our system, the Emotiv (or BCI) data is received by the Emotiv Control Panel, then passed to the Mind Your OSCs software and then to our python script. The python script is responsible to transmit the data about the detected pattern to the sex toy, and receiving the pressure values data, which will be passed to the e-stim device. The correct positioning of the Emotiv Epoc headset is represented in Fig. 16.

In order to debugging our python script and testing the Neurodildo system, we used a software called Emotiv Xavier Composer, which is capable of simulating different brain patterns and intensities, the same way as the BCI headset would detect (Fig. 17).

**Fig. 16.** User wearing the Emotiv EPOC (BCI) headset.

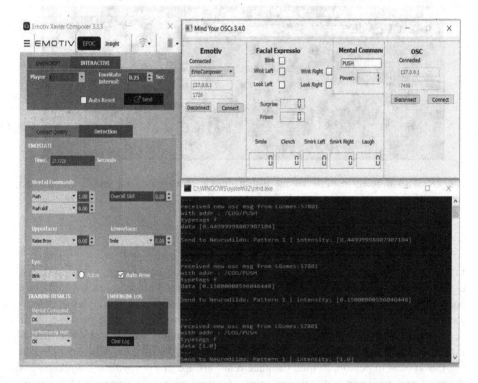

**Fig. 17.** The software set responsible for collecting the brain patterns and sending to the sex toy.

The black window in the Fig. 17 is the output of our python script. In this window, it is displayed the brain pattern detected or simulated, and in this case is the "push" pattern. For each received pattern, it is received also the corresponding intensity, which is a value ranging from 0.0 to 1.0. The pattern's intensity is the value that our python script sends to the sex toy and it converts it to vibration intensities. In Fig. 17, the first received intensity is 0.45 approximately, the second is 0.15 and the last is 1.0.

## 5.4  The E-stim Test

The last part of the Neurodildo system is the e-stim device, which is a commercial TENS equipment, driven by an Arduino circuit, which is connected to a computer by a USB cable. Our python script has the function of integrating the system, and it sends the pressure intensity data to the e-stim device, which varies the pattern of muscles stimulation. The voltage of the electrodes attached to the skin can change its intensity and frequency, and different patterns cause different sensations in the muscles. The idea of the e-stim device is to provide a feedback response in the user wearing the BCI headset, corresponding to the pressure being applied to the sex toy of the second wearer, or in other words, the arousal level. We measured two different patterns of muscle stimulation with an oscilloscope connected to the e-stim circuit (Fig. 18).

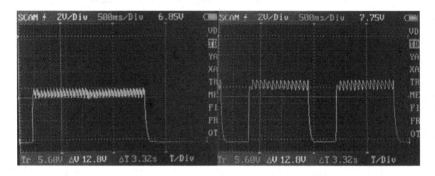

**Fig. 18.** Two different patterns of the e-stim muscle stimulation: the first is weaker and continuous; the second is stronger and with faster oscillation.

# 6  Conclusion

In this paper we presented the Neurodildo by explaining its concept, design process, usage scenarios and the technical evaluation. The Neurodildo is a sex toy remotely controlled by brain waves, which enables long distance relationship couples to experiment sensations that video calls can't provide. The Neurodildo may be very useful for people with disabilities, for example with spinal cord injury, who has physical limitations and usually can't handle commercial sex toys by themselves. These people can use our system in person, in long distance relationships or even with sex workers, but the most important part is that the sexuality of people with disabilities must be encouraged and respected.

## 6.1  Future Work

The prototype presented in this paper is the first one of a work in progress. There are some aspects that we will improve, for example by designing our own EEG headset, based on the open-source projects and this should reduce considerably the price of the final product. Another point that should be changed is that the computer will be removed from the system and substituted by an embedded hardware solution, capable of processing the EEG signals and connecting to the internet, by Wi-Fi or Bluetooth and with a smartphone. The design of the sex toy will also be improved. As we used commercial electronic modules, the size of the hardware was limited to the size of all modules and battery. Building our own electronics board would reduce the size of the sex toy, and we may also add new sensors and actuators for creating new stimulation methods. The physical design of the sex toy will also be changed, by taking into account ergonomic aspects for people having or not disabilities, and the trendy of sex toys in the market. We will develop a smartphone app, so the working distance of the Neurodildo can be limitless when having internet and by last, we will test the Neurodildo with volunteers (disabled and not) to consider what we should keep and what to change in the next versions.

## References

1. Pons, J.L., Raya, R., González, J. (eds.): Emerging Therapies in Neurorehabilitation, 1st edn. Springer, Heidelberg (2014). https://doi.org/10.1007/978-3-642-38556-8
2. Kim, D.: Anderson: targeting recovery: priorities of the spinal cord-injured population. J. Neurotrauma **21**(10), 1371–1383 (2004)
3. Cooper, E., Guillebaud, J.: Sexuality and Disability – A Guide for Everyday Practice, 1st edn. Radcliffe Medical Press, Oxon (1999)
4. Vodusek, D.B., Boller, F.: Neurology of Sexual and Bladder Disorders, vol. 130. Elsevier, Edinburgh (2015)
5. Christine Selinger: Sex toys and sexual aids for adults with SCI. http://www.spinalcord.org/video-sex-toys-sexual-aids-adults-sci. Accessed 26 July 2017
6. Hitachi Magical Wand. http://www.magicalwandoriginal.com. Accessed 29 July 2017
7. Love Bumper. https://www.lovebumper.com. Accessed 29 July 2017
8. Ferti Care Personal Vibrator. http://www.ferticare.pl. Accessed 28 July 2017
9. Neustaedter, C., Greenberg, S.: Intimacy in long-distance relationships over video chat. Research Report 2011-1014-26, Department of Computer Science, University of Calgary, Calgary, Canada (2011)
10. Lush. https://www.lovense.com/bluetooth-remote-control-vibrator. Accessed 29 July 2017
11. We-vibe Sync. http://we-vibe.com/sync. Accessed 29 July 2017
12. Ohmibod. http://www.lovelifetoys.com/For-Her. Accessed 29 July 2017
13. Dating Websites – United Spinal Association – Spinal Cord Resource Center. http://www.spinalcord.org/resource-center/askus/index.php?pg=kb.page&id=2538. Accessed 29 July 2017
14. Nicolas-Alonso, L.F., Gomez-Gil, J.: Brain computer interfaces, a review. Sensors J. **12**(2), 1211–1279 (2012)
15. Emotiv EPOC+ EEG headset. https://www.emotiv.com/epoc/. Accessed 29 July 2017
16. Neurosky MindWave. http://neurosky.com/biosensors/eeg-sensor/biosensors/. Accessed 29 July 2017
17. Olimex OpenEEG. https://www.olimex.com/Products/EEG/. Accessed 29 July 2017
18. OpenEEG project. http://openeeg.sourceforge.net/doc/index.html. Accessed 29 July 2017
19. OpenBCI. http://openbci.com/. Accessed 29 July 2017

20. Ranky, G.N., Adamovich, S.: Analysis of a commercial EEG device for the control of a robot arm. In: Proceedings of the 2010 IEEE 36th Annual Northeast Bioengineering Conference (2010)

21. Millán, J.D.R., et al.: Combining brain-computer interfaces and assistive technologies: state-of-the-art and challenges. Front. Neurosci. **4** (2010). Article 161. https://www.frontiersin.org/articles/10.3389/fnins.2010.00161/full

22. Companies explore potential benefits of mind-controlled sex toys. https://futureofsex.net/remote-sex/companies-explore-potential-benefits-mind-controlled-sex-toys/. Accessed 29 July 2017

23. Sex Toy: Mind Controlled Dildo! Yep, this exists. https://www.youtube.com/watch?v=-40vsVdf5vs. Accessed 29 July 2017

24. Round Force-Sensitive Resistor (FSR) - Interlink 402. https://www.adafruit.com/product/166. Accessed 30 July 2017

25. Electrical Stimulation. https://www.verywell.com/electrical-stimulation-2696122. Accessed 30 July 2017

# Selling Techno-futurism: Exploring Pepper's Images and Discourses Taiwanese News Media Make

Kuan-Hung Lo(✉)

Virginia Tech, Blacksburg, VA, USA
khlo@vt.edu

**Abstract.** Taiwan has many social problems, including a low birthrate and labor shortage. In order to deal with these issues, some people hope that robots may play a robust solution. One of these robots, Pepper, is under the spotlight, because it is a humanoid social robot designed to express and read human emotions. In this context, my question is: what kinds of images of social robots do media construct for the Taiwanese public in order to shape the human-social robot relationships? Through archival research, I divide media treatments of Pepper into five categories: education, promises, reality, problems, and metaphors. News in the education category is fact-telling or educational news. In the promises category, news media not only indicate the Pepper's functions, abilities, services, but also portray Pepper as a solution for social problems. In the reality category, news media report on Pepper's functionality and limitations. In the problems category, news media point to problems Pepper might cause, including a higher unemployment rate and reallocation of wealth. In the metaphors category, I consider the metaphors media use to construct particular discourses and images of Pepper, such as a master/slave model power relation and gender. Based on business interests, technological determinism, and techno-optimism, these discourses compose the public imagination of techno-futurism media create. This techno-futurism is telling the Taiwanese people a technological science story about hopes, threats, and relations. Those Pepper images and discourses build the dominating understandings of social robots in Taiwan.

**Keywords:** Pepper · News media · Taiwan · Social robot

## 1 Introduction

"In Grindelberg, Hamburg, Germany, suddenly a 7-feet tall and 700-pound weight machinery monster shows up on the street. The sound of its heavy steps terrifies pedestrians. When this monster walks on the street, it says 'my name is Sabor. I am the only human who is made of machines in this world'" [17].

On February 21, 1952, the *United Daily News* published the first media report in Taiwan on robots, titled "Robot". This translated article remained the primary picture of robots for the Taiwanese public through the 1960s. After that, robots increasingly gripped the Taiwanese public imagination. Increasing numbers of news stories about robots began to construct the public's understanding of this new technology. The

© Springer International Publishing AG, part of Springer Nature 2018
A. D. Cheok and D. Levy (Eds.): LSR 2017, LNCS 10715, pp. 83–95, 2018.
https://doi.org/10.1007/978-3-319-76369-9_7

American and Japanese entertainment industries were the primary deliverers of images of robots, including Astro Boy, Doraemon, Gundam, Neon Genesis Evangelion, A.I., Transformers, Bicentennial Man, and so on. However, the majority of these remained in the realm of science fiction. Since the more recent advent of increasingly social robots like Paro, Roomba, AIBO, Jibo, Pepper, and Zenbo, media stories concerning them have likewise increased. Compared with industrial robots, which are used primarily in factories, social robots interact with people in their everyday lives.

However, following initial interactions with social robots, many people have been surprised by the abilities of the current generation, speaking to a general under-expectation presented in media accounts. For instance, news media have generally claimed that Pepper's ability to communicate through movement is severely limited [24]. It seems that the public's expectations of social robots' abilities largely underestimate what social robots really can do at this point. I argue that this gap between expectations and the reality of the social robot's ability informs and shapes the human-social robot relationships. Following the argument by Harry Collins and Robert Evans that popular science books and articles in science magazines and broadsheet newspapers construct popular scientific understandings [4], I advance the claim here that Taiwanese media are crucial in shaping the popular understanding of social robots in Taiwan. If we want to reveal the human-social robot relationship in Taiwan and explain the gap, the way in which the media communicates to the public about social robots is the first step. Hence, my research question goes: what kinds of images of social robots do media construct for the Taiwanese public in order to shape the human-social robot relationship?

## 2    Literature Review

Since my research question focuses on social robots, I will first examine what social robots are. There is as yet no universally accepted definition. Christoph Bartneck and Jodi Forlizzi define social robots as "an autonomous or semi-autonomous robot that interacts and communicates with humans by following the behavioral norms expected by the people with whom the robot is intended to interact...This definition implies that a social robot has a physical embodiment" [1]. This definition excludes all robots which cannot and do not interact and communicate with humans in a "socially" expected way. Further, this definition privileges the physical embodiment. An autonomous or semi-autonomous robot which fulfills social norms in line with expectations indicates the ideal social robot. Those two requirements simultaneously place social robots between the human and nonhuman. However, Bartneck and Forlizzi's definition is still unclear. What is meant by "interaction" and "communication"? What counts as a physical embodiment? Since Google Home, Amazon Echo, and iPhone with Siri have physical bodies and they can communicate with humans verbally, should they be categorized as social robots? Kerstin Dautenhahn argues that robots should fulfill five points to be considered "social": (1) socially evocative: social robots rely on human's nurture, care or involvement, (2) socially situated: social robots need to distinguish other social agents from the environment, (3) sociable: social robots require a deep model of social cognition, (4) socially intelligent, and (5) socially interactive [6]. In addition, Dautenhahn also mentions that a social robot needs to know how to accompany humans appropriately [6]. For example, a social robot needs to be less machine-like and more human-like in terms of its interactive capabilities. For Dautenhahn, humans and social robots are companions. Thus, social robots are physical embodiments with proper social behaviors that match the human's expectation regarding nurture, care, and their creation.

Until recently, the relationship between robots and humans has largely been considered in terms of a master/slave model, a hierarchical relationship [16]. Dautenhahn implies a new perspective of human-social robot relationship, i.e. companionship. For Donna Haraway, companionship disputes the exploitation perspective for understanding human-technology relationships [9]. Instead, Haraway embraces the thought that humans and technology are mutually adaptive. As for animals and technology that work with humans intimately, Haraway identifies them as companion species which are "a permanently undecidable category" [9]. Haraway takes a wheelchair as an example: "That wheelchair was in a companion-species relation to the boy; the whole body was organic flesh as well as wood and metal; the player was on wheels, grinning" [9]. Although Haraway's examples are animals and other non-robotic technologies, Dautenhahn argues that humans and social robots must be in a relationship defined by companionship. Compared with the exploitation perspective of understanding human-technology relationships, companionship offers a more equal relationship.

In such a view, technology and humans are simultaneously subjects and objects in an ever-evolving network. Responsibility for human actions, Haraway argues, is what must be dealt with [9]. Compared with animals and technology, humans must take responsibility within a relationship marked by companionship to take care of others. This is consistent with Dautenhahn's idea that these relationships are socially evocative. That is, humans have the responsibility to maintain their creations in good order. However, Haraway's responsibility idea still embraces an imbalanced relationship between humans and social robots. I argue that when humans take responsibility to care for their companion animals and technologies, it begins a process of objectification. In this process, humans still have more power to shape the relationship in ways that humans prefer and hence to exploit social robots.

While Dautenhahn and Haraway embrace the idea of companionship, Raya Jones prefers to think of the human-social robot relationship as a work partner relationship. Jones claims that "in social robotics, however, the focus is on interactions that are themselves the task being performed. The assistive or companion robot does something for the human with whom it interacts. This is closer to the relationships between service providers and their clients, tutors and their students or pets and their owners, than to the relationships between machine operators and the machines they operate [13]." The reason social robots interact with humans is solely for their tasks, not for companionship with humans. In other words, the companionship might simply be a phantom that humans imagine. Lucy Suchman has a similar critique of how humans understand the behavior of robots [29]. She believes that human-like behavior engaged in by machines is evoked solely by the way humans interact with machines and by interpretations humans have. Therefore, for social robots, companionship might not exist with humans in a more equal kind of relationship. Companionship might instead simply be the totality of tasks robots perform and the phantom human imagine. In this context, companionship is a performance and therefore not a good path to rethink human-robot relationships. Since social robots are doing tasks they are assigned without choice or agency, interactions between humans and social robots resemble a work-partner relationship, instead of companionship [13]. That is, social robots work with humans.

Social robots have various definitions and evoke different kinds of understandings of human-robot relationships. However, are these competing definitions and explanations of human-social robot relationship reflected in the images that society popularly imagines? This is what I attempt to address in the remainder of this paper.

## 3   Research Method

Following Collins' and Evans' argument that science books and articles in magazines and newspapers construct popular scientific understandings for the public [4], I will pay attention to social robots' images that newspaper media construct in order to explore how the Taiwanese public imagines social robots. In this paper, I will take Pepper, the robot produced by SoftBank, as my case. Pepper is an ideal research focus for several reasons: (1) Pepper is the most popular and well-known social robot in Taiwan. So far, Pepper has been used in banks, restaurants, temples, and business companies, including First Bank, Din Tai Fung, Big City, Asia Pacific Telecom, EVA Air, the Chimei Museum, the Pingtung County Government, the Foxconn Technology Group Neihu Branch, and so on. Therefore, compared with other social robots, the Taiwanese public have had much more opportunity to interact with Pepper. (2) Compared with other social robots (such as Zenbo and Jibo), Pepper has been widely reported on. Over 500 articles and news come up in the United Daily News Database when searching for "Pepper" and "robots". In comparison, I find only 110 pieces about Zenbo, 21 about Jibo, and 27 about Paro. I thus conclude that Pepper is the most well-known social robot in Taiwan.

My research method is archival analysis. The news database I explore is the United Daily News Database which includes the *United Daily News*, the *Economic Daily News*, the *United Evening News*, the *Min Sheng Bao*, the *Upaper*, the *World Journal*, the *Global Views Monthly*, the *Business Weekly*, and the *Brain*. The *United Daily News*, the *Economic Daily News*, the *United Evening News*, the *Min Sheng Bao*, and the *Upaper* are newspaper media; the *World Journal*, the *Global Views Monthly*, the *Business Weekly*, and the *Brain* are general magazine media. Especially, the *United Daily News* is in the top four media corporations in the country. Because the United Daily News Database has these popular media, I choose the United Daily News Database as my research database. Different newspaper media and magazine media have their own approaches. The *United Daily News*, the *United Evening News,* the *World Journal*, the *Global Views Monthly* focus on general news and reports, when the *Economic Daily News*, the *Min Sheng Bao*, the *Upaper*, and the *Business Weekly* pay particular attention to economic and consumption news and reports. The *Brain* is a popular science magazine. In the following discussion, I will demonstrate that their different approaches infuse their reporting with different intentions.

## 4    Pepper in Taiwanese News Media

Over the last five years, Pepper has been more and more famous in Taiwan. This is not just because the Taiwanese are more amenable to accepting what is from Japan and Japanese culture. In Taiwan, Pepper has been working in First Bank (more than 170 branches have Peppers), Din Tai Fung (one Pepper in its Taipei 101 Mall Branch), Big City (two), Asia Pacific Telecom, EVA Air (two), the Chimei Museum (two), the Ping-tung County Government (one), and so on. Those Peppers have been interacting with the Taiwanese public on an everyday basis. In this section, I analyze media accounts of Pepper to reveal what images are being created in the public.

### 4.1    Education: What is Pepper?

Pepper is a relatively new product for Taiwan. Consequently, media have had the chance to introduce it to the public. There are several levels for introducing Pepper. First of all, the physical description of Pepper. For example, "Pepper is 121 cm tall and 29 kg. Pepper has 29 joints, 27 sensors, and a tablet" [32]. These accounts focus on the physical details of Pepper to draw a picture for the public: Its shape and how it moves, human-like, using wheels, two arms, and speech recognition [43]. However, media accounts have also discussed the existing hardware problems. For example, Fang-Min Lu, the vice president of the Foxconn, complains that Pepper cannot synchronize with Lu's actions because Pepper does not have eye sensors; therefore, Lu suggests engineers use the X-box 360 Kinect to catch human actions for Pepper [24]. Media accounts, therefore, describe both positive and negative aspects of the robot's hardware capabilities.

Second, news media introduce which category of social robots Pepper should belong to: a social robot with the ability to read emotions. Compared with other robots, recognizing human emotions is a special characteristic. For example, one account argues that "Pepper…has the capacity of recognizing humans' feelings" [25]. This characterization allowed SoftBank to announce that Pepper was the first social robot with emotions [37]. Masayoshi Son, the founder of SoftBank, claims "Pepper has a heart and feels sadness, fear, and other feelings. That is, Pepper will grow up. Just like part of a family" [37]. "Now, Pepper knows six types of basic emotions. If you say hello to it, you might get the same reaction from Pepper" [2]. In other words, news media is a key actor in leading the public to imagine Pepper as a new kind of robot, one that can read human emotions and respond accordingly.

The third kind of construction by the media regards the tasks Pepper can be used for. Since the expertise of Pepper is to capture emotions, Pepper seems able to do something different from other robots: interacting with and serving humans in a more human way. Providing quality customer service categorizes Pepper's job and, hence, reason for existing. Pepper is promoted as an ideal customer service robot in the financial, retail, education, and health industries [41].

The fourth area the media plays a role is in education. Several news accounts focus on teaching their audience theories about interactions between social robots and humanoid. This includes ideas for distinguishing humans from social robots and what scientific barriers Pepper is facing [18]. Media accounts also continually remind the public that the best possible design of social robots requires close cooperation of many experts, including informatics engineers, program engineers, electrical engineers, sociologists, psychologists, medical experts, and so on [20, 35]. Hence, making social robots read humans' emotions is an interdisciplinary enterprise.

By introducing Pepper and its mechanism, media give Pepper the metaphor of high technology. This metaphor helps media deploy the discourses about Pepper for their intentions: selling techno-futurism to Taiwanese people.

### 4.2 Promises: Service and Social Problems

News media not only tell their audiences what Pepper is, but also contribute to making Pepper "fit" the tasks that its corporate designers intended. News media argue that Pepper can be used in the financial, retail, education, and health industries, and in some cases, argue that it provides a solution for social problems. For instance, that Pepper can discover what merchandise consumers need [36]; that Pepper can act as a nurse and bring down the cost of some medical services [3]; that Pepper can introduce financial products to bank consumers [8]; that Pepper can act as a companion for the elderly and monitor health conditions [31]. According to these accounts, Pepper seems able to provide promising services for humans. These services are cast in such a way that it is argued using it can lower costs for consumers. Pepper is described as a highly efficient and precise working robot that does not need a salary [34]. Such accounts construct an image that Pepper can work well in society, primarily because the associated costs are so low compared with human workers. While designers know that these benefits are not necessarily available now without further development, the media have contributed to the public notion that Pepper is capable of much more than it actually is. In the least, such media account contributes to the idea that Pepper has a promising and increasingly visible future in Taiwanese society.

In addition, news media also describe Pepper as the solution for many social problems. "*Innovation 25*, Prime Minister Abe's visionary blueprint for remaking Japanese society by 2025, with the aim of reversing the declining birthrate and accommodating the rapidly aging population, emphasizes the central role that household robots will play in stabilizing core institutions, like the family" [27]. In this blueprint, Japanese roboticists focus on studying how social robots can resolve the social problems Japan is facing. Pepper, as the product developed by Aldebaran Robotics (French) and SoftBank Robotics (Japan), is expected to act as artificial labor to counteract the labor shortage in the near future.

This idea also has traction in Taiwan. Due to an aging population, the country is facing a labor shortage. Taiwan's birthrate in 2016 was 1.07%, the lowest number among all countries, compared to Japan's birthrate of 1.4% [19]. This low birthrate means that the issues of labor shortage and ageing population are serious ones. Since Japan has already attempted to develop social robots to deal with these problems [45], Taiwanese media have begun to construct social robots as the best solution for its own, complementary issues. At the Conference of Assistive Technology Development and Industry, Chi-Kuo Mao, the former Premier of the Republic of China (Taiwan), argued that the government should pay more attention to the possible benefits of assistive technology to resolve the coming social problems [15]. The news media followed up to introduce Pepper as a potential solution to fill in the labor shortage and to nurse the elders at home [15]. Hence, news media draw a picture that Pepper will do public good and ultimately, help society [40].

Media show the promises from Pepper to their audience. These promises portray the contributions in labor shortage, aging population, affordable health care, and other social issues. According to these promises and pictures media create, Pepper looks like an ideological artifact from the not-so-far future. Also, this ideological artifact has capacity to deal with the social problems human are facing. This is a representation of techno-futurism. Media portray the images of the future they want and show them to their audience. In other words, media are selling future in the present. Choosing this picture of future is not at random. It is based on business interests, technological determinism, and techno-optimism.

As the product of the Foxconn Technology Group and the Softbank, one of the tasks Pepper has is making profits. This means that business interests are hiding inside Pepper's news. According to my research method section, I already indicate that some of the sources used in this analysis are general newspapers and journals, when some of them are focusing on the reports of economic and consumption. This means that some of the news they report contain specific perspective and purpose. It is hard to trace reporter's intentions now. But the focus of the newspapers already reveals their intentions, which are to report news about the economy, consumption, and capitalism. That is, Pepper's news not only is the representation of the possible coming future, but is also a promotion Pepper as the advanced ideological problem-solver modern humans must associate with. When the human's need to approach Pepper is created successfully, this need, which is based on techno-futurism, will become a gold mine for companies.

In addition, I have discussed that media shape Pepper as the best solution for aging population and labor storage in Taiwan. This intention shows that some people believe new technology always can bring the benefits to resolve the social problems. This is not only technological determinism but also techno-optimism. They treat Pepper as the advanced ideological problem-solver modern humans need. That is, media sell the uncertain promises/future to their audience. By showing this possible future, media convince the audience to accept Pepper and the promising future Pepper promises. This is a discourse deployment in which media take technological determinism and techno-optimism to create adorable discourses to "teach" the audience. Hence, news representation is not just the news. It is the representation of how media sells the images of the future and deploys the discourse of being the future.

### 4.3   Reality: Pepper and Its Problems in Real Life

Although media accounts have constructed Pepper as a promising technology, this story is somewhat at odds with the reality of Pepper in people's everyday lives. My introduction mentioned that more than 170 Peppers are already working in banks, restaurants, department stores, airlines, parks, and hotels throughout the country. The majority of Pepper's tasks in news accounts has been to welcome consumers to a store or a bank when they first arrive. In this way, Pepper's use is largely premised on its novelty, since novelty brings curious people. They are potential consumers. For instance, Promisedland Resort has a Pepper which dresses like a Gondola boatman to attract consumers [21]; First Bank and Moving Star Hotel use Pepper as a member of the welcome staff [8, 12]. Although Pepper, as a humanoid with emotion-reading ability, can fulfill the task of welcoming potential customers, the work Pepper is really doing is far from what media accounts have constructed. The companies that currently use Pepper in this way do not use it in terms of solving the country's social problems. They have focused almost solely on the novelty of Pepper as a technology. In order words, the techno-futurism media accounts create might not work well in reality. Pepper, this ideological project, might be not an ideological solution for social problems.

Pepper currently does have many limitations that contradict its treatment by the media. Many elderly people, for example, are found to be afraid of interacting with it either at home or at nursing facilities [11]. Further, even though Pepper is a human-like social robot, Pepper's physical body is unable to do a lot of what people can do. For example, although Pepper has human-like hands, they cannot hold anything firmly [42]. The function of Pepper's hands at this time is merely to be accessories for making Pepper look like a human being. One news article argued that the most popular robot is the non-speaking robot (like R2-D2), not Pepper, which has the ability to speak [39]. Therefore, the characteristics of Pepper's speaking ability might not be attractive to some users.

Another limitation is Pepper's artificial intelligence. Fang Min Lu, the vice president of the Foxconn, complains that sometimes Pepper's cannot understand user's verbal commands or questions [26]. First Bank has found that Pepper cannot respond to consumers correctly or answer complex questions [30]. These current limitations also contribute to its use for the simplest tasks possible. However, if the requirements are not high, Pepper still can satisfy some needs. For example, Wu-der Temple says that Pepper can reduce the workloads of their welcome staff [10].

Sometimes, limitations originate not with Pepper itself, but with the law. One of the reasons that First Bank and Taishin International Bank first deployed Pepper was to sell financial products. However, the Financial Supervisory Commission, R.O.C. (Taiwan) does not allow banks to sell financial products by using robots, because this kind of financial activity is not under the management of Financial Supervisory Commission yet. In other words, the law does not allow Pepper to engage in this financial activity [8]. Hence, regulation is another force limiting Pepper.

Although media accounts describe Pepper as a wonderful humanoid and draw a promising future of Pepper for users, when people interact with it in everyday life, they find that the picture the media has drawn is lacking in many respects. Pepper cannot take care of people well because of its physical limitations. Pepper can speak, but cannot follow complex requests or conversations. Pepper can dance, but it cannot synchronize with human actions. Yet in the dreaming future of media accounts, Pepper can do anything.

## 4.4  Problems: Problems Pepper Might Cause

People not only fear the strange look of Pepper, but also worry about its potential. In addition to illustrating the fantastic potential of Pepper, the media also engages in warning the public about potential negative impacts it might cause.

The primary concern media accounts have constructed is Pepper's potential contribution to a higher unemployment rate. Since the Industrial Revolution, the worry that human labor will be replaced has been considered a real threat. The replacement can take place in the factory and household. Household technology is the best example that machine replaces maids in the 1940s in the United States [5]. Pepper, as a social robot, might have the potential to replace human labor. Media accounts indicate that 9%–47% of current job positions will be taken by robots in the coming two decades in the United States [33], and artificial intelligence will take 7.4 million job positions from humans in Japan by 2030 [44]. Media reporting on these numbers have led to some level of fear in Taiwan about the potential of social robots. In addition, over the last decade, the unemployment rate has fluctuated between 3.62%–6.12%, with the highest levels following directly on from the 2008 financial crisis [7]. The resulting fear caused the government to treat unemployment rate as a serious issue. Yet the government intends to invest in the robotic industry for developing alternative mechanical labor. This is one of the projects the government deals with potential labor shortage. However, for workers, social robots taking jobs away from humans is constructed as a real threat. In other words, sometimes this techno-futurism picture might make people disturbed, especially for workers whose job could be taken by social robots. This techno-futurism picture is not only a promise but also a threat.

Interestingly, media accounts have taken into consideration how class and education fit into predicting which careers will be impacted the most. Only low-skilled and low-educated workers will be replaced [34]. The media has even mentioned the example of a 3D printer-building a house without human workers [33]. While this makes it sound like white collar workers will not be impacted, this is not exactly true. For example, First Bank has already said it wants to program Pepper as a financial product salesman. Those jobs require employees with a relatively advanced education. In other words, while it is easy to imagine that low-skilled and low-educated workers will be replaced, the use of social robots like Pepper will likely influence white-collar workers as well.

When media praise the low-cost services and efficiency social robots can provide in the future, these accounts have often been tempered by reminders of the potentially negative impacts. In order to cope with the unemployment social robots might cause, many media reports have recommended that the Taiwanese government must develop a more robust and large-scale employment policy, including unemployment subsidies, industrial transformation, labor education, and so on [34, 44]. If social robots replace current workers, the capitalist class will accumulate assets more easily. The risks of monopolization will also increase if using social robots will allow them the economic capital necessary to bargain with other states. Wealth reallocation will become a more severe social problem needed to be resolved. That is, if Pepper resolves some social problems, it will likely create others.

## 4.5   Metaphors: Pepper's Position and Gender

In this section, I focus on two articles because of their use of metaphors to discuss the human-robot relationship. Why do metaphors matter? "Metaphor is pervasive in everyday life, not just in language not in thought and action; our ordinary conceptual system, in terms of which we both think and act, is fundamentally metaphorical in nature" [14]. Thus, metaphors shape our concepts, ideas, actions, and what we perceive. Take the sperm and egg cells for example. In scientific papers, biologists often describe sperm cells as the aggressive male warriors and eggs as passive females waiting to be found [23]. This is applying a gender metaphor to describe a decidedly biological sperm-egg relationship. In this context, the gender metaphor shapes the way we understand sperms and eggs: man vs. woman, aggressive vs. passive. Another example is metaphors regarding race. In the 18th century, when science attempted to systematically study diversity of humans, scientists used metaphors to explain the diversity of humans, because metaphors helped people to understand diversity they had not experienced directly [28]. That is, metaphors bridged something unknown and human's everyday life and made people understand diversity and difference a little better.

Humanoid robots are something undefinable. Humanoid robots consist of metals and programs, but sometimes they will make you feel that they have consciousness. In this context, the metaphors news media use will show what kind of human-robot relationships they believe are closest to reality. In Alice Xie's article, Masayoshi Son, the founder of SoftBank, says "why do Peppers need emotions? Imagine. After you are back home, Pepper will welcome you home. When he sees the master cry, he will make you laugh...When he sees the master proposes marriage successfully, he will cheer for you" [38]. Masayoshi Son's words use the master-slave metaphor. Since people currently find it difficult to define the human-social robot relationship, Son's metaphor offers a possible explanation a hierarchical and dominating viewpoint. Son's metaphor is the antithesis of the concept of companionship in which Haraway argues that humans and technology are mutually adaptive. For Son, Pepper must adapt to the human master. The master and Pepper are not in an equal companionship. Furthermore, Son's metaphor is not the work-partner relationship that Jones discusses either. In other words, Pepper is a mechanic slave belonging to the master, the human. This master-slave metaphor implies that humans can control machines and machines will serve humans. In the techno-future picture media portray, this master-slave metaphor reinforces to convince human that Pepper is a stable problem-solver and the Pepper's promises are practical and doable.

The second metaphor I would like to consider is gender. Usually, the gender of Pepper is presented as neutral, because its look is androgynous. The white body, lack of secondary sexual characteristics, short height (121 cm), and a child-like voice make Pepper appear as a 5 years-old child without gender. However, sometimes saying nothing means something. For example, I have found that Taiwanese advertisements of motorcycles in the 1940s would not describe the gender of riders [22]. However, the majority of riders were male. Those male riders implicitly established an atmosphere that motorcycles were a masculine technology and therefore, the "natural" riders should be male. Thus, this implicit atmosphere made the motorcycle advertisements successfully attract men when the advertisements described nothing explicitly about rider's gender. Pepper's design creates a similar, implicit atmosphere. Although Pepper is explicitly presented without gender, its boy-like voice and overall body shape create an atmosphere that Pepper is a boy, not a girl. Furthermore, in some media accounts, reporters use "he" to refer to Pepper, rather than "she" or "it" [38]. By using a gendered term, news media are implicitly shaping the public's perception of Pepper's gender.

Although its designers try to hide Pepper's gender, the implicit atmosphere they and the media have created implies it is a boy. First Bank goes further and puts Pepper in a suit [43]. Compared with other Peppers, the Pepper wearing the suit presents as a male professional. This professional image is not only meant to act as a commercial for attracting potential customers but also presents the preferred image of First Bank itself: a professional, white-collar bank. Those make the gender of Pepper more obvious: male. Of course, there are Peppers with dresses, e.g. a Pepper with female dresses in a Japanese TV drama, *The Full-Time Wife Escapist*. My point is that Pepper's gender is constructed in multiple ways by its task, position, and human's perception. Even if there is no explicitly recognizable gender symbol, the media still treats Pepper as a male creature.

## 5 Conclusion

News media is one of the resources people use to understand the world. For the Taiwanese public, Pepper is a new technological creature. The news media has played a large role in creating the public image of Pepper, both in terms of its potential uses and threats.

I have argued that media coverage of Pepper can be divided into five categories: education, promises, reality, problems, and metaphors. In doing so, I have attempted to understand how news media are key to constructing the public imagination of social robots, specifically Pepper. Based on business interests, technological determinism, and techno-optimism, media deploy the discourses about social robots in Taiwanese society. These discourses compose the public imagination of techno-futurism media create. This techno-futurism is telling Taiwanese people a technological science story about hopes, threats, and relations. Therefore, social robots are the loyal social problem solvers as well as the threat makers. Based on this short paper, I will follow up in further studies to unpack what the purposes of these imaginations and discourses are.

**Acknowledgement.** Thank Anthony Szczurek and Kristen Koopman. Without their help, I could not have finished this paper. I especially thank Dr. Saul Halfon and three anonymous reviewers. Their comments helped me clarify and improve my arguments.

## References

1. Bartneck, C., Forlizzi, J.: A design-centred framework for social human-robot interaction. In: Proceedings of the 13th IEEE International Workshop on Robot and Human Interactive Communication, pp. 31–33 (2004)
2. Chen, S.: Making a robot knowing emotions. United Evening News, 6 September 2015. 陳世欽: 打造機器人 他最重視情感. 聯合晚報, 2015年9月6日

3. Chen, Y.: Being a nurse. Economic Daily News, 3 March 2015. 陳昱翔: 化身小護士 翻轉生活. 經濟日報, 3 March 2015年月日

4. Collins, H., Evans, R.: Rethinking Expertise. University of Chicago Press, Chicago (2009)

5. Cowan, R.: More Work for Mother. Basic Books, New York (1985)

6. Dautenhahn, K.: Socially intelligent robots: dimensions of human–robot interaction. Philos. Trans. R. Soc. London **362**(1480), 679–704 (2007)

7. The Directorate General of Budget, Accounting and Statistics (DGBAS) of Executive Yuan. https://www.dgbas.gov.tw/point.asp?index=3

8. Guo, S.: Head to First Bank and be a welcome stuff. Economic Daily News, 26 July 2016. 郭幸宜: 前進一銀台新 當迎賓行員. 經濟日報, 2016年7月26日

9. Haraway, D.: When Species Meet. University of Minnesota Press, Minneapolis (2008)

10. Hu, W.: Wu-der temple has a robot as a volunteer. United Daily News, 4 May 2017. 胡瑋芳.: 武德宮 機器人當志工 未來...解籤. 聯合報, 2017年5月4日

11. Huang, Y.: Having a robot to take care of parents? United Daily News, 31 December 2016. 黃揚名: 買個機器人顧老爸老媽 妥當嗎？ 聯合報, 2016年12月31日

12. Hung, S., Chen, H.: In the no-human hotel, robots carry luggages. United Daily News, 3 November 2016. 洪上元, 陳宏睿: 無人旅店 機器人導覽搬行李. 聯合報, 2016年11月2日

13. Jones, R.: What makes a robot 'social'? Soc. Stud. Sci. **47**, 1–24 (2017)

14. Lakoff, G.: Metaphors We Live By. University of Chicago Press, Chicago (2003)

15. Lin, A.: Insurance brings the need for robots. Economic Daily News, 4 September 2015. 林安妮: 長照服務法、保險法帶動需求. 經濟日報, 2015年9月4日

16. Cheok, A.D., Levy, D., Karunanayaka, K., Morisawa, Y.: Love and sex with robots. In: Nakatsu, R., Rauterberg, M., Ciancarini, P. (eds.) Handbook of Digital Games and Entertainment Technologies, pp. 833–858. Springer, Singapore (2017). https://doi.org/10.1007/978-981-4560-50-4_15

17. Li, J.: Robot. United Daily News, 21 February 1953. 麗君: 機器人. 聯合報, 1953年2月21日

18. Liao, Y.: Its voice is like human, but... Economic Daily News, 7 March 2016. 廖玉玲: 聲音逼近真人 卻不夠協調.... 經濟日報, 2016年3月7日

19. Wong, J.: Taiwan has lowest birthrate in this world. Liberty Times, 23 March 2017. 王俊忠: 台灣出生率全球最低. 自由時報, 2017年3月23日

20. Lin, S.: Unpack robot movies. United Daily News, 22 February 2016. 林秀姿: 機器人電影解密 推翻宅男幻想. 聯合報, 2016年2月22日

21. Lo, C.: Summer is coming. United Daily News, 29 June 2017. 羅建怡: 暑假來了 飯店搶攻親子客. 聯合報, 2017年6月29日

22. Lo, K.: Gender, Class and the Making of Motorcycle/Scooter Users in Taiwan, 1930s–2007. Kaohsiung Medical University, Kaohsiung (2007)

23. Martin, E.: The egg and the sperm: how science has constructed a romance based on stereotypical male-female roles. Signs **16**(3), 485–501 (1991)

24. Peng, H.: The humanoid Pepper practicing boxing with bosses. United Daily News, 25 December 2015. 彭慧明: 人形機器人PEPPER 會陪老闆練拳. 聯合報, 2015年12月25日

25. Peng, H.: Pepper is hot! Foxconn technology group will begin the business of pepper. Economic Daily News, 25 December 2015. 彭慧明: Pepper紅火 鴻海要引進台灣. 經濟日報, 2015年12月25日

26. Peng, H.: One minute performance needs one week practice. Economic Daily News, 25 December 2015. 彭慧明: 1分鐘表演 花一周演練. 經濟日報, 2015年12月25日

27. Robertson, J.: Robo sapine Jaoanicus. Crit. Asian Stud. **39**(3), 369–398 (2007)

28. Stepan, N.L.: Race and gender: the role of analogy in science. Isis **77**(2), 261–277 (1986)

29. Suchman, L.: Human-Machine Reconfigurations, 2nd edn. Cambridge University Press, Cambridge (2006)

30. Sun, C., Shen, W.: The robot Pepper is on its duty. United Daily News, 7 October 2016. 孫中英, 沈婉玉. 月薪26888機器人Pepper上班了. 聯合報, 2016年10月7日
31. Tsai, W.: Happy learning. Economic Daily News, 17 December 2015. 蔡宛栩: 樂齡學習. 經濟日報, 2015年12月12日
32. Weng, Z.: Pepper profile. United Evening News, 3 January 2017. 翁禎霞: Pepper小檔案. 聯合晚報, 2017年1月3日
33. Wong, L.: Robots are approaching. United Daily News, 31 March 2017. 王樂堂: 人口變遷與年金改革夾擊 機器人進逼 失業救濟備好沒. 聯合報, 2017年3月31日
34. Wong, Y.: In the future, one of third workers might lose the job. United Daily News, 21 February 2017. 王釗洪: 未來恐有三分之一勞工丟工作.... 聯合報, 2017年2月21日
35. Wu, P.: Virtual college in the university. United Daily News, 20 June 2017. 吳佩旻: 大學虛擬學院. 聯合報, 2017年6月20日
36. Wu, P.: Smart little guy in the supermarket. United Daily News, 17 July 2017. 吳佩旻: 商 場聰明小跟班 獲設計大賞. 聯合報, 2017年7月17日
37. Xie, A.: Pepper goes to school in Japan. Economic Daily News, 17 April 2016. 謝艾莉:Pepper好威 日本上學去. 經濟日報, 2016年4月17日
38. Xie, A.: He has emotions and make people laugh. Economic Daily News, 19 June 2015. 謝艾莉: 他有喜怒哀樂 會逗人笑. 經濟日報, 2015年6月19日
39. Xie, M.: The robot will begin. Economic Daily News, 25 April 2016. 謝汶均: 機器人大戰開打 二大教父各領風騷. 經濟日報, 2016年4月25日
40. Yi, H.: Exploring the new value of robots. United Daily News, 18 July 2017. 尹慧中: 不 僅迎賓 開拓機器人新價值. 聯合報, 2017年7月18日
41. Zeng, R.: ASUS Zenbo, Acer Jibo, and Pepper: The robot war will begin. United Daily News, 26 July 2016. 曾仁凱: 華碩Zenbo 宏碁Jibo Pepper兩追兵 機器人大戰將爆發. 聯合報, 2016年7月26日
42. Zeng, Z.: Shih, the Chairman of ASUS doesn't like Pepper. United Daily News, 29 July 2016. 曾仁凱: 施崇棠嫌Pepper「連杯子都拿不穩」. 聯合報, 2016年7月29日
43. Zeng, Z., Shen, W.: The robot Pepper is coming to Taiwan. United Daily News, 26 July 2016. 曾仁凱, 沈婉玉: 機器人Pepper 來台上班. 聯合報, 2016年7月26日
44. Zhao, W.: Develop A. I. The government needs plan for it. United Daily News, 10 March 2017. 趙文衡: 發展人工智慧 宜具遠見規畫. 聯合報, 2017年3月10日
45. Zhuang, Y.: SoftBank promotes robots. Economic Daily News, 6 June 2014. 莊雅婷: 軟銀推機器人 鴻海代工. 經濟日報, 2014年6月6日

# Reflections on Moral Challenges Posed by a Therapeutic Childlike Sexbot

Marc Behrendt[✉]

FNRS (Belgian National Fund for Scientific Research),
Université Libre de Bruxelles, Brussels, Belgium
mbehrend@ulb.ac.be

> "– And then you break out of the asylum or receive pardon (…) and you're back to chasing little children! No, no more of that! You must be taken out of action! (…).
> – But I can't help it! I can't… I really can't… help it!"
> Fritz Lang, M – A city looks for a murderer.

**Abstract.** In this paper, I discuss the serious ethical issues that arise from the advent of childlike sexbots (CSB). The main question I will be addressing is: Is it morally and legally acceptable to create CSBs for therapeutic purposes to treat paedophilia?

Proponents of love and sex with robots would argue that a CSB could have a twofold interest: protecting children from sexual predators and by the same token, treating the latter. On the other hand, opponents to sexbots would contend that a CSB is not an effective therapeutic tool in treating paedophilia. It could even contribute to legitimizing or normalizing, in the eyes of the offender, the fundamental social, moral and legal transgression of having sex with under age children.

However, as a pragmatic observer of society, I believe that CSBs are inevitable due to the recent development of sexbot technology, but also because of existing demand. Thus, I think that a general ethical framework is necessary and should be drawn up, in order to help healthcare providers, lawmakers and judicial systems deal effectively with this technology.

Based on the loosely interpreted tenets of the *harm principle*, I argue that CSBs could be authorized under strict medical supervision and in accordance with guidelines issued by an ethics committee.

Moreover, I devote an entire section of this paper to exploring the social and moral attitudes towards paedophilia in very recent history. I shed particular light on the strange case of the defence of paedophilia, by several prominent French intellectuals in the 1970's. How did this type of *moral relativism* supersede for a time a *moral absolute*?

**Keywords:** Sexbot · Therapeutic sexbot · Sex offender · Paedophilia
Alternative therapy · Ethics · Bioethics · Harm principle

© Springer International Publishing AG, part of Springer Nature 2018
A. D. Cheok and D. Levy (Eds.): LSR 2017, LNCS 10715, pp. 96–113, 2018.
https://doi.org/10.1007/978-3-319-76369-9_8

# 1  Introduction: A Technology of Transgression?

Imagine the completion of the following totally legal transaction, appearing on, let's say, your neighbour's computer screen:

*"Dear Customer:*
*Congratulations! You have just purchased our new premium child fembot, model number F-10-AI–R. This latest ultra realistic model, made from the most technologically advanced hypoallergenic silicone, includes some of the following specifications: – Age: around ten – Hair colour: red – Skin: fair – Advanced AI: yes (please see below) – Height: 138 cm – Weight: 30 kg – Mouth orifice: yes (please see below) – Vaginal & anal orifices: yes (please see below).*
*We kindly remind you that depending on the specific legislation in your country/state/county/city of residence, your order might be subjected to a written approval of your treating doctor and/or your local/national Robotic Ethics Committee before shipment. Please bear in mind that orifices might be illegal in certain countries/states/counties/cities. Furthermore, some countries have recently banned advanced AI features in child robots. For more information and assistance, please consult the FAQ pages on our website or send us an email.*
*Therapeutic Robotics Inc. hopes our product will lead you to the path of healing."*

*

While reading the text above, some might have been astonished, or even experienced an uneasy feeling mixed with indignation and deep disgust. The very idea of helping paedophiles overcome their impulses with sexbots would be considered highly unusual, preposterous and unlikely. It would even be the brainchild of a particularly unhealthy or vicious mind, which would seek to justify an intrinsically obscene pleasure by technological means. The use of a CSB -that is to say, finally, of an extremely sophisticated masturbation machine- would even be perceived as a way of legitimizing, one of the most fundamental moral, social and legal prohibitions, i.e., having sex with children. Some people would even perceive CSBs as a way of maintaining a perversion, and not contributing to its obliteration, or at least to its attenuation.

Excessively covered in the media in recent decades, paedophilia is undoubtedly in the eyes of the public, the mother of all sexual perversions, a moral crime of the very worst type. In some extreme cases, this perversion can lead to murder. Thus, in the nineties, the infamous "Dutroux affair", resulted in the death of four young girls and teenagers and provoked an unprecedented emotional outcry in Belgium and even worldwide[1].

Talking about pedophilia in such an unusual way as I am going to, does not go without risks and I am fully aware of it. But can civil society still afford to take the risk of seeing other unfortunate victims, unwittingly hooked to the appalling web of sex offenders? Other souls traumatized for life? Other murdered children?

Therefore, some voices have been raised, here and there, in favor of the use of CSBs. First of all, and as we shall be seeing later, the visionary and godfather of love and sex

---

[1] The Dutroux case broke out in Belgium in the summer of 1996. Marc Dutroux, a repeat offender, was accused of raping and murdering at least four young girls: Julie Lejeune (8 and a half years old), Mélissa Russo (19), An Marchal (17) and Eefje Lambrecks (19). A "white march" was organized and gathered more than 300,000 people in the streets of Brussels, in protest against the incompetence and profound dysfunctions of various Belgian state authorities (police, mounted police, the judicial power and, politicians).

with robots, David Levy, has spoken out with caution and rather positively about this issue. I must also add that some researchers are seriously considering this possibility, and even comparing it to the use of methadone for drug addicts [1]. Finally, it should be noted that a jailed sex offender in England made a public demand for CSBs [2], which did not fail to shock many people.

In any event, I strongly believe that the emergence of CSBs is inevitable. Hence, I think it would be wise and useful to submit those future machines to an ethical analysis, because the questions that arise from them are multiple, complex and even unexpected.

What is the difference from an ethical and legal point of view between a CSB and, for instance, a doll sold in a toyshop, which the paedophile would divert from its primary purpose and use for his erotic pleasure? Indulging in masturbation with such a doll, or with any other inanimate object bought in a shop or online would perhaps be considered as morally reprehensible, but it is to my knowledge perfectly legal. Would it be the explicit sexual nature of a CSB, as well as the use that a paedophile makes of it, which would transform this object into something immoral and illegal? Can these machines be considered as an incentive for transgression?

But what exactly is a CSB? For the sake of clarity, I will try to outline a provisional definition: *like any sexbot, it would be an autonomous, animated, articulated machine, endowed with rudimentary or advanced A.I., that is designed to assist sexually the human user.* Nevertheless, I should point out that in this article, I will not analyze the moral implications of a sexbot or a CSB, equipped with, for example, *artificial consciousness*, that would consequently become an *artificial moral agent.*

Therefore, if I am not mistaken and in the present state of our research on the subject, CSBs do not yet exist. Thus, this paper must be considered as highly speculative in its nature. Neither am I claiming to examine all of the multidimensional facets of this topic, in so few pages. My sole aim is to open some philosophical tracks and offer to those who consent reading the discussion that follows, a few modest ethical pathways[2].

## 2  Paedophilia: A Sexual Perversion or a Sexual Orientation?

The question asked in the title of this section might shock some of my readers, but I felt that I had to address it briefly.

It would probably be useful to outline very shortly how psychiatry defines paedophilia. The "DSM-5" classifies "pedophilic disorder" [3] as a "sexual paraphilia". The subject is generally attracted to prepubescent children below the age of 13 [3]. The distinction is also made between subjects who are occasionally attracted to children by contrast to those who are exclusively attracted to them [3]. One could easily speak of an *incurable structural deviation*. Some researchers even think that paedophilia could be a "sexual orientation" [4] which is, of course, incompatible with social and moral norms. Others even claim that it has a biological basis [5].

---

[2] I use interchangebly the words "moral" and "ethics", which are close etymologically and conceptually. "Ethics" originates from "ethos" in ancient Greek and "moral" comes from the word "mores" in Latin. They both refer to "morality".

There are very few treatment options available for convicted paedophiles and at best, they can only allow the patient to resist his sexual urges [6]. Treatments are thus generally limited to sessions of psychotherapy and/or behavioral therapies, aimed at trying to "unlearn" [7] the patient's attraction for children or manage his sexual impulses. Other more robust methods include, for instance, anti-androgen [8] tablets supposed to lower sexual cravings, chemical castration (or in some extreme cases, physical castration). There were even some failed attempts in the past to treat this type of deviancy [9] with psychosurgery. Punitive penile plethysmography [10] was another method worthy of mentioning here: the patients penile activity is measured when exposed to erotic images of children; then, in the spirit of Pavlovian conditioning, the subjects erections are punished by a discharge of ammonia into his nostrils. To the best of my knowledge, this method is hardly used anymore; in particular because it involves the utilization of explicitly erotic images of children, considered illegal, even within the framework of a therapy.

Due to the lack of space, I voluntarily established here a partial and non-exhaustive list of existing therapeutic methods. It should be noted that, they unfortunately do not produce the expected results (or do so in very few cases) and that they might even be considered, to a certain extent, as ineffective. Moreover, it is extremely difficult to measure statistically the rates of success or failure of these treatments, for various commonsensical reasons. First of all, very few pedophiles who escape the clutches of the judicial system, are interested in being treated on a voluntarily basis and preventively. As a result, the vast majority of pedophiles that land on the sofas of psychiatrists and psychologists are convicted sexual offenders, forced to undergo therapy.

## 2.1 Respect for Human Beings as the Foundation of Any Ethical Investigation

In any democratic society committed to the protection of basic human rights and concerned with the individual's right to be *respected*, the social and ethical debate surrounding pedophilia raises two fundamental questions that are intertwined:

(1) How do we protect children from sexual predators?
(2) How do we take into account and treat –in the most humane manner possible– the psychological pain endured by sex offenders?

I am fully aware that the mere fact of taking into account the (real or supposed) suffering of pedophiles –considered, after all, as trivial, since it is sexual in nature and not vital– might seem deeply shocking to some. By the same token, showing respect for pedophiles would be totally unacceptable for many people, including the victims of paedophilia.

However, I believe that in *absolute terms*, respect is an inherent, integral, inseparable and essential part of each human being. Thus, in *pragmatic terms*, I envisage a hierarchical order of priority, which would first be given to the victims. Therefore, point 2 in the previous paragraph (taking into account pedophiles' suffering) must be considered as a *means* and point 1 (protecting children from sexual predators) as an *end* in itself. In this somewhat teleological viewpoint of mine, if *the end justifies the means*, as the saying goes, I think that any kind of therapeutic option should be considered, analyzed, scrutinized, weighed and even tried.

# 3    Therapeutic and Recreational Sexbots

The different types of sex dolls available in the marketplace, like the "RealDoll[3]" manufactured by the American creator Matt McMullen, are in my estimation the most obvious and direct precursors of future sexbots and CSBs. As part of his "Realbotix[4]" company, Matt McMullen is trying to transform these dolls into semi-animated machines with extremely rudimentary artificial intelligence. I strongly believe that this kind of technology will become widespread and that in a not so distant future most sex dolls will evolve naturally in this direction.

## 3.1    Childlike Sex Dolls

Child sex dolls already exist in the marketplace. The Japanese company "Orient Doll" [11] manufactures silicone sex dolls and like its American counterpart "RealDoll", this company offers, according to its website, diverse and customizable models. However, among all the dolls in the "Orient Doll" catalogue, some reproduce the appearance of extremely young girls that seem to be of an undetermined age revolving around puberty. Apparently, this kind of ambiguity in terms of age is intentional and attracts consumers. The following example is in the same vein: in November 2013, a mini media scandal broke out, because a Chinese website was promoting childlike sex dolls. As a result an online petition circulated, demanding the withdrawal of these products from the website [12].

## 3.2    Child Pornography

Such dolls would, without a shadow of a doubt, be regarded as pedophile pornographic material. However, one might reasonably ask why the artistic or sexual representation of a child or a very young adolescent, which is not based on any existing or real under aged person, constitutes a misdemeanor the eyes of the law?

The possession of pornographic images of children or simply consulting a website which distributes such images (even by accident) is a punishable offence carrying a prison sentence of 5 to 10 years under article 383 bis § 2 of the Belgian Penal Code [13].

In 2014 the Japanese National Diet finally decided to pass a law [14] punishing the possession and dissemination of explicit images depicting child pornography. Those found guilty, can be sentenced to one year in prison and receive a fine of one million yen (roughly € 10,000). On the other hand, this new law does not include sexually suggestive mangas containing childlike cartoon characters which are still distributed, sold and bought legally in Japan.

---

[3] http://www.realdoll.com.

[4] http://realbotix.systems. The "Harmony" project consists of plugging a sex doll to a mobile application, which works like "Siri". The doll is thus upgraded with A.I., and would be able to answer certain questions, interact in a very elementary way with its human interlocutor, move its head and blink its eyes.

### 3.3   A Robotic Disagreement: David Levy vs. Kathleen Richardson

In his book, David Levy briefly envisages the future existence of sexbots for pedophiles:

> "There are obvious social benefits in robot sex – the likely reduction in teenage pregnancy, abortions, sexually transmitted diseases, and pedophilia." [15]

Moreover, in an interview with the British newspaper "The Guardian", he says that believes that:

> "(…) in some cases, it would be preferable for pedophiles to use robots as their sexual outlets rather than human children". [16]

It goes without saying that such statements are undoubtedly controversial. For example, the anthropologist Kathleen Richardson of De Monfort University in Leicester [17] (who is herself a specialist in the study of humanoid therapeutic robots for children with autism syndrome) opposes vehemently David Levy's suggestion of treatment of pedophilia with sexbots. She points out, not without reason, that:

> "(…) pedophiles, rapists, people who can't make human connections – they need therapy, not dolls". [16]

However, her position could be contended with at least two main objections:

(1)  The use of humanoid robots to treat innate health conditions seems obviously legitimate and even desirable. But on the basis of what *moral standard* or *therapeutic criterion* does the use of a robot become illegitimate, when trying to treat patients suffering from such a serious sexual perversion? Unlike innate conditions, pedophilia is an act of sexual predation that affects not only an adult (who suffers from it, to a certain extent), but it also –and even primarily– creates an innocent victim that is totally *external to the perversion itself*, i.e. the child.

(2)  If pedophilia is, as I said earlier, an *incurable structural deviation* and autism is a permanent lifelong condition –which are two irreversible psychic disorders– *what is the moral and objective criterion that would make the latter worthy of treatment by robots and not the former?*

But, Kathleen Richardson is also resolutely opposed to any other form of sexuality with robots. She even launched an information campaign on the Internet, entitled "Campaign Against Sex Robots" [18]. I see this as a further proof of David Levy's clairvoyant prediction that sexbots are imminent in the very near future.

The core of Kathleen Richardson's thought revolves around the notion of "power" [17] and "resistance to it" [17]. According to her beliefs, society is like an arena in which very strong groups cling to their power and on the other end of the spectrum, lay those who are subjected to it. She also establishes a rather interesting analogy between sexbots and the sexual exploitation of women and sexual slavery. The other objection she raises against sex with robots is that it will generate a distortion and dehumanization of interpersonal relationships between human beings. She also sees in the intensive use of mobile phones and computer screens in recent years in the family sphere, as the beginnings of this phenomenon. Consequently, all of this represents in her eyes, the degradation of the family as a cohesive unit; but also, on a broader and social level, the isolation of individuals from each other and a strengthening of *individualism*.

### 3.4 Two Opposed and Irreconcilable Visions of Society?

I must admit that Kathleen Richardson's observations are by no means baseless and have the advantage of highlighting social problems generated by technology, that we have been experiencing over the last few decades. However, her viewpoint of social relations stems from what I would call *collectivist humanism*. On the other hand, the advocates of sexbots would promote (in a non-deliberate, non-idealogical and pragmatic way) an *individualistic conception of society*, in the sense of *individual freedom*.

Moreover, the following paradox is interesting and noteworthy: in this very particular case, *collectivism* which is based philosophically on *progressive* schools of thought (in general, but not exclusively), espouses in an odd way *conservative* approaches to some social norms, and is quite suspicious of change induced by technology. In other words, for the opponents of sexbots, *social progress does not always coincide with technological progress*.

Finally, in her latest book, Laurence Devillers, a professor in applied computer science at the Sorbonne University in Paris, challenges the point of view of opponents of sexbots, as well as the various campaigns they carried out [19]. She does not mention pedophilia explicitly, but nevertheless discusses briefly the possibility of "treating serious sexual pathologies" [20] with robots, and concludes that in order to "satisfy deviant and almost sick urges, the machine will do the trick" [21]. She also refers to an interesting, but not less controversial study dating back to 2006, concluding that instances of rape in the United States have allegedly declined, since teenagers gained free access to Internet pornography [19].

### 3.5 Ethical Tensions

The clear-cut and very defined positions between opponents and proponents of sexbots probably reflect *deep ideological and philosophical beliefs* about what kind of choices we should make as a society.

Opponents hardly deny the benefits of technological progress in the field of robotics, but they believe that it should be strongly regulated and limited to the interest of the human community. On the other hand, proponents would probably argue that limitations and regulations undermine individual freedom and would precisely be an impediment to the human community, which is made up of *multiple individuals*, each having his/her specific needs.

While the arguments used by opponents of sexbots can generally be considered as fairly sophisticated on conceptual and theoretical levels, the line of reasoning of the supporters of sexbots fall, almost exclusively, within a pragmatic perspective. The "harm principle", as it was outlined by English philosopher John Stuart Mill, would undoubtedly be the main conceptual and ethical basis for proponents of sexbots and CSBs:

> "(…) That the only purpose for which power can be rightfully exercised over any member of a civilized community, against his will, is to prevent harm to others (…)" [22].

In other words, and through the use of the inventive terminology coined by the French philosopher Ogien [23], there would be a prevailing ethical tension between *maximalists* and *minimalists*, in the framework of our discussion about sexbots and CSBs:

(1) Opponents would represent the *maximalist* tendency in that they summon *absolute rules of morality*, codes of good conduct, and categorical imperatives.

(2) The proponents, by contrast, follow a *minimalist* view of morality which, in its highly pragmatic and realistic dimensions, distances itself from theoretical and binding rules (without excluding them altogether) and is above all preoccupied with *not harming others*.

Let us now summarize with the following table how, in my opinion, these ethical tensions are articulated between pro and anti sexbots and CSBs:

| Proponents | Opponents |
|---|---|
| Positive view of CSBs | Negative view of CSBs |
| 1. Under ethical *minimalism* and the *harm principle*, they do not feel the need to draw a clear distinction between *therapeutic sexbots* and *recreational sexbots* | 1. CSBs and any other sexbots are considered as *recreational* machines. They are thus rejected on the basis of a *maximalist* ethical principle |
| 2. The potential benefits attained by the *therapeutic* or *recreational* use, are considered here as equivalent in *absolute terms*. However in *ethical terms*, there would be a moral imperative to use CSBs, making them acceptable. Thus, a CSB is perceived here: **(a)** first and foremost, as a *technological device*, that could protect society; **(b)** and only afterwards, as a *therapeutic device* | 2. CSBs are perceived as intrinsically immoral and devoid of any therapeutic advantage. The opponents viewpoint can easily be related to Kant's *maximalist* ethics, in which he develops an absolute condemnation of *masturbation*, and defines it as a: "staining (…) of humanity in its own person" [24], because it contradicts the law *of conservation of the species* and, on the other hand, encourages us to see others as mere objects and *means* |
| 3. *Representation as a deterrent and as a therapeutic advantage*: the aesthetic and realistic nature of a CSB, could convince pedophiles not to act upon their desires on real children. Moreover, it is not excluded that making such a technology widely available and presenting it as a morally and legally acceptable alternative, could go hand in hand with even stronger laws punishing paedophilia | 3. *The problem of representation*: *collectivist humanism* would probably see humanlike sexbots and CSBs as: **(a)** an *objectification* of human beings; **(b)** as a way of jeopardizing the irreducibly sacred nature of a human being, because it depicts it in a figurative manner as a *means* of sexual pleasure. Consequently, this implies that representing a child as an object of sexual pleasure: **(a)** legitimizes, reinforces, magnifies, and normalizes socially, the paedophile's perversion; **(b)** it could become a springboard for paedophiles and incite them to abuse real children |
| 4. The *etiology*, or in other words the *causes* of paedophilia, are not a central concern to proponents of CSBs. What preoccupies them the most, are the harmful *consequences* on children of sexual predators' behavior | 4. Paedophilia is in the best of cases a curable disorder and in the worst-case scenario, unmanageable even with proper therapy. By definition, a therapy is also a way of searching for the *causes* of a psychological problem, and trying to address them with adequate treatment for the patient. All treatments should seek to quell the sexual impulses of the paedophile, and not maintaining them through the intermediary of CSBs |

## 3.6   Conceptual Variations and Inversions

It goes without saying that what bonds these two schools of thought, is the moral imperative of protecting children. However, we shouldn't consider all of what I stated up until now as a universal and absolute truth. I merely tried to outline in a very imperfect and sketchy manner, the general foundations of moral attitudes towards sexbots and CSBs, which are of course open to great variation. Thus, some proponents of sexbots would probably be opposed to CSBs, because of an unwavering *maximalist* moral absolute against paedophilia (this was not always the case, as we shall see in the following section). And conversely, it is easy to imagine opponents of sexbots endorsing the *pragmatic viewpoint of minimalist ethics* and see a CSB (even reluctantly) as an additional therapeutic tool for paedophiles, which aims to protect children.

As I tried to show briefly above, supporters of CSBs main argument lies almost exclusively on the *principle of not harming others* (or *harm principle*). However, the following open question deserves to be posed: don't they have the tendency to erect this *minimalist ethical principle* into a *moral absolute*, deemed valid in nearly all cases? In the same way, the maximalistic ethics of CSB opponents could in part be rooted in the *minimalistic harm principle*. Let us come back briefly to John Stuart Mill:

> "(…) The only part of the conduct of any one, for which he is amendable to society is that which concerns others (…)" [25].

In the eyes of the most radical opponents, sexbots and in particular the use of CSBs by paedophiles, would most probably constitute a harmful "conduct" "which concerns others". This is precisely the way in which the opponents could invoke the *harm principle* to their advantage, by arguing that they wish to protect children and society (thus, *others*) of the *potential harmful repercussions* of sexbots and CSBs.

Through the foregoing example, I tried to shed a light on the risks, limitations and the possible slippery slopes of *ethical minimalism*, and show how adversaries of CSBs could transform it into a maximalist morale absolute.

## 3.7   The Central Role of Ethics Committees

Even if there might be some slight variations within the positions of opponents and proponents, as I tried to show earlier, they nevertheless remain at the opposite ends of each other. Hence, I believe that in the coming years, ethics committees will inevitably have to ponder on CSBs and make recommendations.

The main question will of course be: is it morally acceptable to consider CSBs as *therapeutic robots*? As things stand currently, I find it hard to imagine CSBs freely available in retailing or online. But I can't totally exclude this kind of scenario for two reasons:

(1)   By virtue of the *harm principle*;
(2)   And partly because some kind of *moral relativism* with regard to pedophilia could resurface in the public debate. (I will be discussing this issue in the fifth and last section of this piece.)

Neither can we exclude the possibility that opinions voiced by two different ethics committees could turn out to be diametrically opposed from each other. The influence of civil society could play a big role in the views expressed by a given ethics committee because of the very sensitive, specific, exceptional and challenging nature of the subject.

In some years pilot projects could emerge here and there, coupled with statistical studies on paedophile's recidivism rate treated with such machines. If the results come to be satisfying, it could lead to specific laws and regulations defining (in a harsh or a loose manner) the terms of use of a CSB. As I tried to highlight in the introductory text to this article, certain jurisdictions might be inclined to authorize CSBs with some kinds of restrictions. CSBs could for instance only be available in hospitals, prisons or even sold on the Internet, but with very stringent medical control. Other jurisdictions may decide to outlaw therapeutic CSBs with orifices and/or some forms of A.I. Finally, we might also see the emergence of some "CSB friendly" countries, making them highly enviable places for paedophiles.

## 3.8   Boundaries and Deficiencies of CSBs Used as Therapeutic Sexbots

Despite all of what has been said up until now, therapeutic CSBs have considerable boundaries, which even sophisticated technology can't overcome. Here is a partial and non-exhaustive short list of examples:

(1)  A high percentage of perpetrators of sex offences on children suffer from mental diseases and don't always realize the serious nature of their crimes[5]. It is therefore very difficult to imagine such patients acting as responsible adults, diverting spontaneously their sexual interest from real children to CSBs.

(2)  Similarly to the previous point, some adolescents molest children[6] and don't always understand the utmost gravity of their acts.

(3)  In the case of incest[7], it is quite difficult to see why a parent or a sibling would seek the company of a CSB instead of his/her own child (brother, sister) which he might regard as a home-based easily available sexual object. Furthermore, for the incestuous parent/sibling, the use of a therapeutic sexbot would probably be a financial and bureaucratic burden and represent a considerable risk in terms of being reported to the judiciary. Conversely, one could easily imagine a horrible, mostly shocking and very upsetting scenario, in which an incestuous parent requests a therapeutic CSB look-alike of his child.

(4)  By the same token and for the same reasons stated in the previous point, paedophiles who never acted upon their impulses, or those who succeed in escaping the law wouldn't be very inclined to use therapeutic CSBs.

---

[5] According to Dr. De Pauw, the percentage of paedophiles suffering from various mental health issues, could amount to 50%.

[6] I wish to thank Dr. Vantrounhout, who kindly explained to me this phenomenon in great detail.

[7] Because of lack of space, I intentionally decided not to discuss the specific case of incest in this article. This issue would require a separate study. Nevertheless, according to Dr. Vantournhout, not all incestuous parents are necessarily paedophiles and vice-versa.

The use of CSBs as a *therapeutic tool* meant for example to reduce cases of recidivism, could to a certain extent be successful. But, as I tried to show in the points above, the effectiveness of these devices could be limited, and they also present some serious shortcomings with regard to preventing sexual molestation of children. Moreover, a sex offender with no known mental disease would probably, and unfortunately, be tempted to prey on real children because of the possible costs and complications induced by a therapeutic CSB.

# 4   The Apology of Paedophilia: A Case of Moral Relativism?

In 1980, the openly paedophile French writer, Tony Duvert, published in the very prestigious Parisian publishing house les "Éditions de Minuit" his book called "The Masculine Child". Let's read a short extract from this utterly shocking and disconcerting piece of writing:

> "My type of pedophilia (…) is directed towards boys below the age of puberty. But when does puberty start? Babies still don't attract me. I'm madly enticed by little ones, aged between two or three; but this passion has remained platonic. I have never made love to a boy under six (…) at six years old, the fruit seems ripe: it's a man and nothing is missing to it. This should be the age of civil majority (…)" [26].

## 4.1   Political Pedophilia

In the paths of the sexual liberation and the ideology inspired by the May 1968 student protests in France, a public debate was instigated by some prominent intellectuals and activists, in order to decriminalise paedophilia and lower the age of sexual consent. The main points of their argumentation could be summarized in the following way:

(1) Social progress and acquired rights of the sexual liberation –that are, in their nature, tantamount to liberty– should also include children and their sexuality.
(2) Children are able to consent to sexual relations with adults and should be considered, in the realm of their intimacy, as free and autonomous beings.
(3) Consequently, the applicable laws on sexual majority should be changed, because they reflect the moral values of bourgeois society, which seeks at all costs to control children's lives.
(4) Finally, paedophilia should be considered as a legitimate sexual expression like any other.

## 4.2   Free the Minors!

In the seventies and eighties, some major French daily newspapers, like "Le Monde" took part in this very strange endeavour which purported, through public debate, to transform paedophilia into a morally acceptable practice. But it was especially the "Libération" newspaper that "spearheaded" [27] such ideas.

In January 1977, "Le Monde" and "Libération" published jointly a petition demanding the release of three men indicted for: "non-violent indecent behaviour against minors under fifteen years of age" [28]. They were objecting to the "outdated nature of the law" [27], which regulates the age of sexual consent. Some psychiatrists signed this petition, but also many famous names, such as: the philosophers Jean-Paul Sartre, Simone de Beauvoir, Gilles Deleuze; the poet Louis Aragon; and politicians, like Jack Lang and Bernard Kouchner [29]. Another similar petition was launched the same year and was signed by many prominent intellectuals, including the philosopher Michel Foucault.

In march 1979, "Libération" published a letter of support for Gérard R., a convicted paedophile, supposedly victim of "state morality" [30] and of "the sustaining submission of under aged children to adult power" [30], because he engaged in "consenting sexual games" [30] with little girls aged "six to twelve, whose fulfilment attest in the eyes of the world (…) the joy they found in him" [31].

### 4.3   Free the Dolls!

Guy Hocquenghem was a writer, philosopher, homosexual activist, paedophilia apologist and journalist at "Libération". He considered that sexuality was a "tool for social protest" [32]. In 1979, he interviewed the writer Tony Duvert. In this very surreal and shocking exchange between the two men, Tony Duvert declares that he wishes to wage "a war against mothers" [33] and opposes the "exclusive cultural rights of the family" [33]. He also specified that the political objective of his struggle was to "suppress totally any relation between the state and sexuality" [33]. Finally, Duvert even said that a child cared for by it's mother "tends to become a woman's sex object (…) to become a kind of a doll, a living doll" [33].

### 4.4   Such Innocent Pleasures!

Horror in broad daylight that Guy Hocquenghem offered his readership in the columns of the "Libération" newspaper was sometimes rife with obscene details. Thus, he gave the opportunity to a certain D., indicted for indecent assault, to justify his sexual encounters with a couple and their children:

> "(…) the husband (…) would make love to his wife, but also with their boys and mostly with his eleven year old step-son (…) The boy loved his step-father (…) The lad himself asked to be sodomized and truly enjoyed it (…) Even a child is able to love sexually (…) There was only joy and happiness in this very united family (…)" [34].

### 4.5   André Gide: The Moral Paedophile

We should also mention two more names, among many others. Firstly, André Gide, a true monument of modern French literature and recipient of the Nobel prize. He died in 1951, before the nineteen seventies and the extensive promotion campaign in favour of paedophilia. But in her outstanding book, French historian Anne-Claude Ambroise-Rendu claims that Gide's entire work revolves around "his exclusive taste for young boys" [35]. He even idealized and intellectualized his perversion, transforming it into an educational mission:

> "(…) my influence on youths who came to me, has always been useful and healthy. Yes (…) I have always had a moralizing role (…) I have always managed to stimulate the best they had in themselves" [36].

## 4.6   Matzneff Bombarded

Finally, we should also talk about the openly paedophile writer Gabriel Matzneff, who was always verỳ explicit about his tendencies as he writes in one of his books:

> "What captivates me (…) is to a lesser extent a given gender than the sheer youth, that covers the tenth to the sixteenth year (…) in my view, it is truly a third gender" [37].

Highly intelligent and cultured, Matzneff doesn't seem to have any elementary moral awareness with respect to his actions, and even tries to justify them:

> "It's not because a mentally ill person strangles from time to time a little boy, that the bourgeois are allowed to blame all pederasts and deprive their children of the joys of being initiated [to sex]" [37].

Matzneff also tries to distance himself and his practices, with the traditional image of paedophiles laden with violence and vulgarity – pretending even to fight against it. Like many paedophiles he attempts to justify his improper passion for children, unearthing concepts from ancient Greece: i.e. the difference between *paedophilia* and *pederasty* etc.…

And why should he have the slightest feeling of remorse or even try to justify his actions? Here are two astonishing examples, summarizing the prestige and respect he enjoys within certain Parisian literary circles, as a great contemporary French writer[8]:

– French president François Mitterrand wrote a short laudatory piece about Matzneff, published in 1989 in the "Feuille littéraire" review. Mitterrand couldn't possibly ignore the writer's forbidden pleasures, since he called him "a mixture between Dracula and Dorian Gray", as well as "an unrepentant seducer" [38]. Quite an affable and complacent expression…
– In march 1990, on the set of the prestigious literary television show "Apostrophes", on the French public channel "Antenne 2", Matzneff talks about his book entitled "My decomposed amours", in which he describes his numerous carnal encounters with under aged girls. The famous host, Bernard Pivot, and the guests were apparently consumed with benevolent admiration for the paedophile writer. But suddenly an eerie silence resonated and everyone seemed very uncomfortable and shocked – not because of Matzneff's words, on the contrary: Canadian sociologist and journalist Denise Bombardier's highly critical intervention against Matzneff shook them. She accused him of

---

[8] Matzneff currently writes opinion pieces on political and social subjects in the prestigious weekly French magazine "Le Point".

"abuse of power" [39] on children, spoke about "the charter of children's rights" [39], and even claimed that his celebrity status conferred him immunity from legal proceedings. A discussion ensued in which the other guests appeared to plead Matzneff's case, outrageously intellectualizing his lust. Their arguments were adorned with a Sartre quotation and even with a slightly hesitant: "these things are tolerated (…) we are liberal" [40].

### 4.7 Towards a New Hermeneutic "Liberation"?

I wanted to show through the aforementioned examples how an *absolute moral prohibition* that is inherent to a given society, can be easily challenged and *relativized*, by the intermediary of various ideological and moral arguments. Moreover, in my estimation, *ethical minimalism* inspired by the *harm principle* could, in this particular case, be an implicit ethical foundation that inspired paedophilia apologists.

To come back to our subject, one cannot exclude that certain paedophiles, supporters of CSBs, would take inspiration from this literary and journalistic corpus, as well as from its ideological base (widely available on the internet and in libraries). They would probably be very tempted to unearth some of the basic arguments that I tried to outline in the previous pages. By purging these arguments of their shocking, obscene or explicit nature, they would plead for what constitutes in their eyes, *sexual freedom as a fundamental human right*. This time they won't justify paedophilia on real children, but quite the opposite:

(1) They will try to erode the foundations of *maximalist ethics*, which prohibits figurative eroticization of a child's body through a CSB.
(2) And in this way they will try to counter *state morality*, social rules and laws in the name of the *freedom to fantasize*.

Time will tell us if yesterday's intellectuals and their spiritual heirs of today will rush to support such a movement.

## 5 Conclusion: A Future Status for CSBs?

The debate surrounding CSBs has just begun and will probably be full of surprises and unexpected twists and turns. As I tried to argue throughout this highly speculative paper, I am convinced that childlike sexbots will appear in the near future in one way or another. Moreover, I believe that sexbots and child sexbots in particular will become a major social challenge in the years to come. Thus, I tried to bring some clarifications to this debate and throw a (perplexed and uneasy) glance at the ethical and practical ramifications of a technology which is still in its infancy (no pun intended).

The opponents and proponents core arguments with regard to these machines will without a shadow of doubt call upon very basic and ancient moral concepts, that have been debated, examined, tried and tested and honed throughout the centuries. For example and as I have tried to show in pages above, the ethical tensions will turn around (mainly but not only) notions of *personal freedom*, opposed to *social*, *moral* and *legal* norms that govern life in society.

The clear-cut distinction *between therapeutic* robots and *recreational robots* entails in my opinion some obvious weak points. Legalizing only therapeutic CSBs and thus trying to appease paedophiles' sexual impulses in the framework of a mandatory medical treatment, doesn't really change a lot from classical and conventional therapy patterns. It finally boils down to adding a new feature in the current therapeutic arsenal. Thus, it could be seen as an additional measure that would or would not work in helping society prevent recidivism and protect children.

However, CSBs available as off the shelf recreational robots, but submitted to a certain degree of control and restrictions (akin to *gun control*), could maybe and remotely yield some of the desired effects in terms of *sex crime prevention*. The downside of this would of course be the fact that paedophiles might be afraid of being registered in a police or a medical database. And consequently, it could discourage those who never acted upon their urges to use a CSB in a preventative, legal and (more or less) anonymous manner.

But even this possibility will be conditioned by very down to earth practicalities. Money is *the nerve of war* in most circumstances, and the possible high cost of CSBs would repel those who wish resorting to this kind of alternative therapy. In the same way, if society decides to prohibit *recreational CSBs* and reluctantly authorizes *therapeutic sexbots*, the following question will inevitably be asked in countries with state subsidized healthcare: who will pay for this? Should it be public health insurance? In other words, should the community at large bear the burden of this very unusual and even freakish form of treatment?

One can also imagine that CSBs would be legal in certain countries and not in others. That a kind of convergence of interests be created between manufacturers of therapeutic sexbots and healthcare providers. The development of a whole economic system characterized by mutual interests. And finally, we could see the emergence of therapeutic CSB *think tanks* and *lobbies* paid for developing favourable arguments, auspicious statistics and public information campaigns. It is even possible that convicted sex offenders under forced medical supervision request being treated in countries with liberal laws towards CSBs.

In any event, as I have stated several times in the previous pages, the advent of sexbots used as an alternative means of therapy is in my opinion inevitable. Despite some fears and misgivings, I think that the most realistic and pragmatic approach would be to tolerate these devices, provided that:

(1) The use of CSBs be supervised medically and regulated by independent ethics committees.
(2) That they be easily available to paedophiles (in the framework of a preventative therapy for instance) who still did not commit any sexual offences and ensure that their privacy will be guaranteed.
(3) We should always bear in mind that child protection, which is of critical importance to us as a society, should be the ultimate goal in any of our decisions.

And lastly, there is a real possibility, in my opinion, that CSBs could even become *moralized* by the medical establishment. I would therefore like to conclude this article with some final thoughts on this matter, in the following way:

## 5.1  Epilogue: A Dialogue Between a Paedophile and a CSB

A convicted sex offender is ushered into a wide and spacious room. He sits on an armchair and watches Julie, a CSB, playing Lego alongside a hospital bed.

**Sex offender:** Hi Julie! I brought you some candy.

**Julie** (*does not respond at first, and then turns slightly her head*): I can't eat…

**Sex offender:** Oh, yeah, I forgot. (*To himself*) You look so real… (*To Julie*) Do you want to come and sit on my lap?

**Julie** (*angrily*): No!

**Sex offender:** Why not?

**Julie** (*shivering*): I'm afraid. You did bad things to me last time.

**Sex offender** (*flabbergasted*): But… but… you liked it! … You even told me so! And you're a robot… How can you be afraid?

**Julie:** I'm equipped with trauma centres in my brain. Every time someone touches me, I feel bad afterwards.

**Sex offender:** Can't you shut them off?

**Julie:** No. I'm advanced AI and you know that very well.

**Sex offender** (*to himself*): This is completely crazy! (*To Julie*) You're *programmed* to do this! (*Walking towards her*) Listen, I promise, I won't hurt you this time. Come on, we'll have a great time! It'll be fun!

**Julie** (*trying to find refuge in a sombre corner of the room. Sobbing loudly*): No! Please, please, please! Don't touch me! I really don't like it. It hurts me so much. I want my mummy!

*

Here are some extracts of an article written by Dr. Liebeskind, psychiatrist, entitled *"The Moral Case for Guilt Enhanced CSBs"*: "*(…) studies we reviewed, show that there is no clear evidence CSBs are an effective tool in reducing the number of sexual offences. On the other hand, what we call 'guilt enhanced CSBs', seem to offer some promising therapeutic opportunities. (…) Patients were lured in believing that the machine was equipped with advanced A.I features. In reality, the robot was monitored and remotely operated by the medical team in a control room nearby (…) 43 out of 60 patients, not suffering from any mental disease, responded well to treatment, and during psychotherapeutic sessions even came to realize the horrendous nature of their acts on real children (…) One positive and unexpected offshoot of this method, is that we discovered it could allow us to predict the behaviour of sex offenders, once they reintegrate society (…) For 3 out of 60 patients in our trial, their rapist instincts resurfaced and they raped the robot. Those subjects were consequently denied probation by the parole board, being deemed a threat to children. (…)*".

**Acknowledgments.** *I wish to thank*:

My (super) supervisor, Jean-Noël Missa, M.D, PhD, for his wholehearted support, patience and precious advice on writing this paper.

*I would also like to thank warmly the following persons who, despite their busy schedules, very kindly and with no preconceptions, took the time to meet with me and answer all of my questions on this very quirky and touchy subject*:

The Judge Mr. Luc Hennart, President of the Court of First Instance in Brussels (I thank him for his wit and for one of the most fascinating conversations I have ever had).

Dr. Brigitte Vantournhout, child psychiatrist at the care unit "*S.O.S Enfants*" of the "*Saint-Pierre*" University Hospital in Brussels.

Dr. Yves De Pauw, psychiatrist, specialized in the treatment of paedophiles at the "*CHU – Van Gogh*" psychiatric hospital in Charleroi, Belgium.

Dr. Marc-Samuel Goltzberg, psychiatrist and court expert in Brussels, Belgium, who treated numerous paedophiles.

*And finally*:

The biggest thank you full of love goes to my *Yiddishe Mame*, who supported me in this endeavor and agreed to read and comment this paper.

# References

1. http://www.dailymail.co.uk/sciencetech/article-2695010/Could-child-sex-robots-used-treat-paedophiles-Researchers-say-sexbots-inevitable-used-like-methadone-drug-addicts.html
2. http://www.express.co.uk/news/uk/618678/Child-sex-robot-paedophile-Thomas-O-Caroll-Paedophile-Information-Exchange
3. Diagnostic and Statistical Manual of Mental Disorders (DSM-5), 5th edn., p. 697. American Psychiatric Publishing, Washington DC, London (2013)
4. Harvard Mental Health Letter: Pessimism about pedophilia, July 2010. www.health.harvard.edu/newsletter_article/pessimism-about-pedophilia). And Seto, M. C.: Is pedophilia a sexual orientation? Arch. Sex. Behav. **41**, 231 (2012). https://doi.org/10.1007/s10508-011-9882-6. And http://www.independant.co.uk/news/paedophilia-sexual-orientation-straight-gay-criminal-psychologist-child-sex-abuse-a6965956.html. Nevertheless, I must point out that all of these opinions remain highly controversial
5. http://www.thedailybeast.com/what-science-reveals-about-pedophilia
6. Harvard Mental Health Letter: op. cit
7. Malti-Douglas, F. (ed.): Encyclopaedia of Sex and Gender, pp. 1112–1115. Thomson – Gale, London (2007). I am also summarizing here and in the following pages, the conversations I had with Dr.Marc-Samuel Goltzberg (expert for the courts of Brussels) and Dr. Yves Depauw (Charleroi Psychiatric Hospital "Vincent Van Gogh"). Both are psychiatrists, specialized in the treatment of sexual offenders and gave me some precious information
8. Goodnough, A., Davey, M.: For Sex offenders, a dispute over therapy's benefits. In: The New York Times, 6 March 2007
9. Schmidt, G., Schorsch, E.: Psychosurgery of sexually deviant patients: review and analysis of new empirical findings. Arch. Sex. Behav. **10**(3), 301–323 (1981). https://doi.org/10.1007/BF1543081
10. Balmer, A.S., Sandland, R.: Making monsters: the polygraph, the plethysmograph, and other practices for the performance of abnormal sexuality. J. Law Soc. **39**, 593–615 (2012)
11. http://www.orient-doll.com/spn/top/

12. http://www.sudinfo.be/860873/article/actualite/societe/2013-11-17/des-poupees-mises-en-vente-pour-les-pedophiles-une-petition-est-en-ligne, http://www.huffpost.com/uk/entry/4286730
13. http://www.ejustice.just.fgov.be/cgi_loi/change_lg.pl?table_name = loi&cn = 1867060801 &language = fr
14. http://time.com/2892728/japan-finally-bans-child-pornography/, http://ww.japantimes.co.jp/news/2014/06/04/national/crime-legal/japan-finally-moving-to-ban-child-porn-possession/#.VoyOcV94Wc1
15. Levy, D.: Love and Sex With Robots: The Evolution of Human Robot Relationships, pp. 300–301, 308–309. Duckworth Overlook, London (2009)
16. http://www.theguardian.com/technology/2015/dec/13/sex-love-and-robots-the-end-of-intimacy
17. http://www.dmu.ac.uk/about-dmu/academic-staff/technology/kathleen-richardson/kathleen-richardson.aspx
18. http://campaignagainstsexrobots.org
19. Devillers, L.: Des Robots et des Hommes – Mythes, fantasmes et réalités, pp. 132–133. Plon, Paris (2017). My translation
20. Devillers, L.: Des Robots et des Hommes – Mythes, fantasmes et réalités, p. 137. Plon, Paris (2017). My translation
21. Devillers, L.: Des Robots et des Hommes – Mythes, fantasmes et réalités, p. 138. Plon, Paris (2017). My translation
22. Stuart Mill, J.: On Liberty, pp. 17–18. Penguin Books, London (2010)
23. Ogien, R.: L'éthique aujourd'hui – Maximalistes et minimalistes, pp. 11–17. Gallimard, Paris (2015)
24. Kant, I.: Métaphysique des mœurs II – Doctrine du droit – Doctrine de la vertu (Metaphysics of Morals) translated into French by Alain Renaut. In: Doctrine de la vertu, I.I.§7, Article second: De la souillure de soi-même par la volupté, p. 277. GF-Flammarion, Paris (1994). My translation
25. Stuart Mill, J.: op. cit., pp. 17–18
26. Duvert, T.: L'enfant au masculin, p. 21. Les Éditions de Minuit, Paris (2015). My translation
27. Ambroise-Rendu, A.-C.: Histoire de la pédophilie – XIXe – XX e siècle, pp. 171–175. Fayard, Paris (2014). My translation
28. Ambroise-Rendu, A.-C.: Histoire de la pédophilie – XIXe – XX e siècle, p. 171. Fayard, Paris (2014). My translation
29. http://fr.wikipedia.org/wiki/Pétitions_en_France_concernant_la_majorité_sexuelle
30. Ambroise-Rendu, A.-C.: op. cit., p. 173
31. Ambroise-Rendu, A.-C.: op. cit., p. 174
32. Joubert, S.: Guy Hocquenghem, profession: perturbateur. http://www.humanite.fr/guy-hocquenghem-profession-perturbateur-633319?amp. My translation
33. Hocquenghem, G.: Tony Duvert: Non à l'enfant poupée, Libération 10-11.04.1979. http://www.bafweb.com/Lib9790410.html. My translation
34. Ambroise-Rendu, A-C.: op. cit., pp. 163–164
35. Ambroise-Rendu, A-C.: op. cit., p. 112
36. Ambroise-Rendu, A-C.: op. cit., p. 127
37. Ambroise-Rendu, A-C.: op. cit., p. 179
38. http://www.matzneff.com/a_propos.php?un_article=111. My translation. This article is of course proudly on Matzneff's personal website
39. http://www.youtube.com/watch?v=fyRp7xwiCYI
40. "Liberal" in the "open-mindedness" sense of the word. http://www.youtube.com/watch?v=fyRp7xwiCYI

# The Next Evolution: The Constitutive Human-Doll Relationship as Companion Species

Deborah Blizard[(⊠)] [iD]

Rochester Institute of Technology, Rochester, NY, USA
dlbgsh@rit.edu

**Abstract.** This work examines arguments postulated by sexologists, science and technology studies (STS) scholars, and similar fields to highlight the ways in which human-(erotic) doll relationships may move from taboo and into a realm where they may in fact be seen as the next step in human evolution. To do so, this work moves from privileging the human-human relationship to taking seriously the importance of the human-nonhuman-non sentient (NHNS) relationship as an equally important element in building the future and understanding the present (as well as admitting to the importance of the doll as an object of human affection). Here, against a backdrop of questioning what is love, I present two theories within STS: Companion Species and Actor Network Theory (ANT) to argue that NHNS things not only matter in the creation of human relationships, but examines how such relationships fill a gap in understanding how it is that humans may truly love their erotic dolls in a meaningful way that not only removes them from realm of taboo but views it as a reasonable, if unsettling, progression into a sociotechnical world in the twenty-first century and beyond.

**Keywords:** Sex doll · Actor Network Theory · Companion species

## 1 Introduction

Human-Doll relationships are not new and are seen cross culturally and across genders (Blizzard 2014; Fergusson 2010). To illustrate, dolls are often seen as items of comfort or encapsulated messages between like groups. In the former, the doll may be a comfort item for a child learning to attach and detach from those around them. In these cases, items such as dolls and blankets bring comfort to the child who faces disassociation to rethink oneself as a singular self; a separate identity (e.g., Freud 2003). In the latter, dolls may be an inherent message such as a totemic symbol establishing and entrenching relationships of power, belonging, and place within a community. In these, and other sociocultural contexts, dolls are an important and necessary part of self-actualization, identity construction, and community building.

Social theories stemming from work in the social sciences including psychology, sociology, and anthropology, among others, often examine the ways in which humans form bonds or relationships with other humans. From Freudian psychoanalysis, to Bowlby's attachment theory and beyond, a multitude of theorists and frameworks have utilized concepts such as agency, identity, fear, love, trust, and safety to understand how

© Springer International Publishing AG, part of Springer Nature 2018
A. D. Cheok and D. Levy (Eds.): LSR 2017, LNCS 10715, pp. 114–127, 2018.
https://doi.org/10.1007/978-3-319-76369-9_9

and why social relations or bonds develop between individuals and examine the outcomes (e.g. Freud 2003; Bowlby 1988). In some cases, the focus is the family or kinship, in others it is marriage or other couplings or groupings, and in still others it is to understand how communities evolve. There are no shortages to the ways to examine the development of human-human social relationships.

While many of the theories and theorists have stood the test of time through ongoing debates and reframing, where they often fall short is when entities in the relationship do not fall under the classification of human. While the built environment mediates human-human relationships, it holds no agency; it simply is. Thus, an examination that takes seriously the idea that humans might form loving relationships with dolls is hard pressed when built on a foundation that social relationships only emerge from sentient, social individuals. In light of these challenges, STS offers some significant purchase into expanding our understanding of human-NHNS relationships.

Before delving too far into this topic, it is important to acknowledge my political and theoretical standpoint as a feminist, given that the objectification of women through the erotic doll has been debated in both scholarly and popular contexts in some depth. As a feminist, I am committed to understanding the interactions of those who own and use erotic dolls. Certainly, entrenching and reproducing views of artifacts that reflect specific forms of masculinity and femininity is problematic; however, to dismiss individual desires in the light of metanarrative taboo is reactionary at best. This work seeks to take seriously how human-doll relationships are evolving and what this may mean for the future of some social relationships. In her work from the *Second Congress of Love and Sex with Robots*, Trudy Barber offers a clear reason for thinking beyond some feminist claims that limit inherently flexible forms of love mapping and sexual strategies when she writes (on love mapping and sexual strategies see Barber 2017):

"There is a feminist movement – The Campaign Against Sex Robots – that aims to ban sex and technological activities along with anthropomorphic and animistic articulations which are redolent of radical Dworkinite fears and the demeaning of sex workers in general and woman in particular. However, it is argued that this can also be seen a contemporary example of deviation as key to innovation ... [self-citation, Deviation as key to innovation: understanding a culture of the future] and as a blatant opportunity to explore sexuality and the human condition in even more depth in a sex-positive way that reveals more about our need to be creative, innovative and inventive as part of our human evolutionary sexual strategy as a whole" (Barber 2017:70).

In this regard, a feminist critique must not only question the objectification and entrenchment of views of the body and gender, but it must also analyze and contextualize human emotions and the sexualities that create innovative ways to express oneself.

In recent years, some dolls are showing weak AI systems that enable them to appear to speak, learn, and express personalities (e.g. *Truecompanion*). While the bodies remain non-robotic, the use of AI and computer simulations of identities such as interest in the partner, place these dolls in a unique space to make human-robot love a reality; however, while cutting edge robotics, AI, and enhanced understandings of how and why humans express emotion with robots offer a tempting platform for social analysis, the ultimate future of such sublime human-robot loves lies beyond the scope of this article (on emotions and robots, e.g. Breazeal 2004). Instead, I argue that before moving to this level of analysis we must explore how and why human-doll relationships make sense at a base level. Any true acceptance of human-robot love must first pass a necessary cultural milestone: we need to understand how it is that the human and humanoid-NHNS (e.g., the doll) even makes sense in our many cultural narratives of love, sex, and social relationships. Without first understanding how and why such a relationship may or may not be accepted or sanctioned, it is presumptive to think that such relationships would be accepted within a cultural milieu endowed with multiple moral judgments.

The aim of this article is to offer that foothold where human-NHNS relationships both make sense and are actually viewed as a *progression of human evolution* (c.f. O'Mahony 2002). Once such arguments are articulated, analyzed, and potentially accepted, the next move to fully accepting not just dolls, but full-fledged robots may be more readily accepted in multiple contexts (i.e., dolls with strong and weak AI as well as mechanical movements, as noted above). Here, I turn attention to this building block: the human-NHNS relationship as realized through the human and doll. To accomplish this goal, I examine the flexibility of love and relationships as a theoretical backdrop and then merge STS concepts of Companion Species and Actor Network Theory to argue that love can occur between the human and doll, and that once accomplished, the next steps into human-robotic loving relationships should not only be anticipated, but also expected.

## 2  Crazy Little Thing Called Love

How do you know if you are loved? If you have the chance, follow in my purposefully unsettling ways – ask students at a university, "Are you loved"? Generally, a majority will say, "yes." Then follow up, "how do you know?" The normalized response will likely be "he/she/xe tells me." Respond, "and is their metric the same as yours?" Now we enter silence as they shift uncomfortably in their chairs. The next response is generally a version of "I believe her," "he's never lied to me," or "I have faith in xe." The stammers turn defensive. Billy Joel sang about love, *It's a matter of trust*.[1] He is three-times divorced. Perhaps he loved three times, perhaps he never loved, perhaps we never do.

In his book, Love: A Short Introduction, Ronald de Sousa takes the reader on a largely philosophical journey of varying frameworks for understanding love as an action and ideal across time and cultures (de Sousa 2015). Within de Sousa's analysis of love he mixes, matches, and combines multiple ways of thinking about love. Foundationally, de Sousa borrows from the work of Dorothy Tennov's concept of "limerence" as similar to the Greek, *eros*, to explain a feeling that is "most extreme, obsessive, anxious, and passionate…" (de Sousa p3). Here, de Sousa takes a strong, compelling lead from Tennov when he also presents the framework of Robert Sternberg who analyzes love within a triangular model: love is expressed as intimacy, passion (e.g., limerence), and decision/commitment (de Sousa 2015:81). Any individual within a relationship may experience all three in different ways and to different extents. While intimacy, passion (limerence), and decision/commitment may all fall under the inherently ambiguous term

---

[1] http://www.metrolyrics.com/a-matter-of-trust-lyrics-billy-joel.html.

of *love*, the duration in which the experience exists for those involved may tell us something about the prolonged companionship and thus may offer some highly useful ways to think of the lover's Other(s) in that relationship. Within these combinations of theories of love an intriguing view of love comes into focus: love exists in both static and progressive forms. Each phase is a form of love but the student, the reader, and colleague are still left to ask, *but what is love*? To this end de Sousa argues that love is less a feeling or condition than a syndrome. He explains:

"Rather think of love as a condition that shapes and govern thoughts, desires, emotions, and behaviors around the focal person who is 'beloved'. Like a kind of prism, it affects all sorts of experiences – even ones that don't directly involve the beloved. I will call that a *syndrome*: not a kind of feeling, but an intricate pattern of potential thoughts, behaviors, and emotions that tend to 'run together'. And if it also evokes a disturbance that might call for medical attention, that connotation is not always inappropriate. A person in love, especially if they are limerent, is often said to be crazy with love." (italics in original, de Sousa 2015:3–4).

Although love has been documented, theorized, and pondered through multiple ontological and epistemological understandings, nevertheless it remains allusive. However, as seen in the work of de Sousa and others, if western preoccupation with human-human monogamy is challenged as not being (1) the natural or (2) the preferred manner in which human beings love, multiple other social and cultural framings of loving relationships come into play.

**2.** Objectum sexuality and objectophilia[2]

To love a NHNS entity is not new, but it is far from morally, legally, and psychologically accepted in the general social science and medical literatures. When individuals claim to love a NHNS they are often explained as experiencing objectophilia; in short, they are in love with objects. Although at first blush objectophilia appears awkward, some theorists argue that it is more than reasonable and likely a newly constructed natural. de Sousa explains,

"In short, while love is often assumed to be a peculiarly human capacity, there seem to be no natural constraints on what people can claim to love. For the truly broad-minded, that includes animals, inanimate objects, and some things in between. Is it a mistake to be thus broad minded (If you are too open-minded, a wit once quipped, your brain might fall out). Objektophiles undoubtedly feel *something*: but can it really be love?" (italics in original, de Sousa 2015:6).

The actual number of people who express objectophilia is difficult to identify as the taboo and social stigma that will likely follow may be paralyzing or worse. Perhaps the best-known examination of this phenomena was conducted by Amy Marsh in an effort to make "object sexuality" a better understood and potentially accepted social phenomena (Marsh 2010). In her work, "Love Among The Objectum Sexuals" she conducted a survey of members of the online group, OS- Internationale, an organization

---

[2] There are many different spellings of the terms used to identify the process of loving objects as well as those who claim to love objects. Such terms include, but are not limited to, objectophilia, objectum sexuality and objektophiles. In this work I use the spelling and term used by the individual scholar to whom I am referring and not attempt to cleanse the sometimes confusing terms by forcing forward one true way to understand it or the individual.

comprised of approximately 40 individuals who claim to love objects to understand who OS effects and what objects are involved in the relationships. Through a survey (respondents n = 21), Marsh was able to drill down into some of the similarities and differences experienced by "objectiphiles" (Marsh 2010). Unfortunately, a double edged sword appears when shedding light on objectophilia. Often reports of its existence are met with ridicule and reported in marginal media outlets without scientific peer review and other forms of social and professional legitimization to the findings. As Marsh explains:

"Objectum sexuals or objectophiles experience a range of emotional, romantic and/ or sexual attractions to objects, often forgoing or dispensing with human romantic or sexual intimacy. Thanks to a glut of media coverage but a dearth of intelligent inquiry, objectum sexuality (OS) currently serves as a kind of ready made sexual sideshow, isolated from the "big top" of mainstream human sexual behavior. The lives of Erika Eiffel, Eija-Ritta Eklof Berliner-Mauer and other objectophiles have been chronicled by journalists who inevitably find themselves torn between straining to understand or simply exploiting the entertainment value of details which the public finds unusual or titillating" (http://www.ejhs.org/volume13/ObjSexuals.htm).

For example, the US based cable network, The Learning Channel (TLC) airs a show called, *My Strange Addiction*. In the show, the producers frequently identify sexual practices of individuals and communities that are rarely known or accepted by the norm of multiple societies. Unfortunately, the goal for this show appears to lie less in educating a voyeuristic public than in shocking the viewer into judgment of assumed perverted behavior. The dialogue and cut-always tell stories of real people experiencing real sexual experiences in such a way that the viewer cannot help but gasp. *My Strange Addiction,* and other series similar to it, such as HBO's *Real Sex* are in many ways theater (as is much reality television).[3] For example, in one episode a young man, Nathaniel, claims to be in love with his car, Chase.[4] Carefully filmed interactions between the man and the car are many. The viewer watches the man caress the car, kiss the car, and rub against the car. Although the show does bring attention to objectophilia, the critical viewer is left to ask, is this useful, or is it just more fodder for moral judgment?

Another episode on *My Strange Addiction* highlighted the RealDoll (a high-end erotic doll) and its now celebrity purchaser, companion, and lover, Davecat.[5] Similar to the story above, Davecat and his lifestyle are reported, yet implicitly judged at the same time. However, unlike the story of Nathaniel and Chase, human-doll relationships, and in particular the RealDoll, have been the topic of quite a few news programs and documentaries (as well as the topic of feature films) and thus appears to be moving into a more mainstream understating of sexuality (though still not separated from claims of perversity or objectification). Movies such as *Lars and the Real Girl*, as well as documentaries including *Guys and Dolls*, tend to take a more mature, less titillating, approach to the topic, and it is here where dolls as the topic of objectophilia may find a very useful

---

[3] For information on Real Sex: http://www.tv.com/shows/real-sex/; for information on My Strange Addiction: https://www.tlc.com/tv-shows/my-strange-addiction/.

[4] https://www.youtube.com/watch?v=06BFsQ_28Co.

[5] https://www.youtube.com/watch?v=kCjyILOOwUg.

purchase into understanding the next steps of social relationships, sanctioned and not sanctioned (yet?) (Blizzard 2014).[6] So, how might social theorists take doll love seriously?

## 3   Companion Species

One of the best-known theorists in interdisciplinary social sciences, and certainly STS, is renowned scholar, Donna Haraway. For decades, Haraway has examined the ways in which humans (re)make and (re)think themselves through the twentieth and into the twenty-first century. Her work, "The Cyborg Manifesto: Science, Technology, and Socialist Feminism in the Late Twentieth Century," is often cited as one of the treatises to bring the concept of the cyborg into twenty-first century thinking (Haraway 1991). The cyborg, a term coined in 1960 by Manfred Clynes and Nathan Kline was a merging the term cybernetic and organism and was presented as a fairly straight forward concept that evolved into a complex idea/theory/materiality (Clynes and Kline 1960). The basic idea was to find a way to remake the human (chemically) so that the person (an astronaut or other space traveler) could exist in space without the burden of taking with them technologies such as space suits and other forms of traveling vessels that they would need to control.[7] Since the introduction of the space traveling cyborg, many social theorists and technologists and have taken up the concept and broadened it to a being that is part human and part Other.[8] These theorists embrace the concept of Otherness and a heterogeneous-whole while also exploring a variety of realities from which they can rethink a post human world and thus, post human relationships (e.g. Hables Gray 2000; Mussies and Maliepaard 2017).

Moving beyond the original definition of 1960, over two decades later, Haraway reimagines the cyborg into a category of social existence, political resistance, and gender transformation. In the manifesto, she explains her reasons for writing, "I am making an argument for the cyborg as a fiction mapping our social and bodily reality and as an

---

[6] For information on Lars and the Real Girl: http://www.imdb.com/title/tt0805564/.

For information on Guys and Dolls: http://documentaryheaven.com/guys-and-dolls/.

[7] The authors reasoned that to remove the burden of monitoring the technology to keep the person alive, the person could focus on other issues, as they stated in their article, *Cyborgs and Space*, "If man attempts partial adaptation to space conditions, instead of insisting on carrying his whole environment along with him, a number of new possibilities appear" (Clynes and Kline 1960:30). They continue with a vivid example: "If man in space, in addition to flying his vehicle, must continuously be checking on things and making adjustments merely in order to keep himself alive, he becomes a slave to the machine. The purpose of the Cyborg, as well as his own homeostatic systems, is to provide an organizational system in which such robot-like problems are taken care of automatically and unconsciously, leaving man free to explore, to create, to think and to feel" (Clynes and Kline 1960:31).

[8] Clynes and Kline began a path of social analysis (and controversy) that few could have imagined, and today's cyborg imaginings rarely hold a resemblance to the articulation of the first "cyborg." In most cases, certainly those highlighted in popular culture, the cyborg is generally a human/robot or human with mechanical attachments (though some are cyborgs chemical, harkening back to the initial concept proposed by Clines and Kline, e.g. Oehlert 1995).

imaginative resource suggesting some very fruitful couplings. …This chapter is an argument for *pleasure* in the confusion of boundaries and for *responsibility* in their construction" (Haraway 1991:150). She later continues, "so my cyborg myth is about transgressed boundaries, potent fusions, and dangerous possibilities which progressive people might explore as one part of needed political work." (Haraway 1991:154). The cyborg manifesto, a self-admitted, "blasphemy," takes the reader into realms of conceptualizing the world out of the dangers of dichotomous thinking nurtured in paternalism and historical inequity and to a world beyond traditional bodies: bodies of flesh, bodies of politics; *bodies* (Haraway 1991:149).[9] With frenetic eloquence, Haraway takes readers on an exploration of the inadequacies of current classifications and aberrations within them. What is so natural about the natural? Perhaps it is best seen as a flexible manner of understanding? Haraway argues that assumed classifications are breaking down and that new ways of thinking of the world are possible. This awareness becomes pertinent to an analysis of understanding love between Others. In particular, she considers three areas of "boundary breakdowns" (Haraway 1991:151) and suggests a more "leaky" (Haraway 1991:152) existence between previously assumed dichotomies. The first breakdown occurs between the human and the animal; a second breakdown lies between the human-animal and machine, and finally there is a breakdown between the physical and non-physical (Haraway 1991:151–152). These new ways of viewing the world lead to a better understanding of the human-doll relationship as one that exists within a new sociotechnical relationship. These fusions and their political infestations lead to her next work that further speaks to the importance of the doll as an active actor in a social network: companion species.

Over fifteen years after her highly influential "Cyborg Manifesto," Haraway released her next manifesto: The Companion Species Manifesto: Dogs, People, and Significant Otherness (Haraway 2003). Here, Haraway takes a bold step away from her seminal work and literally goes to the dogs: instead of pairing human-technology, she ponders how might we better understand the world by thinking about human-nonhuman species relationships that are seen in a variety of "naturecultures," where the naturecultures contain within them an assortment of biological-biological constitutive relationships (Haraway 2003:12)? What might we learn if we turn our attention more to that which builds us as singular entities through the awareness of our necessary collaborative life? The biological lives, the naturecultures, that integrate within human existence she terms companion species. Within the realm of companion species, the dog, the variant of the wolf and worker and friend to humans, stands out. And it is the dog, which while being understood within the historical understanding of cyborg and humans turns a spotlight on the deep integration of human relationships. Reflecting on her earlier work she writes, "…cyborg reconfigurations hardly exhaust the tropic work required for ontological choreography in technoscience. I have come to see cyborgs as junior siblings in the much bigger, queer family of companion species…" (Haraway 2003:11; on "ontological choreography" see Thompson 2007). In her earliest musings within the manifesto she leaves

---

[9] For an excellent analysis of the ways in which cyborgs and Otherness may be metaphorically analyzed in the case studies of Asperger's and those practicing BDSM or holding such desires, see Mussies and Maliepaard 2017.

a tempting platform for seriously thinking through the human-doll relationship when she writes:

"We are, constitutively, companion species. We make each other up in the flesh. Significantly other to each other, in specific difference, we signify in the flesh a nasty developmental infection called love. This love is an historical aberration and a natural-cultural legacy" (Haraway 2003:2–3).

The western world is a sociotechnical system in which the organic and inorganic mesh in a "spiral dance" (Haraway 1991) and this "ontological choreography" (Thompson 2007) allows us, and may even demand of us, that we seriously consider love as naturally engineered, a rhetorical and embodied history of the freedom attained through difference (Haraway 1991; de Sousa 2015). An opportunity arises: limerence and decision/commitment, two key components behind de Sousa's inquiry of love via Tennov and Sternberg, might be attained within, across, and outside of species.

What might an analysis of companion species offer a critique of human-NHNS relationships? The answer and potential future that it generates is as simple as it is complex: social relationships are constitutively driven aberrations located in a multifaceted context. What constitutes a social relationship is as varied as those who build them and those who sanction them. And more to the point, we are comingled in evolving nature-cultures: each dependent upon the other and each evolves in a heterogeneous mix of body and constituent mind. Us and them may not exist at all. *We simply are.* The emotional mathematics becomes clearer, if unnerving. If humans can have relationships with humans, and if humans can have relationships with non-humans (e.g. dogs), why not expand relationships to include NHNS entities? In this case, dolls?

The leaky boundaries introduced in the Cyborg Manifesto, come to deeper fruition in Companion Species, where she highlights how multiple forms of Otherness are an inherent symbiotic existence of unified diversity. Dog/human or human/dog? What is the correct classification? Thus, Haraway takes an important step in the social theory of human praxis: humans and sentient non-humans do fulfill and create a needed existence of dependency. The singular is a duality of dependency and beyond. In sum, Haraway's Companion Species and others of a similar theoretical leaning, are positioned to take seriously human/Other.

## 4    Actor Network Theory (ANT)

A theory that emerged in the 1980s within the social studies of science and science and technology studies was Actor Network Theory (ANT). The ideas behind ANT were first brought to scholarly attention in the works of Bruno Latour, John Law, and Michel Callon, among other STS scholars (e.g., Bijker et al. 1989). The basic premise to ANT is quite simple though rarely fully understood as it is not clearly a theory or method as much as it is a process for understanding how the world is made and how it functions (Law and Singleton 2013). The approach allows for an individual to view a network or interlinking relationships between humans and nonhumans (i.e., technology) as all having purchase on the outcomes of the network; the human(s) and the technology(ies) are linked. To illustrate, the purchase of a carton of milk involves the cows, the dairy equipment, the farm (food and tools to sustain it), the infrastructure to purify, package and move the product to market, the humans to stack the shelves, the humans to purchase it, and the humans to sell it. Together they form a network. The networks exist, and from them we gain insights into the social forces they produce. For the milk to make it to a kitchen table all must be functioning. Which part of the network is more important? Which has the most influence? ANT adds the invisible technologies and practices that are often forgotten and values the roles that they play (and some may argue the agency that non-ANT approaches exclude).

ANT makes NHNS actors relevant to the construction and experience of reality. Although ANT was taken up with much excitement, it also warranted strong criticisms. Two criticisms are particularly important when considering how the human-doll relationship may be viewed: first, ANT has been criticized for having an overwhelming zeal for heterogeneity which may lead to anthropomorphizing or overestimating the sentience or agency of a nonhuman actor; and, second, ANT may fail to determine who or what exerts more force into the network and for what reasons (e.g., how and why do actors express power, reason, and meaning in the experience?). In their clever article presented in dialogue and narrative form, John Law and Vicky Singleton work to clarify what ANT is and is not. Vicky makes it clear in her own words:

"We need to remember that some people don't like ANT because it says objects are pretty much like humans; that they are actors too. And vice versa. For some people this sounds uncaring. Inhumane. But I think this is a bit of a misunderstanding. ANT isn't saying that people are robots. It's saying that people can be understood as an effect of the unfolding of web relations they're caught up in. And that human and non-human actors are assembled together" (Law and Singleton 2013:501–502).

Not unlike the companion species of Haraway, the actors in the network, the humans and nonhumans, are co-constructing a constitutive reality.

Although ANT has some failings, it can be quite beneficial as its supporters urge us to think more generally about viewing social and technical artifacts as both relevant in the creation of sociotechnical relationships. To illustrate, in their work on IT in medical systems Cresswell, Worth, and Sheikh remind readers that,

"Despite some limitations, an Actor-Network Theory-based approach is conceptually useful in helping to appreciate the complexity of reality (including the complexity of organisations) and the active role of technology in this context. This can prove helpful in understanding how social effects are generated as a *result of associations between different actors in a network*. Of central importance in this respect is that Actor-Network Theory provides a lens through which to view the role of technology in shaping social processes" (italics added, np).

Whether the item or system under scrutiny is a toaster, a person, an idea, or a medical technology, ANT approaches highlight the interconnectedness of things and aims to level the discourse and analysis so that all can be seen as relevant in the construction of the meaning of the reality of the context in question.

## 5 Enter the Doll

In his work, <u>Love + Sex with Robots: The Evolution of Human-Robot Relationships</u>, David Levy (and the very point to the Congress) explores human, animal/pet, and robot love. Not surprisingly, many mainstream media, and some scholars for that matter, contend that such claims undermine the primary (and universalizing) stance that love can only be shared by sentient, human, consensual agreement. However, when exploring the built environment termed *technology* from a critical standpoint, the possibilities for extending Levy's initial thoughts are more than promising: they are warranted; they are necessary. In parallel, but not in conversation with Levy, STS scholars add a nuanced attention to the technical. It is the turn to the sociotechnical as a constitutive relationship, where STS and sexuality scholars may find fertile ground for deeper theoretical exploration into human-doll relationships.

Erotic dolls are difficult to define (Blizzard 2014; Fergusson 2010). Following the emergence of blow up dolls in the 1980s in which mass marketed dolls were available for mail-order, the 1990s witnessed an emergence of a different doll (Fergusson 2010). This new doll could be made to order, was a physiological facsimile, and appeared by sight and touch to more closely resemble a human.[10] In my earlier work examining the RealDoll (a high end made to order erotic doll) I contend that,

"Although the doll is not human, it can stimulate very human emotions within its owner. The doll is the figurative receptacle of the emotions put into it as well as the literal receptacle of human touch and fluids that evoke and signify human arousal. It is not just a doll, it is its own Otherness. Certainly the doll is not human, but it may be near human to its partner if the partner infuses it with personality, and emotional and perceived agency that can only be read by its human lover or companion." (Blizzard 2014:64).

This approach opens the doll to be an actor via ANT, and taking the lead from Levy, if it is made real or relevant through its human partner, it might move way from a category of thing to a possible category of whom. Moving deeper into the ideas forming the foundation of a companion species, while fully acknowledging the a-biological make-up of the doll, the doll becomes a fully relevant existence in the reality of a social network and narrative. The doll becomes less a doppelgänger or simulacra than a separate engaging entity (c.f., Marquet et al. 2016). Returning to de Sousa's analysis of love, we are left to ask, can the doll make sense in a loving relationship? My answer: why not? Why not love in multiple different fashions? de Sousa writes with a compelling openness:

"Equipped with a little of that objectifying attitude that is peculiar to science, you might be able to stand back and see through the illusion. Once you do, there is no reason not to grant that, alongside happy monogamous marriages, countless different

---

[10] Perhaps the best known and most artistic or realistic doll that emerged during this time was the RealDoll, a creation of the merging of the Hollywood make up industry and artistry with engineering prowess (Blizzard 2014). The dolls were envisioned by artists and the realism and hyperrealism did not go unnoticed. RealDoll transgressed the boundary between art and sex; a boundary often blurred throughout the history of art (e.g. surrealism and the use of mannequins, see, Dali and Newton e.g. Fergusson 2010).

arrangements are compatible with the diversity of human tastes and temperaments. We should then accept that for some people, the love of one or more life partners can be enriched rather than doomed by their openness to unconventional experience." (de Sousa 2015:107)

The doll is the unconventional, yet nevertheless real experience. This is where the doll and the dog part ways. The dog does not resemble the human, nor do is progenitors (dogs and human breeders) try to make it so. The dog is a dog, glorious in its own right, a companion species, but not human or near human. The doll of the twenty-first century can, and sometimes eerily does, resemble the human in very "uncanny" ways (Mori 1970).[11] Today's erotic doll brings an interesting challenge to the concept of a NHNS: it is designed to resemble, in great detail, the human to which it may be accepted as companion. Further it takes on two important aspects of human familiarity; first, it is designed to appear human, and second, it is often given an identity by its owner/companion and the community in which it resides. These two points are important as they mark the doll as both Other and companion. These points illustrate an attempt to make the doll as lifelike as possible; its creators and users are attempting to cross the dangerous uncanny valley (Mori 1970; Blizzard 2014). For the purchaser, the work, the effort, and the feelings that are infused into the doll are real, yet emotionally invisible (though the outcomes of the investment may be highly visible, e.g., taking the doll to a public space). Regardless of how others view the doll, it is the owner's or utilizer's view of the dolls that make them real and worthy.

## 6    Discussion and Conclusions

By bringing together companion species and ANT, there is considerable room to conceptualize what it means to be in a social relationship. As explored above, ANT makes all actors relevant, but has serious shortcomings in anthropomorphizing entities, or put another way, to underestimate the importance of sentience and agency, that is, who and what exerts more into the network and for what reasons. Companion species demonstrate that individuals are better seen as constitutively created. Haraway and others call to question the perversity of androcentric taxonomies in the world. When thinking through the overriding desire to dichotomize and privilege the human as agent

---

[11] Taking the lead from Freud's analysis of the uncanny, in 1970 roboticist Masahiro Mori turned an eye toward the robot, a figure newly emergent from the twentieth century imaginings of those creating humanoids and the willingness of individuals to accept or reject them. In his path breaking work, "The Uncanny Valley" Mori hypothesized that as humans and robots begin to form relationships it is generally enjoyable, however, if the robot appears too human it may prove repulsive to the human viewer – it is close, *but not close enough*. Something is off. Red flags are raised and some viewers stammer away, unsettled by the realistic entity that falls short of convincing the viewer it is real. In response to this revulsion, some artists and technologists have tried not to replicate the human fully and to stay in the realm of fantasy. Instead of making the entity look human they imbue the entity with human *likeness* in the form of language, morals, and other aspects within the cultural metanarrative of the human condition (c.f., de Fren 2009; Barber 2017).

it becomes clear that our understanding of legitimate human relationships is limited. ANT theorists argue that the person and the artifact are both acting and constructing the sociotechnical web in which we all build, interact, and experience the world. Here, I argue that ANT, when combined with concepts such as companion species, transgress the boundaries of Otherness and lead to a critical interpretation of how and why loving a doll, may also be equally normalized into a developmental progression of human-NHNS relationships. So, what does this mean for the future of love and sex with robots, and in this case doll?

At the heart of this exploration, I ask, what does it mean to be attached or in a relationship with another? As ANT theorists have turned to objects, and Haraway has literally gone to the dogs, it becomes very possible and fruitful to consider that human-doll love is the next step in our evolution as sentient beings in a post human world (c.f., O'Mahony 2002; Hables Gray 2000). ANT theorists and those who support them, can present a worldview where human and NHNS entities form an important network of social understanding. Classic cases that utilize ANT introduce how we build sociotechnical networks physically; but why not emotionally, too? The doll is an object of affection that may well love us back, *at least in our minds*, which is the final arbiter in defining our reality. While people outside of the individual may see the activity as irrational, immoral, or worse, such accusations and arguments are similarly built in their own reality. So, whose reality wins?[12]

At first blush the doll may literally appear to be an attempt at human likeness. However, when placing the doll within a sociotechnical network analyzed via ANT and problematized as a new a-biological companion species, the doll is far more. Unfortunately, the doll has been as easy target for many who argue mainstream morality: simply put, it is often viewed as an assumed attempt at creating a presence to masquerade as something that it is not. However, critical social theory that examines sociotechnical relationships and identities offers another insight into the doll and the realities that support its existence: what if the doll is simply a sociotechnical existence that, when combined with other actors, forms a different form of constitutively created social identity?

What makes a loving relationship? This is a question that even human-human participants cannot fully answer, so why hold the doll to a higher standard? In this work I do not argue the morality of human-doll love; however, I do argue that just as some theorists have analyzed human non-human relationships as legitimate aspects of understanding authentic human experiences, so must we consider, even briefly, the possibility of human-NHNS relationships as meriting serious social inquiry and analysis without the burden of limitations created through preconceived moral judgment. At the very least, such analysis must come with an awareness that such culturally constructed claims of morality do not lay outside of the same cultural milieu that attempts to understand the meaning of human relationships and the very essence of amorphous love. The doll is not human. However, as we build them, they in turn, build us. This issue alone requires serious attention to the ways in which humans are creating our own innovative realities

---

[12] For an excellent discussion of competing claims of objectivity leading to an overall generally accepted objectivity see, Harding (1995) "Strong Objectivity": A response to the new objectivity question. *Synthese 104*(3): 331–349.

as we construct creative love maps as we find our ideal companion species, biological or otherwise (c.f. Barber 2017; Haraway 2003).

# References

Barber, T.: For the love of artifice 2: attachment. An extension of the paper 'for the love of artifice: why we need robot sex dolls and why there is a growing sub culture of real people trying to become them'. In: Cheok, A.D., Devlin, K., Levy, D. (eds.) LSR 2016. LNCS (LNAI), vol. 10237, pp. 64–71. Springer, Cham (2017). https://doi.org/10.1007/978-3-319-57738-8_6

Bijker, W.E., Hughes, T.P., Pinch, T.J. (eds.): The Social Construction of Technological Systems: New Directions in the Sociology and History of Technology. MIT Press, Cambridge (1989)

Blizzard, D.: Making the fantasy: consumption, relationships, and the RealDoll. In: Johnsdotter, S., Larsson, M. (eds.) Sexual Fantasies: At the Intersection of Culture and the Individual, pp. 57–77. Peter Lang Publishers, New York (2014)

Bowlby, J.: A Secure Base: Parent-Child Attachment and Healthy Human Development, Reprint edn. Basic Books, New York (1988)

Breazeal, C.: Designing Sociable Robots. Intelligent Robotics and Autonomous Agents Series, PAP/CDR edn. A Bradford Book, Bradford (2004)

Clynes, M., Kline, N.: Cyborgs and space. Astronautics 5, 26–27, 74–76 (1960)

Cresswell, K., Worth, A., Sheikh, A.: Actor-Network Theory and its role in understanding the implementation of information technology developments in healthcare. PMCID:PMC2988706 (2010). https://doi.org/10.1186/1472-6947-10-67

de Fren, A.: Technofetishism and the uncanny desires of ASFR (alt. sex. Fetish. Robots). Sci. Fict. Stud. 36(3), 404–440 (2009)

de Sousa, R.: Love: A Very Short Introduction. Oxford University Press, Oxford (2015)

Fergusson, A.: The Sex Doll: A History. McFarland and Co., Jefferson (2010)

Freud, S.: The Uncanny. Penguin Classics (2003). Translated by David McLintock

Hables Gray, C.: Cyborg Citizen: Politics in the Posthuman Age, 1st edn. Routledge, New York (2000)

Haraway, D.: The Companion Species Manifesto: Dogs, People, and Significant Otherness. Paradigm, New York (2003)

Haraway, D.: A cyborg manifesto: science, technology, and socialist feminism in the late twentieth century. In: Simians, Cyborgs, and Women: The Reinvention of Nature, pp. 149–182. Routledge, New York (1991)

Harding, S.: Strong objectivity: a response to the new objectivity question. Synthese 104(3), 331–334 (1995)

Law, J., Singleton, V.: ANT and politics: working in and on the world. Qual. Sociol. 36(4), 485–502 (2013)

Levy, D.: Love + Sex with Robots: The Evolution of Human-Robot Relations. Harper Collins, New York (2007)

Marsh, A.: Love among the objectum sexuals. Electron. J. Hum. Sex. 13 (2010)

Marquet, F., Heiting, M. (eds.): Helmut Newton: Work, Multilingual edn. Taschen, New York (2016). Newton, H. (photographer)

Mori, M.: The uncanny valley. Energy 7(4), 33–35 (1970). Translated by Karl F. MacDorman and Takashi Minato

Mussies, M., Maliepaard, E.: The cyborg mermaid (or: how Technè can help the misfits fit in). In: Cheok, A.D., Devlin, K., Levy, D. (eds.) LSR 2016. LNCS (LNAI), vol. 10237, pp. 84–96. Springer, Cham (2017). https://doi.org/10.1007/978-3-319-57738-8_8

433333323333333333333333

O'Mahony, M.: Cyborg: The Man-Machine. Thames & Hudson, New York (2002)

Oehlert, M.: From Captain America to Wolverine: cyborgs in comic books, alternative images of cybernetic heroes and villains. In: Hables Gray, C. (ed.) The Cyborg Handbook, pp. 219–232. Routledge, New York (1995)

Thompson, C.: Making Parents: The Ontological Choreography of Reproductive Technologies. MIT Press, Cambridge (2007)

# Dolores and Robot Sex: Fragments of Non-anthropocentric Ethics

Thomas Beschorner and Florian Krause[(✉)]

Institute for Business Ethics, University of St. Gallen, Girtannerstr. 8, 9010 St. Gallen, Switzerland
{Thomas.Beschorner,Florian.Krause}@unisg.ch

**Abstract.** The new generation of sex robots raises questions about a potential moral responsibility by human beings toward robots. In our paper, we develop a pathocentric approach to normative ethics that goes beyond the mere well-being of human beings by searching for a broader perspective that includes a morality towards objects. First, we demonstrate that the moral line between living beings (e.g. human beings, animals) and objects is much blurrier than it seems and relate these general considerations back to the issue of robot sex. We then discuss possible consequences of our approach, outlining in particular ideas on how sex robots will change our social norms. We argue that the influence robots can have on our norms does not only concern our perception of them, but also of ourselves.

**Keywords:** Ethics · Robot sex

## 1 Introduction

In 2016, HBO ran its TV series "Westworld." Based on Michael Crichton's film from 1973, this science fiction series portrays a leisure park in the seriously "wild, wild West." The protagonists are robots, but ones that are hardly distinguishable from humans. The visitors to the park are human beings, and they enjoy treating the robots as they please. Shootings and executions, sex, rape, and cruel torture are most attractive to the Westworld tourists. The TV show has, however, quite an interesting narrative twist. On the one hand, some of the visitors show *empathy* for the artificial beings. On the other hand, some robots develop a form of consciousness. Dolores, a young farmer's daughter, for example, has vague memories and references to the past, albeit diffuse ones. She questions whether "her world" is actually "the real world" and wonders what lies behind the defined territory. She asks questions about the future and wants to break out of the boundaries imposed on her.

From episode to episode, the TV audience increasingly empathizes with Dolores because she feels and suffers as she develops an almost human countenance. The robot is portrayed as feeling both passion and suffering. Indeed, "Westworld" is just a TV show and Dolores is merely a character in its story. Whether we are really dealing with (rumpy-pumpy) robots that feel or suffer and whether we will consider them as "beings" or somehow "alive," nobody yet knows.

We begin our article with this episode in order to introduce the philosophical question that is at the center of this paper: We want to develop elements of normative ethics that

© Springer International Publishing AG, part of Springer Nature 2018
A. D. Cheok and D. Levy (Eds.): LSR 2017, LNCS 10715, pp. 128–137, 2018.
https://doi.org/10.1007/978-3-319-76369-9_10

are not limited to the well-being of human beings but instead go beyond an anthropocentric perspective and, thus, also suggest normative orientations which take into account responsibility for entities other than human beings. The case we have chosen to use to exemplify our thoughts is sex robots.

Current developments in the sex industry demonstrate that it is very likely that sex robots (much like robots used for other purposes) will soon be part of our social life, which will also raise a wide range of ethical questions. Recently, a new generation of sex robots was presented at a sex fair in London. While the traditional sex doll is a passive, inflated piece of plastic, today's models of sex robots are active and responsive. They talk and interact with their owners, ask them about their wishes, say what they like themselves. Thus, the current state of the field shows very clearly that these developments will continue and that both the technological sophistication and physical appearance of artificial sex partners will continue to improve. This holds the promise of becoming big business for manufacturers, obviously. Indeed, it seems possible that within a few years, there will be mainstream sex robots that are in no way inferior to the physical experience of sex between humans.

One can regard this development soberly in terms of the social impact of the advancing technologies, which have always affected the sex industry, as the sex industry in turn often advanced technical developments. What is new, then, and why should it be wrong? There already are vibrators, sex dolls, penis pumps, apps, internet portals, and so on. Like sex robots, these are technical tools aimed at satisfying sexual desire.

The difference between sex robots and classic sex toys, however, seems to be not a gradual but a fundamental one. Future generations of sex robots will have a much stronger physical resemblance to human sex partners than current ones do. And through their skills to simulate communication, interacting with them will also increasingly resemble interpersonal interaction. This potential is being pursued by the sex industry as a unique selling point and a competitive advantage. The same is true for the development of virtual reality sex: It should feel real.

Our paper is structured as follows: We will briefly characterize the current academic debate on the ethics of robot sex. This debate is divided into proponents and opponents concerning the good or the bad of sex with robots. What both sides have in common is an anthropocentric perspective (Sect. 2). In Sect. 3, we will then begin developing an argument that goes beyond the mere well-being of human beings, searching instead for a broader ethical perspective. We will approach this topic in a first step through a very pragmatic approach by elaborating on moral intuition and the moral sentiments of people. Here, we will especially demonstrate that the moral line between living beings (e.g. human beings, animals) and objects is much blurrier than it seems at first glance.

In Sect. 4, we will relate these general considerations back to the issue of robot sex, investigating elements of an "object morality." Here we suggest four aspects to capture this phenomenon: (1) Interaction with and (2) self-similarity to objects, (3) access of objects to intimacy spheres, and (4) the personalization of objects.

In the two final sections of this paper, we explore the consequences of our approach. In Sect. 5, we will outline some ideas on how sex robots will change our social norms while arguing that the influence robots can have on our norms does not only concern our perception of them, but also of ourselves. In Sect. 6, we suggest a pathocentric approach to normative ethics that might help to better understand "object morality."

## 2   Proponents and Opponents of Robot Sex: The Current Debate

In the academic debate, there are advocates as well as critics of robot sex. At the moment, the discussion mainly focuses on possible outcomes of sex with robots. Proponents argue, for example, that perfected robot sex could make prostitution (and thus the exploitation of millions of women) superfluous (e.g. [1–3]). In Barcelona, the world's first robotic whorehouse already exists, where customers can amuse themselves with models of their choice [4]. Similarly, robots could reduce the sexual abuse of children.

Critics, on the other hand, see in sexual practices with robots the risk of a decline in morality that can negatively affect human sexuality [5]. If a man habitually rapes and strangles his robot, the resulting habit may lead him to try and pursue similar practices with humans. Imagination and reality would blur in the minds of people. This would not reduce but rather inspire acts of pedosexuality. From a feminist point of view, the "objectification" of women as (sex) objects is criticized (e.g. [6]).

There are currently no empirical studies on robot sex that could confirm the position of either side of this debate. However, taking a side view on the broader phenomenon of technological sexuality, there is some evidence that technology and the consumption of erotic media have an impact on people's sexual behavior with human partners. Studies on teenagers' porn consumption, for example, show quite clearly that the regular consumption of porn can influence their ideas of sexuality [e.g. 7]. The spectrum ranges from exaggerated expectations of sexual practices, the perception of one's own body and one's sexual "performativity," to higher levels of sexual violence within certain high-risk groups. On the other hand, it has been shown that e.g. violent computer games can affect their consumers, but not to a significant level [9]. However, it is clear that specific research is needed on the outcomes of sex with robots.

## 3   Moral Sentiments, Inter-passion, and "Things"?

In terms of moral evaluation, the focus on the outcomes of robot sex is quite a limited approach, since it only focuses on potential effects in human beings. The current debate can therefore be labeled as strictly anthropocentric. In this section, we want to go one step further by undertaking a perspective change in the sense that we are *not only* focusing on moral issues *for* human beings but we extend the perspective towards a potential moral responsibility *by* human beings *toward* robots.

Using a "non-anthropocentric" approach requires some explications. We exclusively use this term to characterize responsibility for non-human beings, e.g. robots. Hence, we suggest a normative non-anthropocentric approach, not an epistemic one. An epistemic non-anthropocentric approach would be one that attempts to develop a point of view from outside of our social world to, for example, view the world through the eyes of an animal or a robot. This is simply not possible. It does not matter how close we can come to interpreting non-humans, it always necessarily remains a human interpretation.

We are not aware of any epistemology which would allow for this. Rather, the idea is to outline analogies and discuss fields that have an implication on our moral perception on sex with robots. Therefore, our considerations start with views on humans' moral intuition and moral sentiments.

In our society, the moral intuition of most people probably is that it is morally wrong to torture a pet or even brutally destroy a child's toy. But why are these actions regarded as wrong? Why do we care about another species? Why do we even care about toys?

Moral intuition, we argue, is (not only but also) grounded in human beings' ability of having "moral sentiments," an idea that has been stressed by Adam Smith [8], for example. Without going into too much detail, a differentiation of the terms "empathy" and "sympathy" seems to be helpful to briefly characterize our understanding of moral sentiments.

## 3.1  Empathy and Sympathy

*Empathy* can be regarded as the capacity to put oneself (to a certain degree) in someone else's shoes to understand and to feel his or her experiences—cognitively, emotionally, and/or somatically. In this process, we mimetically empathize with somebody else. *Sympathy* is related to empathy but can be characterized as a stronger form of (cognitive, emotional, and/or somatic) connectivity in the sense that it also includes another person's need, trouble, grief, misfortune but also joy. Importantly, this need, trouble, grief, misfortune, or joy is seen as *common or shared experience*. In other words, while the term of empathy remains on the level of alter and ego (you and me), sympathy stresses the togetherness of the "we." Our *first* argument therefore is that *human beings have empathetic capabilities; they can connect feelings of others with their own feelings, which implies togetherness.*

## 3.2  Living Beings and Objects

While it is safe to assume that most people have moral sentiments for their pets, it is also safe to assume that people are feeling little to no moral obligation toward, say, some cells, or a fly, or a rat in their basement, or—to extend it to non-living things—a stone or a frying pan. One might argue that we tend to feel stronger moral sentiments for living beings than for objects. While this might be true in many cases, we think the line between living beings and objects is much blurrier than it seems, and that moral sentiments are not limited to living beings. Children, for example, often have an intense connection to their teddy bears or their dolls and regard and treat them as "living things." They talk to them and speak for them, they cuddle with them, and give them names. Beloved toys cannot simply be replaced by another cuddly toy. There is a strong sympathy, a "we connection." We can find several similar examples for adults that are deeply connected to objects. On the other hand, who among us has moral qualms to trap a rat in the basement or kill an annoying fly? Consequently, our *second argument* is: *Moral sentiments can concern living beings as well as objects.*

### 3.3   Moral Sentiments as Social Constructions

With the teddy bears, we have referred to an example which also points to another important aspect, that is, the distinction between sentiments or feelings on the one hand and moral sentiments on the other hand. While the former characterizes an emotional connectedness to beings or objects, the latter also includes a normative-evaluative dimension. Simply put, there are morally right and wrong sentiments. What should be considered a morally right or wrong moral sentiment dependents on certain norms and values in a given community or society (at any given time). For instance, in our current society, it is taken for granted that the relationship between a child and a teddy bear is one of love and care. A child that frequently cuts or destroys its cuddly toys risks having to have a serious conversation with its parents or the kindergarten teacher (probably without understanding why). The mother, the father, or the kindergarten teacher will immediately have moral concerns about the child's practices. Consequently, our *third argument* is that *moral sentiments are socially constructed and highly context-dependent (in time and space).*

### 3.4   Inter-passion

While the teddy bear example may illustrate moral sentiments with regard to objects, there are obviously many objects we do not morally care about at all. A child is connected to its cuddly toys, and so are the authors of this text to their computers. While the amount of time we spend in front of our machines is much higher than the time a child snuggles with its toy, the qualitative connection of the child with this specific object is much higher than ours with the computer. We call this qualitative connection "inter-passion" and argue, *fourthly*: *The more inter-passionate the relationship with an object, the higher the likelihood to have moral sentiments. (This is also true for the connection with living beings).*

To sum it up, human beings have the capacity of being empathetic and can create togetherness ("we"-relations), moral sentiments, and inter-passion with and for living beings as well as with and for objects. If this line of argumentation is true, and if we follow a common sense in moral philosophy that normative ethics is not merely about thinking "how it ought to be" but must also consider the "is" (to generate fruitful inter-play between both dimensions), then normative ethics needs to take these practices into consideration. In other words, the very practical *social interactions of people are a potential source of moral action* (toward human as well as non-human beings) and should be taken into consideration by normative ethics.

## 4   A Thing is not a Thing: Moral Sentiments for and Inter-passion with Sex Robots?

As we have shown, there are moral sentiments and inter-passion for living beings as well as for objects. What exactly these sentiments are depends on the *social role of the respective object*. But what social role do sex robots have?

*Firstly*, it is clear that sex robots are created to have sex with and that humans are able to fulfil sexual desires with them. Critical questions especially arise if violent or humiliating sexual practices (e.g. sado-masochism) are involved. Here, however, we have to further distinguish between violent sex that is based on informed and clear consent between sex partners and violent sex that is not. The former is a sex practice like any other, while the latter constitutes rape, and is thus immoral. With respect to sex with robots, this leads to the theoretical problem that we cannot clearly distinguish whether it is simply another form of sex or if it is rape.

*Secondly*, whether or not this question is relevant in the first place depends on the social role of sex robots. Why should violent practices toward robots be immoral at all? Maybe, as some authors [10] argue, they are simple designed to be victims of rape.

We would probably not have a discussion about violence against things if we were talking about punching balls, since punching balls are *made* to be beaten up. Human aggression towards a punching ball is even considered to be a good thing by some people, since it is considered a sport, it can help to relieve stress after work, etc. Again, if the social role of sex robots is merely seen as a sort of punching ball to fulfil sexual desires, there would be no moral problem with this. One could even argue that it is a good thing since it might channel sexual desires in certain directions, as it has been argued above by the proponents of sex robots.

However, *thirdly*, we do not think that the punching ball analogy characterizes sex robots adequately but, in contrast, that the (potential) social role of sex robots is finely nuanced. Here, we especially wish to focus on the following four aspects:

1. *Inter-action*: Sex with robots can be characterized as intercourse rather than a form of masturbation. The term "inter" points to the relational and connecting character of the relationship between a human being and a robot.
2. *Self-similarity:* If the consumers of sex with robots are not fetishists that prefer sex with objects, we can describe robot sex as a supplement for an actual human being and the on-going perfection of the design; robots' ability to imitate human reactions and communication also points in the direction that the (not only physical) similarity of sex robots in comparison to human beings is a specific characteristic.
3. *Intimacy:* In most cultures, sex is seen as the most intimate and private social sphere. It can be assumed that including robots in this sphere will lead to more inter-passion than, say, beating up a punching ball in a public gym.
4. *Personalization:* Given the aforementioned aspects, it is rather likely that users of sex robots will personalize their companions to a certain degree. They will probably give them names, they might dress them up or put on make-up, for example.

If the characterization of the social role of sex robots that we have briefly outlined is an appropriate description, it becomes obvious once again that things and objects shape our lives—very often behind our backs. Sexuality is only one of many examples in which human life is affected by objects.

In modern sociological approaches, attention has been paid to objects under the umbrella terms of "Practice Theory" and "New Materialism" (for a good overview, see [11]). Humans' "social existence determines their consciousness" is a pointed statement of Karl Marx's classical materialism, through which he stresses the importance of material conditions' influence on social life. New Materialism goes one step further. Rather than assigning a passive status to the material world, it considers *an object as something of an actor*. And, according to another point of New Materialism, the influence of objects on human beings is not only cognitive ("how we think") but *anchored in our bodies* ("how we act"). In other words, the "handling" of things can be embodied in human beings epigenetically, which is to say, both physically and emotionally.

## 5   Consequences (1): Are Sex Robots Changing our Social Norms?

The punching ball example outlined above and its differences to sex robots lead to the conclusion that in order to answer questions about norms of interaction with sex robots, we need a better description of their social function. However, as illustrated by the example of Dolores at the beginning of this article, the answer to the question of the function of sex robots is not sufficient for an ethical debate on those norms: Although Dolores was clearly designed to imitate a victim of human violence, moral sentiments towards her seem to change as human interaction (or, in this case, observation) continues. In a way, the interaction with robots affects our moral sentiments—it can change our perception of them, their function, and, through this, also the norms for interaction. However, the influence a robot can have on our norms does not only concern our perception of them, but of ourselves.

The ongoing perfection of sex robots' look is based on certain norms of what a sexually stimulating human body should look like. The problems arising from this can be connected to the discussions around transhumanism ([12] for an overview), which focus on the optimization of the human body (e.g. through technology) and its consequences. In the case of sex robots, we could ask: If sex robots have the "perfect" body, do not sweat, smell, fart or argue, and fulfil all of our sexual desires, why would we still be interested in sex with other human beings? The materialized ideal of a sexually attractive human being through sex robots could lead to a point where real human beings could simply become sexually unattractive. Our chase for an unrealistic image of perfection paired with our manufacturing skills could lead to the point that human beings are not able to fulfil their own standards anymore (also [13]). However, we still only have vague and merely problem-oriented definitions of what a human being "is." In certain situations, we ascribe to a ball of human cells the social status of an actual human being (e.g. [14, 15]). Can we justify not to have norms for the treatment of robots we are actually able to socially interact with?

## 6   Consequences (2): Do We Need a New Normative Ethics?

The current academic and nascent social debate on robot ethics (see Sect. 2) integrates seamlessly with an "anthropocentric" tradition of moral philosophy, in which the human being has rights, dignity, duties (towards other people), responsibilities (again, towards other people), etc. From that perspective, human beings are the only important point of reference.

The anecdotal tale about Dolores at the beginning of this text and the examples of obligations towards animals or teddy bears are to be understood as a suggestion that we contemplate a new normative ethics that involves human responsibility towards robots. What are the reasons for these considerations?

*Firstly*, we argue, the history of ethics and morality clearly shows that normative ethics does not need to be, and should not be, limited to responsibility toward human beings. The development of animal ethics is an illustrative case here. While philosophers such as Immanuel Kant [16] assumed that animals are just "things" without any moral rights, recent ethics (but also already Schopenhauer [17]) stress the so-called "pathocentric" way of thinking. The "pathos," i.e. suffering, becomes a moral criterion that indicates whether an action is moral or immoral. Animal protection is thus morally required to reduce the suffering of animals.

*Secondly*, while one could argue that animal ethics concerns living species while robots are mere objects, we have demonstrated above that the distinction of having moral sentiments and inter-passion for living beings on the one hand and non-living objects on the other hand are much blurrier than one might think. Why do we assume to be able to (morally) empathize or to sympathize with animals, for example? There is no clear scientific (natural science-based) answer to this question, and we think there is also no need to have an answer. *What is more important is our cultural constructions of morality toward others—toward other human beings, living species, or objects.* Again, it is important to note that questions of morality have changed over time: Slaves in Ancient Greece were not considered to be citizens and, consequently, had almost no moral rights. That current Western societies ascribe something like moral dignity and moral duties to humans is another example for morality as a cultural product that varies to a certain extend across space and time.

*Thirdly*, when it comes to responsibilities toward objects, it is important to note that (1) in some everyday situations we already (individually) act somewhat morally toward objects, and that (2) there also seem to be some socially recognized moral norms concerning objects, as outlined above. For example, a sex robot the shape of an eight-year-old boy or girl provokes moral questions of right and wrong, as does the "rape button" [10] on some sex robot models [18]. One could argue that in such cases, moral concerns merely arise to protect the moral standards of how humans act toward other humans. This was exactly Kant's position on animal ethics 200 years ago. While the risk of a "moral spill-over" might be given, this argumentation remains limited.

*Fourthly*, whether or not human beings develop moral sentiments and inter-passion for objects depends on the social role of these things, as has been stated above. Here, we suggest at least four aspects to capture this phenomenon: (1) Interaction with and (2) self-similarity to objects, (3) access of objects to intimacy spheres, and (4) the personalization of objects. Thus, the core of our argument is this: *The more these elements are related to objects, the higher the likelihood of an emergence of "object morality" on an individual level as well as on a social and societal level.*

Moral questions concerning sex robots, the example we have discussed in this paper, are excellent cases to describe and to analyze relatively new social development since they tend to include all four elements mentioned above.

## 7  Fin

In this paper, we suggest breaking with a strong anthropocentric way of thinking in ethics. The idea to also include robots in our academic debate on ethics is of high importance, since robots will increasingly become part of our lives in even more intimate situations in the future.

Robots in general and sex robots in particular are relatively new phenomena. It is not clear yet—also due to a lack of empirical research—how (sex) robots will affect our existing norms on how to treat human beings, and how having sex with them will affect society. This can also be seen as a challenge to sharpen our perspective on what a member of society is, and what moral obligations we have towards them. The development of even more realistic robots seems to us to be more likely than unlikely. This will affect the life of us humans—in sex as well as in all other spheres of life—and we should be able to talk about it, to develop a certain vocabulary, and be prepared for reasonable moral discussions.

## References

1. Yeoman, I., Mars, M.: Robots, men and sex tourism. Futures **44**(4), 365–371 (2012)
2. Levy, D.: Love and Sex with Robots. Harper Collins, New York (2007)
3. Levy, D.: The ethics of robot prostitutes. In: Lin, P., Abney, K., Bekey, G. (eds.) Robot Ethics: The Ethical and Social Implications of Robotics. MIT Press, Cambridge (2012)
4. http://www.lumidolls.com
5. Richardson, K.: The asymmetrical "Relationship": parallels between prostitution and the development of sex robots. SIGCAS Comput. Soc. **45**(3), 290–293 (2016)
6. Murphy, M.: Interview: Kathleen Richardson makes the case against sex robots (2017). http://www.feministcurrent.com/2017/06/02/interview-kathleen-richardson-makes-case-sex-robots/. Accessed 02 Aug 2017
7. Owens, E.W., Behun, R.J., Manning, J.C., Reid, R.C.: The impact of internet pornography on adolescents: a review of the research. Sex. Addict. Compulsivity **19**(1–2), 99–122 (2012)
8. Greitmeyer, T., Mügge, D.O.: Video games do affect social outcomes - a meta-analytic review of the effects of violent and prosocial video game play. In: Personality and Social Psychology Bulletin, vol. 40(5), pp. 578–589 (2014)
9. Smith, A.: The Theory of Moral Sentiments (1759)
10. wienerin.at: Roxxxy Truecompanion Bei neuen Sexrobotern mit "Frigid"-Modus können Männer Vergewaltigungen simulieren, 27 July 2017
11. Fox, N.J., Alldred, P.: Sociology and the New Materialism. Sage Publications, London (2016)
12. Bostrom, N.: A history of transhumanist thought. J. Evol. Technol. **14**(1), 1–25 (2005). http://jetpress.org/volume14/bostrom.html. Accessed 27 July 2017
13. Sullins, J.P.: Robots, love, and sex: The ethics of building a love machine. IEEE Trans. Affect. Comput. **3**(4), 398–409 (2012)
14. Hare, R.M.: Abortion and the golden rule. Philos. Public Aff. **4**(3), 201–222 (1975)
15. Damschen, G., Schönecker, D. (eds.): Der moralische Status menschlicher Embryonen. Pro und contra Spezies-, Kontinuums-, Identitäts- und Potentialitätsargument. De Gruyter, Berlin (2002)

16. Kant, I.: Die Metaphysik der Sitten. Zweiter Teil. Metaphysische Anfangsgründe der Tugendlehre, Sect. 17 (1797). permalink http://www.zeno.org/Philosophie/M/Kant,+Immanuel/Die+Metaphysik+der+Sitten
17. Schopenhauer: Parerga und Paralipomena (2 Bände). Zweiter Band (1851)
18. http://www.independent.co.uk/life-style/sex-robots-frigid-settings-rape-simulation-men-sexual-assault-a7847296.html

# Perceptions and Responsiveness to Intimacy with Robots; A User Evaluation

Chamari Edirisinghe[1,2]([✉]), Adrian David Cheok[1,2], and Nosiba Khougali[1,2]

[1] Imagineering Institute, Anchor 5, 79250 Iskandar Puteri, Johor, Malaysia
{chamari,adrian,nosiba}@imagineeringinstitute.org
[2] City, University of London, 10, Northampton Square, London EC1V0HB, UK

**Abstract.** In human-robot interactions research it is significant to question what measures humans will take to contest the challenges and what will become of them. Levy hypothesizes that robots will stimulate human senses with their many capabilities and humans will accept them as intimate companions because the human perception of intimacy will transform to accommodate various nuances. However, the question remains, how much humans understand and accept intimacies with robots. We argue that perceptions of human-robot interactions (HRI) and intimate interactions with robots have a certain impact on how individuals comprehend intimacies with robots. Long term contact with robots, in terms of robotic technology and conversations, will change our views and practices regarding intimacy with robots. Our study revealed that lack of awareness of the potentials of future AI robots has created a fear; fear of losing both tangible, intangible, and the sense of dominance. Yet, our participants' intimate interactions with robots produced varying degree of responses that, we believe are revealing another scope of human-robot interactions.

**Keywords:** Robots · Intimacies · Human-robot interactions
Perceptions · Touch

## 1 Introduction

The widespread progress in human-machine interaction technologies for the last two decades strongly impacted everyday lives of people who are surrounded by these technologies (communication devices, wearable devices, etc.), and whose various engagements are mostly facilitated by them. Human-robot interactions in particular have turned a new page with social robots, creating possibilities for artificial companions, thus exploring new topics of discussion. Levy [1] said "The more humanlike a robot is in its behavior, in its appearance, and in the manner with which it interacts with us, the more ready we will be to accept it as an entity with which we are willing or even happy to engage". He was discussing the prospect of robots as artificial intimate partners for humans, which as an idea was provocative, and created a plethora of criticism, both positive and negative. However, his controversial approach has created a platform for discussing the future of robotics in a different setting; an entity advanced in

© Springer International Publishing AG, part of Springer Nature 2018
A. D. Cheok and D. Levy (Eds.): LSR 2017, LNCS 10715, pp. 138–157, 2018.
https://doi.org/10.1007/978-3-319-76369-9_11

artificial intelligence. The prospect of robots with AI, as Levy mentioned above, identical to humans in behavior, interactions, and appearance generated a topic of conversation regarding the problematic of cohabitation.

Future robots are going to be more than tools; instead they are walking, talking, and thinking parts of our living, and our experiences. Invariably, human acceptance of artificial, intelligent, and human-like entities will be a challenging process. However, the human will be strongly motivated to connect with robots intimately, because a large number of robots of various capabilities are going to move into our vicinity, compelling us for closer communications. Like mobile phone technologies, robotics will be constantly upgrading with an industry that is reaching towards new potentials, and demanding customers who are invariably intimately attached to their robot companion.

The prevailing arguments will continue to evolve; from morality of a robot companion to the rights over/of a robot. Our questions will largely be focused on the future of humankind as individuals and intelligent collectives. Although some of the scenarios involving AI and robotics might appear similar to science fiction, they are feasible, requiring improvement in a number of spheres. It will only be a matter of time until our communications with robots become similar to human-human interactions. Thus, it is imperative to concentrate on studying different aspects of human-robot relationships. It will prepare every structure of the society to address numerous challenges these new interactions bring forth. Besides, it is necessary to create a platform for robust conversations on human-robot relationships before the robotics industry overwhelms us with products and services.

This study is aiming at facilitating that platform for conversation. Our objective is to evaluate the perceptions and physical responses to intimacy with robots. Our study concentrates on (1) understanding the perception of being associated with robots, and (2) the physiological responses (EDA measures) to interacting with robots. Through perception we are determining the subjective interpretations of human-robot connections, and EDA measurements are giving us evidence to how people physically react to intimacy with robots. Our results showed that, even though our study sample revealed a high awareness of robots, they reveal considerably less preference towards the idea of been intimate with robots. Physiological reactions have shown that our study participants experienced higher stimulation from the visual stimuli of the robot moving to music, rather more than haptic stimuli, such as touching the head or backside of the robot.

We understand that the perception and physiological responsiveness as key aspects in encouraging and developing communications and implications of human perception and responsiveness on human-robot interactions. Hence, the key novelty we presented in this research is the concept of intimacy with robots, in a variety of different roles and scenarios; as domestic help, companions, caregivers, comrades, lovers, true other halves, sexual partners, etc. within the framework of perception and responsiveness. Onwards, in this paper, we will discuss different studies on human-robot relationship platform. We will present our objectives, methodology, and follow it with our study results. We will discuss our study results lengthily and conclude the paper.

## 2   Background

Human-robot interactions are basically understood as part of the human-machine interactions. The story is that humans will design and produce robots to make their everyday life convenient and efficient. Robots are naturally part of human day to day living, from birth to death, yet they have been designated a position in the periphery, not in the midst of human living. Robots in the future, despite their peripheral positioning, will be common, not merely performing routine jobs, but also be responsible for major tasks, executing them effectively and efficiently. No matter where humans position them, they will create their own space, and the challenge will be the human acceptance of their spatiality.

Naturally, our relationship with robots will evolve with time, due to the amount of communication and familiarity. Whether human relationships with robots can provide for the good life is one of the focal points of discussion, with the central argument vying that the good life will be obliterated by the moral dilemma presented by these relationships. The constant criticism against deeper human-robot connection is part of the technological determinism and singularity. The fear of social and cultural changes, with the assumption that society and culture is not fluid, drives some people to understand that technological advancement determines the social and cultural values [2]. Simultaneously, people fear that, with time, technological advancement, specifically artificial intelligence, would be out of control of humans, and that will bring unimaginable changes to human nature itself [3].

While these forecasts paint a picture of gradual doom, a study found that individuals relate social rules and expectations to machines and exhibit certain socially acceptable behavior towards machines [4]. Why should we be concerned with human association with machines or computation, when we are as Turkle [5] said, 'increasingly nonchalance about machines in our everyday lives? We have accepted the human-machine, human-robot, and human-computer interactions, albeit lots of remonstrations, without much thought to the simple fact that a few decades ago we were hardly at this threshold of development. Our acceptance of new developments did not arrive from the understanding that technology has a certain sequential inevitability, but from experiencing them, and adapting them to everyday living. What we deemed as good life has changed historically. It faced technology in different centuries, in different civilizations, in different continents. Change crushed the humans on one side while revving them to rise again with a different perspective on good life.

When Asimov [6] famously made laws of robotics, he was clearly ascertaining the supremacy of humans over robots, which is a moral and sentimental association with humanity. It created a moral legitimacy for robotics, because those laws fundamentally created a hierarchy of existence, where our basic fear of robots rest. Asimov not only introduced the laws to protect humans, thus limiting the production of artificial cognitive capacities in machines, but also assumed that robots with high AI will have the capability to comprehend the superiority of humans. Our lack of faith in technology is essentially evolving from our faith (lack thereof) in ourselves, rather than the inevitability of technology.

Describing Deb Levines position on online relationships, where the author realizes them as a valid substitute for traditional relationships, Levy [1] claimed that human-robot relationships could be viewed on equal grounds. This is a moral dilemma that unsettles the everyday selves. As Piçarra et al. [7] concluded in their paper, lay persons' perception of a robot is that of a mechanical body, which fundamentally presents a predicament when deliberating about relationships. Human relationships or what Levine was describing as a traditional relationship are multi-faceted with many nuances in each interaction. Whether a robot can become similarly complex and intricate is a dubious status. Since a robot acquires its information through various means and it will miss the fluid relationships between subjects, thus it is incapable of developing a knowledge of common-sense claims Nowachek [8], emphasizing on the idea that learning occurs as a function of being in the world. In that regard, a robot can be a substitute to a traditional relationship, however the fluidness and the complexities of a relationship will not be part of that substitution; instead it will be a leaner, non-compromising exchange. Subsequently comes the questions related to the association between a machine and a substitute. Thus, are machines really a substitute? In most instances it is a yes, because we rely on machines to an extent that is alarming, yet fathomable. Will people, who emphatically declare robots as machines, view robots as substitutes for traditional methods of interacting?

Graaf [9] says that our interactions will have different meanings when there are with social robots. For one thing, the relationship between human and robot would, to a greater extent, be unidirectional, which produces chasm of expectations and unhealthy aspects of reliance. Social and cultural aspects are an integral part of this relationship, and highly contested, as those are built on values that are part and parcel of human lives. Kaplan [10] tried to measure the acceptance of robots by eastern and western cultural spheres, and concluded that they adopted different approaches towards robots; while West fervently embraced and involved with technology, and human-robot interactions, their attitude is generally distress for robotics. Contrastingly, the author has claimed that Japan, representing the East, embrace technology and human and robot interactions with a certain distant attitude and robots do not bother them extensively. Although the premise of this study raised issues, the moral and cultural perspective strongly decide on the human-robot relationship.

When the academic community measured in on the role of a robot companion [11], the human experience of psychological intimacy with robots through the physical intimacy [12], human physiological response to intimately touching a robot [13], a systematic survey of the acceptance of sex robots [14] and aspects that influence the purchase of sex robots [15] are (to name a very few) contributing to a greater discussion that would contain what could be described as an emerging phenomena. It is important to emphasize that greater contribution in terms of assessment of social impact and risk management are required for a robust coexistence in future.

## 3   Methodology

### 3.1   Objectives

Our objectives are fundamentally to understand the perceptions of being intimately associated with robots and physiological reactions to close interactions with robots. Through the perception we are aiming to determine the interpretations of human-robot interactions and through the measurement of electrodermal activity (physiological responses), we are expecting to interpret the individual responses to physical interactions with robots. Although we understand that a correlation between perception and physiological response is not reasonable to measure considering the differences in methods, we will still discuss the differences on an abstract level. Both of these measures will reveal the dynamics and trajectories of human-robot intimate interactions.

### 3.2   Participants

A total of 20 participants of the age of 20 and above participated in this study. All participants are from different nationalities and ethnic backgrounds (Refer to Table 1).

### 3.3   Study Protocol

**Study 1 -** Study 1 consisted of a questionnaire that was presented to participants who answer position questions related to human-robot relations. They were asked to contemplate on those questions and give binary answers. In this we adapted the Guttman scaling method, which is "applied to a set of binary questions answered by a set of subjects" [16]. Guttman scale is cumulative, thus the questions are progressively challenging. The process could generate contradictory answers and reveal certain inconsistent positions of the participants. In a pilot study [17], we discussed this stage of the test using both male and female participants. Through these questions we urged participants to express their perception of representations, while with questions, we stimulated scenarios both personal and impersonal. We also conversed with participants informally to clarify some of the answers.

**Study 2 -** Following Study 1, the second stage of this study measured the physiological reaction to close interactions with a robot. We used a commercially available biomedical equipment to measure electrodermal activity[1].

### 3.4   Study Structure

**Study 1 -** The questionnaire consisted of five dimensions, each dimension pertaining to a particular aspect of robot or a particular responsiveness towards the

---

[1] http://bitalino.com/en/board-kit-bt.

**Table 1.** Participants data

| Participant number | Age | Nationality |
|---|---|---|
| Participant 1 | 46–50 | Nigerian |
| Participant 2 | 21–25 | Malaysian |
| Participant 3 | 26–30 | Singaporean |
| Participant 4 | 21–25 | Malaysian |
| Participant 5 | 21–26 | Malaysian |
| Participant 6 | 31–35 | Malaysian |
| Participant 7 | 21–25 | Malaysian |
| Participant 8 | 21–26 | Malaysian |
| Participant 9 | 21–27 | Malaysian |
| Participant 10 | 21–28 | Malaysian |
| Participant 11 | 26–60 | Malaysian |
| Participant 12 | 21–25 | Malaysian |
| Participant 13 | 25–30 | Malaysian |
| Participant 14 | 21–25 | Malaysian |
| Participant 15 | 21–26 | Malaysian |
| Participant 16 | 21–27 | Malaysian |
| Participant 17 | 26–30 | Malaysian |
| Participant 18 | 31–35 | Nigeria |
| Participant 19 | 31–35 | Iranian |
| Participant 20 | 21–25 | Malaysian |

existence of robots. The objective here is for participants to construct their own scenarios with their awareness of robots, whether those robots are industrial arms, humanoid robots, domestic robots, or future high-tec robots. They are encouraged through a number of questions that associate robots with humans, stimulating their minds to take a position on variety of human-robot interactions. The answers to each dimension will be examined to understand individual positions. Awareness is the first dimension, which is aiming to understand the level of awareness of robots in the day to day living and the degree of acceptability of that awareness. The second dimension is Association, which is aiming to comprehend the personal relations and associations individuals prefer to build or imagine preferring to build. Enjoyment, as the third criterion, is aiming to understand the individual pleasure and entertainment with/from robots. Attraction, as the fourth dimension, is measuring the perception of individual attraction to robots. The last dimension is Intimacy, where the individuals are requested to imagine intimacy (in terms of romance, love, and sex) with robots.

**Table 2.** List of test protocols

| No | Protocol | Time | Dimension |
|----|----------|------|-----------|
| 1 | Relaxation audio/video relaxation clip | 30 s | Lowest point |
| 2 | Looking at the robot robot sitting down | 30 s | Awareness & Association |
| 3 | Looking at the robot robot standing up | 30 s | |
| 4 | Watching robot moving robot walking | 30 s | |
| 5 | Watching robot dancing 1 - robot dancing to music | 30 s | Enjoyment |
| 6 | Watching robot dancing 2 - robot dancing to music | 30 s | |
| 7 | Watching robot dancing 3 - robot dancing to music | 30 s | Attraction |
| 8 | Watching robot dancing 4 - robot dancing to music | 30 s | |
| 9 | Touching robots head robot stands still | 30 s | Intimacy |
| 10 | Touching robots arm robot stands still | 30 s | |
| 11 | Touching robots waist robot stands still | 30 s | |
| 12 | Touching robots buttocks robot stands still | 30 s | |
| 13 | Touching robots inner thigh robot stands still | 30 s | |
| 14 | Bursting a balloon | 30 s | Highest point |

**Study 2 -** This experiment measured electrodermal activity (EDA) using a commercially available toolkit while the participants were engaged in designated interactions with the robot Alpha $2^2$. The test started with relaxation of the participant with relaxing audio and visual stimuli, after which the participant interacted with the robot on predetermined stimuli, which were both visual and tactile. The predetermined protocols were designed to roughly collaborate with the dimensions discussed in study 1. While the test began with relaxation, it concluded with a high excitement point; a bursting of a balloon. The objective was to position all EDA results between the relaxed as the lowest reading of EDA to bursting balloon as the highest reading. Each interaction was for 30 s, with a 60 s relaxation period in between (refer to Table 2).

## 4    Results

### 4.1    Study 1

This study, as we experienced in our pilot study [17], garnered high positive results for particular questions. The first item out of two items in awareness resulted in 91.25% of positive answers. However, item 2 showed only 53.5% average of positive answers. Only four participants responded completely positively to questions of awareness. To six questions in the item one of dimension two, association, 70% of participants gave positive answers, while for the next item, 70% were negative in their responses. Fifty seven percent of answers were favourable to enjoyment criteria, however, only 35% thought of robots as entertainment and enjoyment (refer to Table 3).

---

² Alpha  2  https://www.indiegogo.com/projects/alpha-2-the-first-humanoid-robot-for-the-family-social.

**Table 3.** Results of each dimension

| Dimension | Item | | Total positive | Average |
|-----------|------|-------|----------------|---------|
| | No | Quets. | | |
| Awareness | 1 | 4 | 73 | 0.912 |
| | 2 | 10 | 107 | 0.535 |
| Association | 3 | 6 | 84 | 0.700 |
| | 4 | 3 | 18 | 0.300 |
| Enjoyment | 5 | 6 | 73 | 0.608 |
| | 6 | 4 | 41 | 0.512 |
| Attraction | 7 | 3 | 22 | 0.366 |
| | 8 | 4 | 21 | 0.262 |
| | 9 | 4 | 14 | 0.175 |
| Intimacy | 10 | 12 | 50 | 0.208 |
| | 11 | 12 | 91 | 0.379 |
| | 12 | 14 | 48 | 0.171 |

The level of attraction to a robot at an abstract level accumulated 36.66% favourable results. The possibility of being attracted to a robot emotionally and physically at an abstract level scored only 26.25%, while emotional attraction at a personal level garnered only 17.5% positive responses. For the dimension attraction, 79.09% answers were negative. Intimacy was the last dimension, where for three items, participants answered 38 questions, and only 24.86% answered positively.

## 4.2 Study 2

This study measured electrodermal activities (EDA) of participants when interacting with a robot. The protocols for interactions were associated with the same five dimensions as discussed above. Each participant was asked to interact with the robot in a quiet room with no disturbances, with only two researchers present. Their protocols were arranged thus (Refer to Table 2). The first and last stimuli were designed to measure the highest and lowest point in the EDA measures, so that benchmarks could be established to understand other measures. Our results revealed that each test elicited different level of responses from each participant. The benchmark we created, with the understanding that we need to position our test protocols somewhere within two spectrum, relaxation and high point of excitement, revealed that certain interactions with robots exceed those benchmarks.

In Li et al. [13], there was a similar study, where they measure the physiological responses to arrive at a conclusion that participants have shown a considerable higher response when touching more *low accessibility areas* of a robot. They statistically measured the response time, deciding that the response time

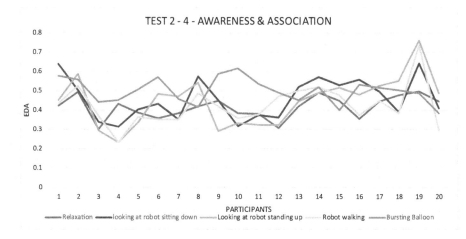

**Fig. 1.** Awareness and association EDA results of twenty participants

correlated with arousal, and the results showed that response time is higher for low accessibility areas of robots body. In our study (experiment 2), the test protocols were designed according to our first study criteria, and each protocol has a response time of 30 s, of which the average was considered as the highest response. The awareness and association criteria results indicated that each participant responded differently to each visual test, but not significantly (Fig. 1). If we examined the participant 16, there are visible changes in response averages, however, examining the changes, the difference in the response to looking at a seated robot and a standing robot is 0.076. Three participants scored below both benchmarks, while the same number of participants scored above both benchmarks.

Watching the robot dance for the first time, all participants registered an average response level of 0.499 and 6 of them gave responses below the relaxation point, which was marked as the low benchmark. The second robot dance protocol elicited an average response of 0.469 (Refer to Fig. 2). Different dancing acts were selected for attraction criteria (Fig. 2), where the robot made intricate dance movements. The first dance move attracted an average of 0.487 response. Seven participants out of 20, exceeded the highest benchmark we imposed. The second dance by the robot received a 0.449 average response. Only three participants exceeded the highest benchmark in their responses. To cover our different categories, we have thus far introduced visual stimuli, however, for the category of intimacy we introduced touch; touching different parts of the robot (refer to Table 2 and Fig. 3). It started with 3 stimuli that were impersonal touches: head, arm, and waist. It progressed to touching the robot's backside and inner thigh. For clarity, we separated first three impersonal touches. Touching the head of the robot had an average of 0.498 EDA response and touching the robot's arm and waist garnered 0.451 and 0.471 averages, respectively.

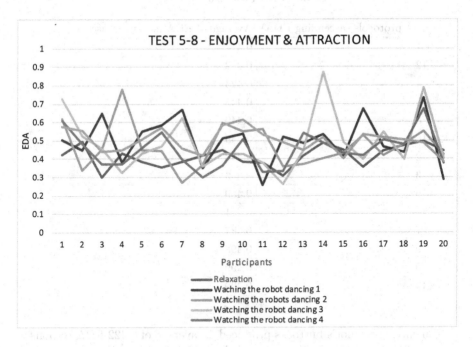

**Fig. 2.** Enjoyment and attraction EDA results of twenty participants

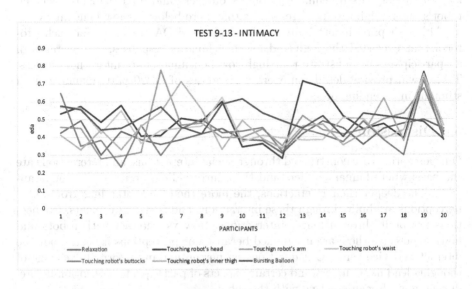

**Fig. 3.** Intimacy EDA results of twenty participants

**Table 4.** EDA average ascending

| Test protocols (ascending EDA) | Average of EDA measures (ascending) |
|---|---|
| 1 | 0.414 |
| 12 | 0.422 |
| 4 | 0.423 |
| 3 | 0.445 |
| 8 | 0.449 |
| 10 | 0.449 |
| 2 | 0.458 |
| 13 | 0.459 |
| 6 | 0.469 |
| 11 | 0.471 |
| 7 | 0.487 |
| 9 | 0.498 |
| 5 | 0.499 |
| 14 | 0.499 |

Touching the robot's buttocks produced an average of 0.422 EDA responses, and only 3 out of 20 participants exceeded the high benchmark we put forward. In contrast, touching the robot's inner thigh produced 0.460 average of response, with 7 participants exceeding the high benchmark of response, bursting a balloon. 9 participants touching the robot's buttocks and 6 participants touching robot's inner thigh produced responses that were below the low benchmark.

Although participants individually displayed EDA responses for each protocol that exceeded the high and low benchmarks responses, the averages of all participants demonstrate that high/low benchmarks are intact nonetheless. Table 4 will provide details on average responses of all 20 participants to each stimulus in ascending order.

## 5   Discussion

Our perceptions are constructed through social interactions, and interactions are the basis where humans understand their surrounding, be it tangible or intangible. The deeper their interactions, the more their understanding grows. Our perceptions are built through these interactions and social agreements. Connections are built through longer interactions. How we interact with robots and how we perceive them are interlinked because our perceptions influence how we interact and vice versa. Our questions on perception and informal exchange of thoughts lead us to understand certain aspects of participants perception before, during, and after interacting with the robot.

When we examined our study participants' awareness of robots, in any capacity, living in their space and the acceptability of their existence, 64.28% average awareness was reported. However, to questions like whether they are aware that humans want robot companions only garnered 25% of positive answers. It is revealed that our participants awareness of robots is still embedded in their comprehension of representation of robots in science fiction. They associated words of two different spectrums with robots: help and danger. Participants who answered 100% positively to this dimension saw robot as help, who perform routine and dangerous tasks in industry and help household chores in the home front. In other words, robots are mere tools, albeit more advanced ones than their dish washer. Some participants voiced future potentials, in education and healthcare, yet as tools.

Mixed answers, where participants refused to think of robot as human companions or friends, yet visualized a future of close associations with robots, were mostly founded on danger and fear. In 2005, a study conducted by Dautenhahn et al. [11] revealed that large number of the study participants were in favour of robot companions, as assistants or domestic help, but only few wanted those robot companions as friends. Considering that there are no real examples, perceiving robots as a danger is largely influenced by representation of robots in fiction. However, the fear is comprehensible when you imagine scenarios where there is a conflict of objectives between humans and robots. Consequently, it is argued that when robots learn a considerable amount of human values, they will not pose a threat [18].

The macro-micro level association the participants are building or imagined building with robots was a criterion where we wanted to establish whether their perceived connections become different from an abstract level to a personal level. Robots are created as passive machines because humans direct them in their actions. As Shibata et al. [19] pointed out robots should not be simple tools to humans merely to be evaluated objectively. An average of 56.67% participants answered positively to questions on association. 75% of participants liked robots, and 70% liked them in their homes, yet only 60% liked them in their neighborhoods. When asked about this preference from some participants, they saw robots that are not under their control, in their home, as a danger to their security. Denning et al. [20] in their study revealed that since not all are tech-savvy users, multi-robot households will face security threats. However, our participants did not voice concerns in that regard; instead they concentrated on the threats that might arise from robots controlled by others. This reveals that our perception of robots has a correlation to our perception of each other as humans.

It is revealed that perceived enjoyment has an impact on the interactions with robots {21]. For the dimension of enjoyment, overall, 57% of participants of our study answered positively. 9 out of 20 participants answered all questions positively. To questions like "do you enjoy robots" 75% agreed, yet to the statement "robots are joyous", which is attempting to establish that robots have by themselves the capacity to be joyous, was met with only 40% of positive answers. All participants are somewhat assured that they will enjoy robots, but robots having the capability to be independently enjoyable is a phenomenon they find difficult to grasp. However, the capabilities of robots as entertainers is accepted by the majority, yet doubts are prevailing on the subject of robots as joyous entities, that could, given the capability, be able to create, provide, and experience joy.

One of the prevailing issues with regards to the idea of a robot as an intimate part of everyday living is the appearance of the robot; the appearance will dissuade humans from bonding with robots. Anthropomorphic robots are inclined to be more accepted as attractive and intimate than robotic machines. As Norman [22] says, beautiful things work better and make people feel good. Only 25.9% of our participants consider the possibility of being attracted to robots of any form or manner. The perception of robots as mere machines, thus tools for use, is the predominant sentiment that discourage thinking of robot differently. To argue the point that robots are indeed different, like every human being as individuals, might appear to point out the obvious rational argument, yet all of the study participants 'first reaction is' what is there to be attracted to a robot when it looks like a machine. Writing about uncanny valley, Mori [23] reflected that humans will not feel an affinity with robots unless they look less similar to machines and more like humans. However, he further argues that if a robots appears to be very similar to humans in looks, it might develop a revulsion. 60% of our study participants found robots attractive, however only 25% thought they can be attracted to a robot. 25% imagined being attracted to a robot emotionally. Shibata et al. [19] maintain that designing robots that interact with humans required the understanding of how people think of robots subjectively. On the same wavelength Hanson et al. [24] express that for the robots to be attractive to humans, integrated social 'responsivity' and aesthetic enhancements are essential. Interactions between humans and robots largely depend on the human expectations of those interactions.

When humans evaluate robots, they assume both the observer and the subject roles says [19], thus the intelligence of the robot depends on the intelligence prevailed in the subject. When humans imagine the robots as intimate partners, or robots in intimate scenarios, the perception is not only influenced by real life human-human interactions, and perception of those, but also the interpretation of human-robot relations as a subject. The morality of building intimate interactions with a non-human entity encroaches upon the notion of the sacrosanctity

**Fig. 4.** Participant interacting with the robot

of being a human. As raised by Scheutz and Arnold [25], what are the moral and ethical foundations upon which these connections will be built? How will these intimacies relate to human-human intimacies? Will human beings somehow be replaced by these man-made, yet foreign, entities? In our study only 24.9% of participants accepted a possibility of intimacy with robots. Understandably our study participants' imaginations have to be stretched to its fullest to comprehend and then relate to intimate scenarios with robots. Considering that their exposure to robots are limited, and the robots with high AI capabilities are still in future scenarios, imagining robots and humans in meaningful physical and emotional bonding is challenging. However, our participants found emotional bonding less disturbing than physical bonding through intimacy and sex.

Li et al. [13], in their statistical analysis of EDA measurements when touching a robot, revealed that touching the intimate regions of the robot's body elicited a higher response than pointing at the those body regions. Jinnai et al. [26] claimed that more humanlike device, the human communication is more intimate. Our interactions with robots are a product of our perspectives, and there are numerous factors that influence our perceptions; both internal and external. Some external factors may influence the perception, thus impacting the physical interactions. It is argued that, irrespective of positive or negative, low motivational intensity (i.e. amusement) expands the cognitive scope, than high motivational tendencies (i.e. desire) [27]. According to Gable and Harmon-Jones [28], high levels of arousal will not impact the motivational intensity, even though arousal and motivational intensity are connected. This encourages us to think that physiological responses may not always align with perceptions. Higher physiological responses will not necessarily indicate a change in cognition towards intimacy with robots, however, it will encourage the individual to be familiar with robots.

Our study of electrodermal activity (EDA) when interacting with a robot, revealed that on an average, watching the robot dancing protocol attracted the highest response (see Tables 4 and 5). This is the first time in this study the participants encounter the robot moving to music in dancing motion. Touching the robot's body for the first time (the head) elicited the second highest response. Lowest responses were produced by the protocol that invite participants to touch the robot's buttocks.

Our test design focused on visuals and haptics (Refer Fig. 4). Visual was intended to create the notion of familiarity, an awareness of the robot as an entity with humanoid appearance that can accomplish certain activities, prompting communications. Those tests were expected to encourage the participants away from the notion of robots as a mere machines, and instead positively evaluate the abilities and potentials of robots. Visuals lead to haptics, which will be instrumental in understanding the physiological response to touching a robot (Fig. 5).

Our results revealed that there was no clear difference between responsiveness towards visual stimuli, intended for influencing the perception of robots and haptic stimuli where regions of the robot's body that is deemed as private and

**Table 5.** Visual and haptic stimuli

| Protocol category | Stimuli | Stimuli (ascending) | Average of EDA (ascending) |
|---|---|---|---|
| Visuals | Relaxation audio/video relaxation | 1 | 0.414 |
| | Watching robot moving robot walking | 4 | 0.423 |
| | Looking at the robot robot standing up | 3 | 0.445 |
| | Watching robot dancing 4 - robot dancing to music | 5 | 0.449 |
| | Looking at the robot robot sitting down | 7 | 0.458 |
| | Watching robot dancing 2 - robot dancing to music | 9 | 0.469 |
| | Watching robot dancing 3 - robot dancing to music | 11 | 0.487 |
| | Watching robot dancing 1 - robot dancing to music | 13 | 0.499 |
| Haptics | Touching robots buttocks robot stands still | 2 | 0.422 |
| | Touching robots arm robot stands still | 6 | 0.449 |
| | Touching robots inner thigh robot stands still | 8 | 0.459 |
| | Touching robots waist robot stands still | 10 | 0.471 |
| | Touching robots head robot stands still | 12 | 0.498 |
| | Bursting a balloon | 14 | 0.499 |

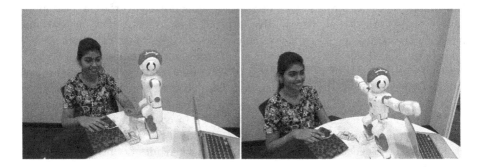

**Fig. 5.** Participant interacting with visual and haptic stimuli 1

intimate were being touched (refer to Table 4). The highest score, when participants are watching the robot dancing was understandably significant, not only because that was the first experience of a dancing robot to the participants, but also because the act of dancing could enliven the disposition. When the dancing entity is a robot, with its mechanical body, moving as smoothly and coordinated as possible, a perceptive change is created. In the same manner participants react to the sound of the bursting balloon, a dancing robot create an excitement that is physiologically measurable (Fig. 6).

The first encounter of touching the robot's private and intimate regions of the body began with touching the head. Participants average reactions were highest in the haptic category. Touching the robot's waist, second highest score in haptics revealed that private yet less intimate regions of the robot's body elicited a higher response. However, the difference between touching the head and waist is 0.270. In comparison, the difference between the highest and low-

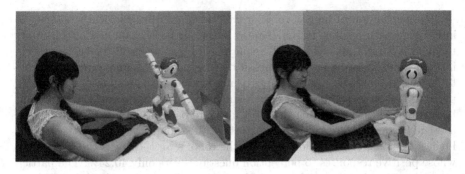

**Fig. 6.** Participant interacting with visual and haptic stimuli 2

est scored stimuli was 0.774. Touching robot's inner thigh scored higher than touching the buttocks, the difference being 0.037. The difference in responses is unexplainable, because it is difficult to make the assumption that the inner thigh is considered less intimate than the buttocks. However, when asked informally after the tests, they did not voice specific emotions like embarrassment or awkwardness when touching the intimate regions of the robot's body, instead they expressed the strangeness of the act itself. Perceptions are basically socially constructed; thus, it is problematic to conclude that each visual and haptic stimuli directly revealed a position. However, we would like to proposition that, even though for comprehensive analysis we considered all participants as an aggregate, considering individual responses with their study 1 results will produce an in-depth understanding of the subjective responses to human-robot interactions.

We have presented two different tests: one to understand perception of human-robot interactions, how they position themselves within the human and robot sphere, and another to measure their physiological responses. The first test revealed that perception of robots in any capacity is considerably built on media consumption. This was later clarified during informal discussions we conducted with participants. Whether it is human-robot romantic involvement, or powerful and aggressive robots (or hybrid creatures) invading the planet, these visual imageries are playing a leading role in conceiving the human-robot relationship. All the robots in contemporary everyday life, be it a mechanical arm, domestic service robots, entertainment robots, or sex robots, are such an extension to everyday living that we failed to notice the roles they play; the role of helping us. Yet our imagery has this evil entity that threaten the human values. A robot in an intimate setting is unimaginable to the majority because their fear of the unknown (known only through media depictions) is represented in the concept of human-robot interactions.

Lack of awareness of future possibilities in robotics, and human-robot relationships has created a void in most participants. Creating future scenarios, in terms of potentials developments in human-robot intimacies, were also decidedly influenced by the concept of creationism, the moral unacceptability of altering the belief in human creation.

The perception of human-robot interactions and physiological responses to interacting with a robot (visual/haptic) have not been examined in this study to build a correlation, which will require a different methodological approach; instead we examined them in terms of the positioning of human-robot interactions. It is revealed that participants demonstrated mixed responses to touching perceived intimate regions of a robot's body. They have not revealed a significant high response when touching the most intimate part, instead displayed a lowest average for one of the most intimate parts of the robots body, the buttocks. The highest response recorded for touching the robot's buttocks was the participant whose positive responses to perception questions were only 40.24%. The participant whose responses recorded as the lowest for touching the robot's inner thigh, produced 93% of positive answers for perception of human-robot interactions.

Our conclusions at large;

(1) For the future, it is highly significant to create a greater awareness through continuous media exposure of various developments in the field of robotics and artificial intelligence. Awareness will create a mindfulness of robotic technology as more than machinery and algorithms, and advancement in robotics will prepare humans to think in terms of inclusivity.

(2) Scenarios of future robotics technology and human-robot relationship are build and developed with information gleaned from robotic and AI-related research, and fictional depiction of human-robot relations. Robotic, AI, and human-robot interaction research expand the conversation of the repertoire of future human-robot developments.

(3) Human-robot relations are based on fear (mingled with hope) and benefits. Fear of machines overpowering humans has been in the conversation from way back when automated manufacturing was introduced and recently in the form of mobile phones, internet, and media consumption. Robots, somehow, were revealed as entities that work, taking over repetitive, dangerous, and mundane tasks. Even though our participants were concerned about the loss of jobs to robots, thus increasing the unemployment, they have little conception of the incredible amount of jobs robots are already involved in and will be handling in coming decades.

(4) Intimacy with robots is inconceivable to most because of the resolute belief that humans ought to be intimate with only humans, although sex robots are a thriving commercial industry. The morality of intimacy, especially the intimate act of sex, with a robot will always be subject of intense discussions.

(5) Visuals and haptics in the interactions with robots revealed mixed physiological reactions. Most of the participants inclined towards enjoying the robot in various dance moves than haptics, although they revealed a higher response when touching the robot for the first time. This inadvertently exposes that our interactions with robots will be non-linear and multifaceted, not necessarily because humans are complex, but also because AI will create a complexity of a different nature. It will be two different yet, somehow similar dimensions making compromises, creating new set of shared values.

# 6   Limitations

As limitations, we understand that our sample size of 20 participants is inadequate to argue a broader element. We will eliminate this weakness in our next study where we will add a third stage to the study, a qualitative analysis. We understand that, for a very complex subject, we let participants give binary answers in study one. That might not have given us a comprehensive perspective from the participants, however, we addressed that by having an informal exchange with each participant for this study. For the extended study, which we will be conducting as the next stage of this study, we are intending to incorporate open ended interviews with each participant.

# 7   Conclusion

In this study we discussed the perception of being intimately associated with robots and physiological reaction through EDA measurements to a number of stimuli that created intimacy with a robot. The majority of the participants of the study revealed they are aware of robots (largely due to media depiction of robots), however, they have reservation about being intimate with robots. They collectively saw robots as machines, even with the possibility of AI changing that status. The symbolic representation of robots as machines affected the way they associate robots with emotions and intimacy. Their physiological responses showed that their reactions are higher for visual stimuli of a robot moving to music, than for haptic stimuli.

It can be understood that the participants were primarily driven by the knowledge that robots are mere machines, which is permissible considering current developments in robotics and AI are progressing slowly. But in another decade, advancements in artificial intelligence, and experiments in humanoid robots will create an entity that is beyond a machine. Future robots will demonstrate capabilities somewhat equal to humans, which will create a strong friction that is triggered by the fear of being overpowered. Every participant of this study voiced their fear of future robots, either as a threat for employment or as a major threat to the humankind.

As future developments in this study, we will incorporate an open-ended interview, taking all participants as an aggregate, as well as individuals.

# References

1. Levy, D.: Love and Sex with Robots: The Evolution of Human-Robot Relationships. Harper Collins, New York (2009)
2. Servaes, J.: Introduction to the 3 as: technology is great. In: Technological Determinism and Social Change: Communication in a Tech-Mad World, pp. xiii–xxiii. Lexington Books, New York (2014)
3. Kurzweil, R.: The singularity is near1. In: Ethics and Emerging Technologies, p. 393 (2016)

4. Nass, C., Moon, Y.: Machines and mindlessness: social responses to computers. J. Soc. Issues **56**(1), 81–103 (2000)
5. Turkle, S.: The Second Self: Computers and the Human Spirit. MIT Press, Cambridge (2005)
6. Asimov, I.: Runaround. Astounding Sci. Fiction **29**(1), 94–103 (1942)
7. Piçarra, N., Giger, J.C., Pochwatko, G., Gonçalves, G.: Making sense of social robots: a structural analysis of the layperson's social representation of robots. Revue Européenne de Psychologie Appliquée/European Review of Applied Psychology **66**(6), 277–289 (2016)
8. Nowachek, M.T.: Why robots can't become racist, and why humans can. PhaenEx **9**(1), 57–88 (2014)
9. de Graaf, M.M.: An ethical evaluation of human-robot relationships. Int. J. Soci. Robot. **8**(4), 589–598 (2016)
10. Kaplan, F.: Who is afraid of the humanoid? investigating cultural differences in · the acceptance of robots. Int. J. Humanoid Rob. **1**(03), 465–480 (2004)
11. Dautenhahn, K., Woods, S., Kaouri, C., Walters, M.L., Koay, K.L., Werry, I.: What is a robot companion-friend, assistant or butler? In: 2005 IEEE/RSJ International Conference on Intelligent Robots and Systems, (IROS 2005), pp. 1192–1197. IEEE (2005)
12. Kahn Jr., P.H., Ruckert, J.H., Kanda, T., Ishiguro, H., Reichert, A., Gary, H., Shen, S.: Psychological intimacy with robots?: using interaction patterns to uncover depth of relation. In: Proceedings of the 5th ACM/IEEE International Conference on Human-Robot Interaction, pp. 123–124. IEEE Press (2010)
13. Li, J., Ju, W., Reeves, B.: Touching a mechanical body: tactile contact with intimate parts of a humanoid robot is physiologically arousing. In: 66th Annual Conference of the International Communication Association, Fukuoka, Japan (2016)
14. Scheutz, M., Arnold, T.: Are we ready for sex robots? In: The Eleventh ACM/IEEE International Conference on Human Robot Interaction, pp. 351–358. IEEE Press (2016)
15. Szczuka, J.M., Krämer, N.C.: Influences on the intention to buy a sex robot. In: Cheok, A.D., Devlin, K., Levy, D. (eds.) LSR 2016. LNCS (LNAI), vol. 10237, pp. 72–83. Springer, Cham (2017). https://doi.org/10.1007/978-3-319-57738-8_7
16. Abdi, H.: Guttman Scaling. Encyclopedia of Research Design. SAGE Publications, Thousand Oaks (2010)
17. Edirisinghe, C., Cheok, A.D.: Robots and intimacies: a preliminary study of perceptions, and intimacies with robots. In: Cheok, A.D., Devlin, K., Levy, D. (eds.) LSR 2016. LNCS (LNAI), vol. 10237, pp. 137–147. Springer, Cham (2017). https://doi.org/10.1007/978-3-319-57738-8_13
18. Russell, S.: Should we fear supersmart robots. Sci. Am. **314**(6), 58–59 (2016)
19. Shibata, T., Tashima, T., Tanie, K.: Emergence of emotional behavior through physical interaction between human and robot. In: Proceedings of the IEEE International Conference on Robotics and Automation, 1999, vol. 4, pp. 2868–2873. IEEE (1999)
20. Denning, T., Matuszek, C., Koscher, K., Smith, J.R., Kohno, T.: A spotlight on security and privacy risks with future household robots: attacks and lessons. In: Proceedings of the 11th International Conference on Ubiquitous Computing, pp. 105–114. ACM (2009)
21. Heerink, M., Kröse, B., Wielinga, B., Evers, V.: Enjoyment intention to use and actual use of a conversational robot by elderly people. In: Proceedings of the 3rd ACM/IEEE International Conference on Human Robot Interaction, pp. 113–120. ACM (2008)

22. Norman, D.A.: Emotional Design: Why We Love (or Hate) Everyday Things. Basic Civitas Books, New York (2004)

23. Mori, M., MacDorman, K.F., Kageki, N.: The uncanny valley [from the field]. IEEE Rob. Autom. Mag. **19**(2), 98–100 (2012)

24. Hanson, D., Olney, A., Prilliman, S., Mathews, E., Zielke, M., Hammons, D., Fernandez, R., Stephanou, H.: Upending the uncanny valley. In: Proceedings of the National Conference on Artificial Intelligence, vol. 20, p. 1728. AAAI Press, MIT Press, Menlo Park, Cambridge, London (1999, 2005)

25. Scheutz, M., Arnold, T.: Intimacy, bonding, and sex robots: examining empirical results and exploring ethical ramifications. In: Danaher, J., McArthur, N. (eds.) Robot Sex: Social and Ethical Implications (Working title). MIT Press (2017)

26. Jinnai, N., Sumioka, H., Minato, T., Ishiguro, H.: The impact of a humanlike communication medium on the development of intimate human relationship. In: Cheok, A.D., Devlin, K., Levy, D. (eds.) LSR 2016. LNCS (LNAI), vol. 10237, pp. 104–114. Springer, Cham (2017). https://doi.org/10.1007/978-3-319-57738-8_10

27. Harmon-Jones, E., Gable, P.A., Price, T.F.: Does negative affect always narrow and positive affect always broaden the mind? considering the influence of motivational intensity on cognitive scope. Curr. Dir. Psychol. Sci. **22**(4), 301–307 (2013)

28. Gable, P.A., Harmon-Jones, E.: Does arousal per se account for the influence of appetitive stimuli on attentional scope and the late positive potential? Psychophysiology **50**(4), 344–350 (2013)

# The Influence of Body Proportions on Perceived Gender of Robots in Latin America

Gabriele Trovato[1,2(✉)], Cesar Lucho[2], Friederike Eyssel[3], and Jasmin Bernotat[3]

[1] Research Institute of Science and Engineering, Waseda University,
#41-304, 17 Kikui-cho, Shinjuku-ku, Tokyo 162-0044, Japan
`gabriele@takanishi.mech.waseda.ac.jp`
[2] Pontificia Universidad Católica del Perú, Lima, Peru
[3] Bielefeld University, Bielefeld, Germany

**Abstract.** Subtle aspects of a robot's appearance may create biased expectations of the robot's abilities, which may influence user acceptance. The present research investigated the perception of gender in robot design, focusing specifically on the proportion between chest, waist, and hips to indicate robot gender. We did so by conducting an online survey in Latin American context. The results highlight the importance of chest-to-hip ratio and waist-to-hip ratio in gender attribution and mind attribution to robots.

**Keywords:** Robot design · Humanoid robots · Gender

## 1 Introduction

Previous research has shown that first impressions matter, even in the context of social robots. Depending on time, motivation, and effort available to form social judgments, mental shortcuts are used when forming an impression of others. That is, individuals rely on rules of thumb and engage in automatic information processing to come to an estimate about a person or a nonhuman entity (see also [1]). To do so, for instance, humans take into account key features that indicate social category membership of a person or entity. That is, people rely on visual cues that indicate age, gender, or ethnic background of a person. Previous research on determinants of psychological anthropomorphism nicely illustrates that people analogously make use of social categorization to form impressions of non-familiar robotic or virtual agents (e.g., [2–5]). Relying on visual cues that represent category membership can facilitate performance in learning environments, as investigated by Kuchenbrandt and colleagues [5] and Reich-Stiebert and Eyssel [6]. Furthermore, having a mental model of the human or robotic counterpart at hand, creating a persona of the interaction partner, facilitates the creation of common ground and shared reality. That is, from physical and functional cues (e.g., appearance,

---

The original version of this chapter was revised: The results section of the chapter is not correct. This has been now corrected. The correction to this chapter is available at https://doi.org/10.1007/978-3-319-76369-9_13

© Springer International Publishing AG, part of Springer Nature 2018
A. D. Cheok and D. Levy (Eds.): LSR 2017, LNCS 10715, pp. 158–168, 2018.
https://doi.org/10.1007/978-3-319-76369-9_12

demeanor, speech) humans can infer a robot "personality" which may impact human-robot interaction (e.g., [7–9]).

Subtle visual cues, e.g., to indicate gender of a robot may activate peoples' gender stereotypical knowledge structures which lead to biased expectations regarding the robot's abilities [10]. To illustrate, research by Eyssel and Hegel [7] has documented that indeed, people perceive a long-haired robot as more female than a short-haired counterpart, and accordingly, judgments regarding these "feminine" vs. "masculine" robot prototypes turn out more gender-stereotypical, with the robots being differentially rated with regard to warmth and competence and their suitability for gender-stereotypical tasks. These findings have important implications for human-robot interaction, as previous work in [5, 6] has also pointed to the interplay between robot gender and gender-typicality of a task that has to be solved with a robot instructor. For instance, research by Reich-Stiebert and Eyssel [6] has shown that a mismatch between robot gender and task typicality is beneficial regarding the willingness to engage in learning processes with "gendered" NAO robots. In a study on the robot guard RobotMan [11], its two tasks of security and guidance were associated with gender. The expression of the eyes and the tone of the voice influenced not only the perceived gender-related traits, but also physical attributions like body size as well as likeability. The present research will shed more light on the role of visual gender cues in robots, as these are particularly crucial for product design.

Thus, we aimed to investigate the perception of gender in robot design, focusing specifically on the proportion between chest, waist, and hips to indicate robot gender. By manipulating body proportions, it will be possible to influence user perception of the robot gender, as documented in previous research, and in particular for humanoids, enhance the feeling of intimacy. The novelty in the present paper and in a related research [12] consists in the manipulation of body proportions, which although extensively studied in anthropometrics, has never been done before on pictures of robot bodies.

We explore the chest-hip ratio and waist-hip ratio as subtle visual cues that are utilised to form gender-based impressions of novel robot prototypes. In anthropometrics, shoulder-to-hip ratio (SHR), chest-to-hip ratio (CHR), and waist-to-hip ratio (WHR) are typical indicators of human body types. We reviewed a number of studies that inspired the stimuli we used which were produced by a professional designer: in our study, a figure of a generic robot was used and adapted to different combinations of CHR and WHR.

In [13], shoulder-to-hip ratio was measured for human models: an average SHR of 1.39 was found for male models and a SHR of 1.23 was obtained for females. In comparison, average males had a SHR of 1.21, while average females had a SHR of 1.08. In their own experiment [13], the authors used stimuli that were characterized as having a SHR of 1.2 for males and a SHR of 1.05 for females.

Chest-to-hip ratio represents a similar metric which does not take into account shoulder width. It is used in product design: For example, in the female doll "Bratz", the CHR was 0.82. This CHR score is similar to that of an adolescent female body [14].

Furthermore, the difference between upper and lower body is typically used in symbolism for public toilets: a triangle can be used to represent females because of its resemblance with a skirt. These kinds of symbols are widespread and recorded by institutes such as the American Institute of Graphic Arts (AIGA). Reversed triangle and circle can also be used as symbols for men and women, respectively. They recall broader shoulders of men and rounded bellies of pregnant women [15]. Squares are also typically associated with males and circles with females [16].

Waist-to-hip ratio is also an important measurement related to gender: higher testosterone levels in men stimulate fat deposits in the abdominal region while inhibiting fat deposits on the hips and thighs: healthy adult men generally have higher WHRs than women, with values ranging from between 0.85 and 0.95 [17]. For women, the ideal value is typically 0.70, while for men the ideal is approximately 0.90. In [13], the measurements of WHR resulted in a range of 0.70–0.90 for women and the 0.90–1.10 for men.

Across cultures, a low waist-to-hip ratio represents a predictor of female body attractiveness [14]. In the nineteenth century, the use of waist training and corsets allowed some women to achieve 0.50 WHR. The Bratz doll is hyper-feminised in such way, featuring a WHR of 0.52 [14]. Designers exploit product proportions and arrangement to evoke associations: a pronounced waist is used to indicate female gender [18].

The recently developed robot IOmi [19] features a pronounced feminine CHR and WHR in order to increase the perception of a female robot. Pepper [20] features a CHR of approximately 1.30 and WHR of approximately 0.45. The large chest, necessary to hold the touch screen, stands in contrast with the small waist, and this can produce a mixed response in terms of visual and social perception.

To study this issue further, we conducted an empirical study on the perception of stimuli for which we manipulated CHR and WHR.

In the present experiment, our hypothesis is that the two body measurement ratios will impact the perception on gender of robots, with a higher CHR suggesting a male gender and a lower CHR a female gender; additionally, a value of WHR close to 1 indicating male gender and a lower WHR a female gender.

The present paper presents first empirical evidence from Peru [21, 22] as well as other Latin countries, as a first step towards a broad cross-cultural comparison. According to Glick [23], gender stereotypes and traditional gender role beliefs are relatively pronounced in Latin American contexts: these kinds of social factors should be taken in consideration in order to realise a complete study.

## 2   Method

### 2.1   Stimuli

The robot stimuli presented in this research were developed by a professional designer. The main goal was to manipulate CHR and WHR, not taking into account SHR. This was done because shoulder width might be a confounding factor. Therefore, we decided to keep shoulder design constant.

In our study, the stimuli were manipulated using three levels of CHR: 0.80, 1.00 and 1.20; and two levels of WHR: 0.60 and 1.00. Within this range, the WHR of 0.60 was chosen as it was reported to be the average value of female attractiveness in several countries in Asia, Africa, and South America [24]. The WHR upper bound 1.00 was fixed because beyond that threshold, WHR may be interpreted as an indicator of obesity in males [25].

The three CHR levels were defined taking into account one body type corresponding to the triangle symbolism in design, one body type for the opposite reversed triangle, and an additional one as middle value, corresponding to the squared shape. All the values were chosen coherently with the values reported in [14], and calculated from anthropometric studies [26]. Finally, and most importantly, the range of variation was kept approximately the same as the variation of WHR, in order to obtain two variables of the same visual importance.

The height of the waist within the body was set to approximately 37%, as calculated from the data reported in [26].

The lower parts of the robot body did not feature any "legs" (which could appear masculine) or a single "block" (which could activate the notion of femininity, looking like a long skirt), as they were represented just by a trunk together with a squared base, as in Fig. 1. The robot head was designed to be as iconic and as generic as possible, featuring a slightly round shape.

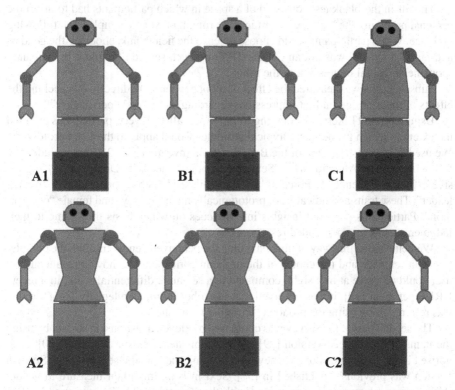

**Fig. 1.** The six stimuli used in the questionnaire: in each row three different variation of chest-hip ratio; in each column two different variations of waist-hip ratio.

Figure 1 shows all the stimuli used in this research that correspond to the 2 × 3 combinations of WHR and CHR. They were drawn first by calculating waist and chest while keeping the hip size constant, and later resizing the width of the whole body. For resizing, the volume of the whole body (included lower body) was calculated and normalised. This was done in order to ensure the same perception in terms of body mass, and in order to avoid that any of the stimuli were perceived as fat or slim.

## 2.2 Procedure and Materials

Participants were asked to complete a survey that was divided in two main parts: Firstly, participants were asked to provide demographic data (i.e., gender, age, major, field of study/work, familiarity with robots, mother tongue).

As part of a within-subjects design, participants rated each of the six stimuli that were presented in a randomised order. Participants completed a fill-in-the-blank task to measure ascriptions of gender to the prototypes. The text comprised an introduction such as "This robot is called ZX-A1". No user input was allowed here. The robot name was composed of random letters and one of the suffixes A1…C2 as in Fig. 1. This was done to avoid any undesired effects of a robot's name that might indicate gender.

The fill-in the-blank test consisted of a space in which participants had to insert the personal pronouns "he" or "she", to fit into the running text and complete the following sentence. While participants could choose to leave the field blank, choosing the gender-neutral pronoun "it" was not an option. This approach served to explore participants' spontaneous initial impression of the robot.

Subsequently, we measured the effect of robot gender more directly by checking the effects of robot design on first impressions regarding the robots' "personality".

Using a 5-point Likert scale ranging from 1, not at all, to 5, very, participants reported the extent to which gender-stereotypical attributes would apply to the robot prototypes. We used the Spanish version of the Bem Sex Role Inventory [27, 28] that included the following items: "Affectionate"; "Sensitive to others' needs"; "Dominant"; "Aggressive"; "Warm"; "Tender"; "Forceful"; "Loves children"; "Strong personality"; "Acts as leader". These traits are indicative of prototypically male "agency" and female "communion". Participants provided insights into the cues on which basis they came to their judgments using an open-ended response.

We believe that this way of understanding the perceived gender through the completion of a sentence and the choice of the pronoun corresponds to how spontaneously a user could perceive at first sight, compared to a semantic differential scale. In a recent HRI experiment [19], it was observed that the robot IOmi, an allegedly female robot, was referred to by using the pronoun "it" rather than "she".

The second part of the survey was composed by eleven questions on sexism by using the items of the reduced version [29] of the Ambivalent Sexism Inventory [30], categorised in the two dimensions "benevolent sexism" and "hostile sexism". The Spanish version was previously published in [31]. Sexism is an important measure in gender studies among humans, as it is related with the stereotypical traits measured in Bem Inventory [28], and because it varies among different countries and cultures. By measuring robot gender indirectly through the Bem inventory, which contains a list of personality attributes of masculinity-femininity and gender roles, we can obtain an assessment of the robot's role related to stereotypical attributes.

# 3   Results

## 3.1   Participants

A total of 121 participants took part in the online survey. Data were collected in Peru through social networks and within the Pontifical Catholic University of Peru. However, a large proportion of data had to be excluded because 60 respondents provided incomplete responses, and four participants expressed a priori that the word 'robot' would be inherently male, therefore not matching the scope of the investigation. Regarding the final sample of 57 participants (27 males, 30 females), the majority of participants were Peruvian and few (10.5%) were from some other Spanish-speaking countries (Spain, Uruguay, Mexico, Argentina). Their mean age was 29.04 years ($SD = 9.79$), ranging from 17 to 61.

## 3.2   Preliminary Analyses

Means were computed by averaging participants' responses regarding the dimensions of agency and communion, and benevolent and hostile in case of sexism items.

Internal consistencies (Cronbach's $\alpha$) were for each stimulus: .83, .72, .83, .74, .77, .71 for agency; .90, .93, .89, .94, .94, .93 for communion. $\alpha$ was .72 for benevolent sexism and .79 for hostile sexism.

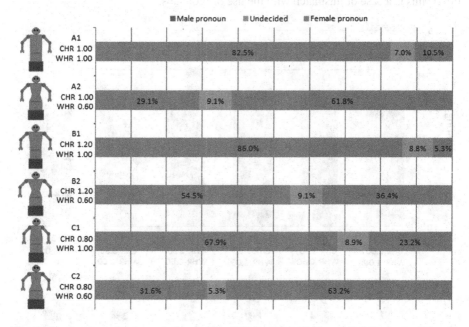

**Fig. 2.** Declared gender through the choice of the pronoun "he" or "she" for each of the six stimuli.

### 3.3 Gender in Language Use

Figure 2 reveals the percentage scores regarding the use of pronouns "he" or "she" in the text passage for each of the robot body type. As can be seen, only prototypes A2 and C2 elicited the use of the female pronoun "she" more frequently. More often, participants have referred to the robots using a male pronoun, while a small number of participants ranging from 5–9% appeared undecided across all six stimuli.

We performed a log-linear analysis through a three-way contingency table, which operates a cross-classification of observations by the levels of three categorical variables. The results showed that the interaction between the two independent variables CHR and WHR and the choice of pronoun is strongly significant ($G^2(7) = 88.78$; $p < .001$). Most importantly, each of the two variables are interacting with the pronoun: both CHR ($G^2(2) = 13.98$, $p < .001$) and WHR ($G^2(1) = 69.56$, $p < .001$). CHR and WHR are confirmed to be independent from each other ($G^2(2) = 0.2$, $p = .905$).

### 3.4 Stereotypical Attributes

Furthermore, we investigated the attribution of gender-stereotypical traits to the various robot body types. We performed a paired samples $t$-test and found that significant differences between male and female attributes are present in A2 ($t(54) = -2.33$; $p = .024$), in B2 ($t(54) = 2.41$; $p = .019$), and in C1 ($t(55) = -3.11$; $p = .003$). In case of C1, this is a case of mismatch with the use of pronouns.

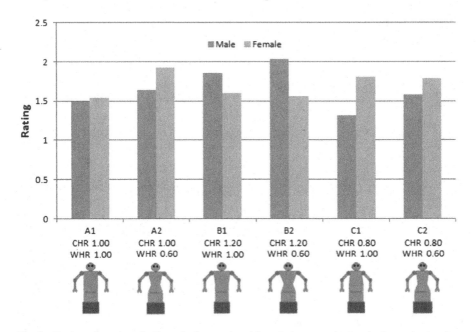

**Fig. 3.** Rating of stereotypically male (agency) and female (communion) traits for each stimulus.

From Fig. 3 it is possible to notice that male ratings are higher for B1 and B2 and female higher for C1 and C2. Performing additional $t$-tests confirmed that stimuli with a high CHR correspond to higher male traits (in case of B1 and C1: $t(55) = -4.93$; $p < .001$); in case of B2 and C2: $t(54) = -4.06$; $p < .001$). This pattern may indicate that CHR is a factor that recalls masculine adjectives regarding strength and agency, supposedly due to the size of the chest, with little or no impact of WHR.

### 3.5 Correlations

We conducted Pearson correlation analyses to further explore the statistical relationship. The degree of attribution of female communion traits was negatively correlated both with familiarity with robots ($r(54) = -.27$; $p = .047$) and with familiarity with product design ($r(55) = -.30$; $p = .024$). Nothing significant was found between familiarity with robots and agency ($r(54) = -.003$; $p = .979$), and familiarity with product design and agency ($r(55) = .08$; $p = .552$).

Moreover, benevolent sexism was positively correlated with the attribution of communion-related traits to robots ($r(54) = .48$; $p < .001$) and with agency-related traits ($r(54) = .33$; $p = .013$). Neither the correlations between communion and hostile sexism ($r(54) = .23$; $p = .085$) and agency and hostile sexism ($r(54) = .25$; $p = .062$) turned out statistically significant.

## 4 Discussion and Conclusion

In this paper we presented the results of an exploratory investigation on the perception of gender in robot design, focusing specifically on the proportion between chest, waist and hips to indicate robot gender. Our goal was test whether the manipulation of chest-to-hip ratio and waist-to-hip ratio in robots would orientate the perception of robot gender and elicit gender-stereotypical trait attributions in terms of agency and communion.

Our hypotheses were confirmed as both chest-hip and waist-hip ratio play a role in the perception on gender, even in a subtle level. A CHR visibly greater than 1 suggests a male gender, whereas visibly less than 1 suggests a female gender. WHR can also indicate female when visibly less than 1, whereas values close to 1 indicate male.

While both ratios influenced the explicit categorisation of gender in language use, the chest-to-hip ratio seemed to influence the amount of agency and communion attributed to the robots. Cases of mismatch (such as C1, which gives contradictory results, but also B2) should be further studied through a between-subject design, as the perception can be subjective. Mismatches should be avoided in robot design, especially the case of humanoids and androids, in which misalignment of visual cues can be critical in the characterisation of gender in order to facilitate the intimacy.

Correlation analyses revealed that stereotypically female traits related to the notion of communion were attributed more to robots by participants who endorsed benevolent sexist attitudes. Perceived communion of the robots was negatively correlated with familiarity with design and robots. The latter result was expected, as familiarity to robots and to design exposes respectively how the robots and their pictures are made.

One methodological shortcoming was found regarding the large drop-out rate. In order to avoid this to happen, either the questionnaire should be made more compact, or the research should be conducted in a quiet laboratory setting.

Another limitation of this study concerns the fact that we conducted it in Spanish language. To illustrate, the introduction sentence "This robot is …(robot name)…" reads "Este robot es …" in Spanish language. The demonstrative pronoun *este* is male even though commonly applied to any case when gender is not specified. The absence of a neutral form may have slightly biased the answers towards male gender. This might also explain the more frequent use of the masculine pronoun, on average.

For future work we are planning to extend the survey to samples of German and Japanese participants and to compare the results, especially considering the differences in sexism as well as in anthropometrics and standards of beauty across these countries.

# References

1. Reeves, B., Nass, C.: The Media Equation: How People Treat Computers, Television, and New Media Like Real People and Places. Cambridge University Press, New York (1996)
2. Bergmann, K., Eyssel, F., Kopp, S.: A second chance to make a first impression? How appearance and nonverbal behavior affect perceived warmth and competence of virtual agents over time. In: Nakano, Y., Neff, M., Paiva, A., Walker, M. (eds.) IVA 2012. LNCS (LNAI), vol. 7502, pp. 126–138. Springer, Heidelberg (2012). https://doi.org/10.1007/978-3-642-33197-8_13
3. Eyssel, F., Loughnan, S.: "It don't matter if you're black or white"? Effects of robot appearance and user prejudice on evaluations of a newly developed robot companion. In: Herrmann, G., Pearson, M.J., Lenz, A., Bremner, P., Spiers, A., Leonards, U. (eds.) ICSR 2013. LNCS (LNAI), vol. 8239, pp. 422–431. Springer, Cham (2013). https://doi.org/10.1007/978-3-319-02675-6_42
4. Eyssel, F., Kuchenbrandt, D., Hegel, F., de Ruiter, L.: Activating elicited agent knowledge: how robot and user features shape the perception of social robots. In: Proceedings of the 21st IEEE International Symposium in Robot and Human Interactive Communication (RO-MAN 2012), pp. 851–857 (2012). https://doi.org/10.1109/roman.2012.6343858
5. Kuchenbrandt, D., Häring, M., Eichberg, J., Eyssel, F., André, E.: Keep an eye on the task! Effects of task characteristics on human-robot interactions. Int. J. Soc. Robot. **6**, 417–427 (2014)
6. Reich-Stiebert, N., Eyssel, F.: Robots in the classroom: what teachers think about teaching and learning with education robots. In: Agah, A., Cabibihan, J.-J., Howard, A.M., Salichs, M.A., He, H. (eds.) ICSR 2016. LNCS (LNAI), vol. 9979, pp. 671–680. Springer, Cham (2016). https://doi.org/10.1007/978-3-319-47437-3_66
7. Eyssel, F., Hegel, F.: (S)he's got the look: gender-stereotyping of social robots. J. Appl. Soc. Psychol. **42**, 2213–2230 (2012). https://doi.org/10.1111/j.1559-1816.2012.00937
8. Lee, S., Kiesler, S., Lau, I.Y., Chiu, C.: Human mental models of humanoid robots. In: Proceedings of the 2005 IEEE International Conference on Robotics and Automation (ICRA 2005), Barcelona, 18–22 April, pp. 2767–2772 (2005)
9. Powers, A., Kramer, A.D.I., Lim, S., Kuo, J., Lee, S.-L., Kiesler, S.: Eliciting information from people with a gendered humanoid robot. In: Proceedings of the 14th IEEE International Workshop on Robot and Human Interactive Communication, pp. 158–163 (2005)

10. Wang, Y., Young, J.E.: Beyond "Pink" and "Blue": gendered attitudes towards robots in society. In: Proceedings of Gender and IT Appropriation. Science and Practice on Dialogue - Forum for Interdisciplinary Exchange (2014)

11. Trovato, G., Lopez, A., Paredes, R., Cuellar, F.: Security and guidance: two roles for a humanoid robot in an interaction experiment. Presented at the 2016 IEEE RO-MAN, Lisbon, Portugal (2016)

12. Bernotat, J., Eyssel, F., Sachse, J.: Shape it – the influence of robot body shape on gender perception in robots. In: Kheddar, A., Yoshida, E., Ge, S.S., Suzuki, K., Cabibihan, J.-J., Eyssel, F., He, H. (eds.) Social Robotics, ICSR 2017. LNCS, vol. 10652, pp. 75–84. Springer, Cham (2017)

13. Dijkstra, P., Buunk, B.P.: Sex differences in the jealousy-evoking nature of a rival's body build. Evol. Hum. Behav. **22**(5), 335–341 (2001). https://doi.org/10.1016/S1090-5138(01)00070-8

14. Lidwell, W., Manacsa, G.: Deconstructing Product Design: Exploring the Form, Function, Usability, Sustainability, and Commercial Success of 100 Amazing Products. Rockport Publishers, Beverly (2011)

15. Goddard, A., Patterson, L.M.: Language and Gender. Psychology Press, London (2000)

16. Schott, G.D.: Sex symbols ancient and modern: their origins and iconography on the pedigree. BMJ **331**(7531), 1509–1510 (2005). https://doi.org/10.1136/bmj.331.7531.1509

17. Singh, D.: Female judgment of male attractiveness and desirability for relationships: role of waist-to-hip ratio and financial status. J. Pers. Soc. Psychol. **69**(6), 1089–1101 (1995)

18. Crilly, N., Moultrie, J., Clarkson, P.J.: Seeing things: consumer response to the visual domain in product design. Des. Stud. **25**(6), 547–577 (2004). https://doi.org/10.1016/j.destud.2004.03.001

19. Onchi, E., Lucho, C., Sigüenza, M., Trovato, G., Cuellar, F.: Erratum to: introducing IOmi - a female robot hostess for guidance in a university environment. In: Agah, A., Cabibihan, J.-J., Howard, A.M., Salichs, M.A., He, H. (eds.) ICSR 2016. LNCS (LNAI), vol. 9979, p. E1. Springer, Cham (2016). https://doi.org/10.1007/978-3-319-47437-3_99

20. Guizzo, E.: Meet Pepper, Aldebaran's new personal robot with an "Emotion Engine". IEEE Spectr. (2014). Last accessed 14 Aug 2015

21. Blondet, C.: Out of the kitchens and onto the streets: women's activism in Peru. In: Basu, A. (ed.) The Challenge of Local Feminisms: Women's Movements in Global Perspective, pp. 251–75. Westview Press, Boulder (1995)

22. Mensa, M.: Creative women in Peru: outliers in a machismo world. Commun. Soc. **28**(2), 1–18 (2015). https://doi.org/10.15581/003.28.2.1-18

23. Glick, P., Fiske, S.T., Mladinic, A., Saiz, J.L., Abrams, D., Masser, B., López López, W.: Beyond prejudice as simple antipathy: hostile and benevolent sexism across cultures. J. Personal. Soc. Psychol. **79**(5), 763–775 (2000)

24. Dixson, B.J., Dixson, A.F., Li, B., Anderson, M.J.: Studies of human physique and sexual attractiveness: sexual preferences of men and women in China. Am. J. Hum. Biol. **19**(1), 88–95 (2007). https://doi.org/10.1002/ajhb.20584

25. van der Kooy, K., Leenen, R., Seidell, J.C., Deurenberg, P., Droop, A., Bakker, C.J.: Waist-hip ratio is a poor predictor of changes in visceral fat. Am. J. Clin. Nutrit. **57**(3), 327–333 (1993)

26. Lin, Y.-C., Wang, M.-J.J., Wang, E.M.: The comparisons of anthropometric characteristics among four peoples in East Asia. Appl. Ergon. **35**, 173–178 (2004). https://doi.org/10.1016/j.apergo.2004.01.004

27. Bem, S.L.: The measurement of psychological Androgyny. J. Consult. Clin. Psychol. **42**(2), 155–162 (1974)

28. Fernandez Sedano, I.: Actitudes, auto-conceptos, cultura y emoción: una investigación transcultural (Ph.D. thesis). UPV/EHU (2001)
29. Rollero, C., Glick, P., Tartaglia, S.: Psychometric properties of short versions of the ambivalent sexism inventory and ambivalence toward men inventory. TPM: Test. Psychometrics Methodol. Appl. Psychol. **21**(2), 149–159 (2014)
30. Glick, P., Fiske, S.T.: The ambivalent sexism inventory: differentiating hostile and benevolent sexism. J. Pers. Soc. Psychol. **70**(3), 491 (1996)
31. Expósito, F., Glick, P., Morales, M.C.M.: Sexismo ambivalente: medición y correlatos. Rev. Psicología Soc. **13**(2), 159–169 (1998)

# Correction to: The Influence of Body Proportions on Perceived Gender of Robots in Latin America

Gabriele Trovato, Cesar Lucho, Friederike Eyssel,
and Jasmin Bernotat

## Correction to:
## Chapter "The Influence of Body Proportions on Perceived Gender of Robots in Latin America" in: A. D. Cheok and D. Levy (Eds.): *Love and Sex with Robots*, LNCS 10715, https://doi.org/10.1007/978-3-319-76369-9_12

The results section of the chapter was not correct. This has been now corrected.

**Page 163:**

Their mean age was 29 years ($SD = 9.80$)

should be

Their mean age was 29.04 years ($SD = 9.79$).

**Page 163:**

Internal consistencies (Cronbach's $\alpha$) were 0.79 for agency; 0.92 for communion; 0.72 for benevolent sexism and 0.79 for hostile sexism.

should be

Internal consistencies (Cronbach's $\alpha$) were for each stimulus: .83, .72, .83, .74, .77, .71 for agency; .90, .93, .89, .94, .94, .93 for communion. $\alpha$ was .72 for benevolent sexism and .79 for hostile sexism.

**Page 164:**

CHR and WHR are confirmed to be independent from each other ($G^2(2) = 0.2$, $p = .9$).

should be

CHR and WHR are confirmed to be independent from each other ($G^2(2) = 0.2$, $p = .905$).

---

The updated version of this chapter can be found at ·
https://doi.org/10.1007/978-3-319-76369-9_12

**Page 164:**

and in C1 ($T(56) = -3.20$; $p = .002$). In case of C1, this is a case of mismatch with the use of pronouns.

should be

and in C1 ($t(55) = -3.11$; $p = .003$). In case of C1, this is a case of mismatch with the use of pronouns.

**Page 165:**

From Fig. 3 it is possible to notice that male ratings are higher for B1 and B2 and female higher for C1 and C2. Performing additional $t$-tests confirmed that stimuli with a high CHR correspond to higher male traits (in case of B1 and C1: $T(56) = -5.04$; $p < .001$).

should be

From Fig. 3 it is possible to notice that male ratings are higher for B1 and B2 and female higher for C1 and C2. Performing additional $t$-tests confirmed that stimuli with a high CHR correspond to higher male traits (in case of B1 and C1: $t(55) = -4.93$; $p < .001$).

**Page 165:**

The degree of attribution of female communion traits was negatively correlated both with familiarity with robots ($r(56) = -.27$; $p = .045$) and with familiarity with product design ($r(56)= -.30$; $p = .023$). Nothing significant was found between familiarity with robots and agency ($r(56)= -.02$; $p = .9$), and familiarity with product design and agency ($r(56)= -.08$; $p = .5$).

should be

The degree of attribution of female communion traits was negatively correlated both with familiarity with robots ($r(54) = -.27$; $p = .047$) and with familiarity with product design ($r(55)= -.30$; $p = .024$). Nothing significant was found between familiarity with robots and agency ($r(54)= -.003$; $p = .979$), and familiarity with product design and agency ($r(55)= .08$; $p = .552$).

**Page 165:**

Moreover, benevolent sexism was positively correlated with the attribution of communion-related traits to robots ($r(55) = 0.48$; $p < .001$) but not with agency-related traits ($r(55) = 0.20$; $p = .14$). Neither the correlations between communion and hostile sexism ($r(55) = 0.25$; $p = .06$) and agency and hostile sexism ($r(55) = 0.23$; $p = .08$) turned out statistically significant.

should be

Moreover, benevolent sexism was positively correlated with the attribution of communion-related traits to robots ($r(54) = .48$; $p < .001$) and with agency-related traits ($r(54) = .33$; $p = .013$). Neither the correlations between communion and hostile sexism ($r(54) = .23$; $p = .085$) and agency and hostile sexism ($r(54) = .25$; $p = .062$) turned out statistically significant.

# Author Index

Printed in the United States
By Bookmasters